M000032110

 Court of Remorse

Critical Human Rights

Series Editors

Steve J. Stern ❦ Scott Straus

Books in the series **Critical Human Rights** emphasize research that opens new ways to think about and understand human rights. The series values in particular empirically grounded and intellectually open research that eschews simplified accounts of human rights events and processes.

In *Court of Remorse*, Thierry Cruvellier offers a nuanced and complex understanding of the International Criminal Tribunal for Rwanda, a central post–Cold War human rights institution that helped to establish a now common pattern of creating justice mechanisms to account for past human rights atrocities. The atrocity in question is the Rwandan genocide of 1994 in which more than half a million civilians were killed. Cruvellier is one of the most knowledgeable outside observers of the court, having watched proceedings and interviewed key actors day after day for nearly a decade. In *Court of Remorse*, Cruvellier draws on these daily observations to render a subtle, eloquent, and intelligent account of the tribunal, and in so doing he helps us understand a critical human rights institution in new and profound ways.

Court of Remorse

Inside the International Criminal
Tribunal for Rwanda

Thierry Cruvellier

Translated by
Chari Voss

The University of Wisconsin Press

Publication of this volume has been made possible, in part, through support from the ANONYMOUS FUND OF THE COLLEGE OF LETTERS AND SCIENCE at the University of Wisconsin–Madison.

The University of Wisconsin Press
1930 Monroe Street, 3rd Floor
Madison, Wisconsin 53711-2059
uwpress.wisc.edu

3 Henrietta Street
London WCE 8LU, England
eurospanbookstore.com

Originally published as *Le tribunal des vaincus: Un Nuremberg pour le Rwanda?*
Copyright © 2006 by Calmann-Lévy

Translation copyright © 2010 by the Board of Regents of the University of Wisconsin System
All rights reserved. No part of this publication may be reproduced, stored in a retrieval system, or transmitted, in any format or by any means, digital, electronic, mechanical, photocopying, recording, or otherwise, or conveyed via the Internet or a Web site without written permission of the University of Wisconsin Press, except in the case of brief quotations embedded in critical articles and reviews.

5   4   3   2   1

Printed in the United States of America

Library of Congress Cataloging-in-Publication Data
Cruvellier, T. (Thierry)
[Tribunal des vaincus. English]
Court of remorse: inside the International Criminal Tribunal for Rwanda / Thierry
    Cruvellier; translated by Chari Voss.
        p.   cm. — (Critical human rights)
        Includes bibliographical references and index.
        ISBN 978-0-299-23674-8 (pbk.: alk. paper)
        ISBN 978-0-299-23673-1 (e-book)
    1. International Criminal Tribunal for Rwanda.   2. Rwanda—History—Civil War,
    1990–1993—Atrocities.   3. Rwanda—History—Civil War, 1994—Atrocities.
    4. Trials (Crimes against humanity)—Rwanda.   5. War crime trials—Rwanda.
    6. Genocide—Rwanda.   I. Title. II. Series: Critical human rights.
KTD454.C7813   2010
345.67571'0251—dc22
2009046343

To
MY PARENTS

Contents

Geographic Landmarks

Historical Reference Points

Colonization and Independence

In 1896, Rwanda, a country where Hutus and Tutsis had lived for several centuries, became a German protectorate and was incorporated into the German empire. In 1919 the World War I victors gave this territory to Belgium. The colonial power based its authority on the royal Tutsi government and reinforced the Tutsi monopoly in administrative and political spheres. In 1959 the monarchy was overthrown by the Hutu social revolution. The first pogroms were carried out against the Tutsi community, causing tens of thousands of Tutsis to flee to neighboring countries. Three years later, in 1962, Rwanda gained its independence. Grégoire Kayibanda, a Hutu from central Rwanda, became the first president. The Tutsi guerilla warfare continued until the mid-1960s. It was accompanied by a new round of anti-Tutsi pogroms within Rwanda, particularly in 1963 and 1964, resulting in a fresh wave of Tutsi refugees fleeing to neighboring Uganda, Burundi, and the Congo. In 1973 General Juvénal Habyarimana, a Hutu from the north, took power following a coup d'état. He created the National Republican Movement for Democracy and Development (MRND), which became the country's single party.

The Civil War

On October 1, 1990, the Rwandan Patriotic Front (RPF), a rebel group consisting primarily of Tutsi refugees who had lived outside Rwanda since 1959, started a civil war by invading Rwanda from Uganda. Within the country, there were massive arrests of Tutsis. In April 1991 the MRND agreed to the principle of reintroducing a multiparty system. In November it started a youth wing called Interahamwe, which progressively morphed into an armed militia group.

In March 1992 approximately three hundred Tutsis were massacred in the Bugesera region, south of the capital city, Kigali. In April a new government was formed that included all the main Habyarimana opposition parties inside Rwanda, and named a Hutu as prime minister. In February 1993 a new RPF offensive in the north resulted in the displacement of a million people in Rwanda. In July the extremist Hutu radio station Radio-Télévision libre des milles collines (RTLM) began broadcasting. That same month a new government was formed, led by opposition leader Agathe Uwilingiyimana. On August 4 the government of Rwanda and the RPF signed the Arusha Peace Accords in Tanzania. This agreement was supposed to end the civil war, organize power-sharing among the various political factions, and enable the return of Rwandan refugees, who had been living abroad for thirty-five years. In October the UN Security Council approved the deployment of 2,500 peacekeepers to form the United Nations Assistance Mission for Rwanda (UNAMIR). On October 21, Tutsi soldiers in neighboring Burundi assassinated the country's first Hutu president, who had been democratically elected four months earlier. Widespread ethnic violence ensued, resulting in tens of thousands of deaths and causing several hundred thousand people to flee to neighboring countries, including Rwanda. Political and ethnic violence in Rwanda continued to escalate. The transition government was not functioning, and the parties were blaming each other for the failure.

The Genocide

On April 6, 1994, Rwanda's presidential plane was shot down by missiles upon its descent into Kigali, killing President Habyarimana, the new Burundian president (Cyprien Ntaryamira, a Hutu) and two of his cabinet ministers, the Rwandan army chief of staff, and the head of presidential security. Starting at dawn on April 7, the presidential guard assassinated Prime Minister Agathe Uwilingiyimana along with several ministers and Hutu personalities from the democratic opposition. Ten Belgian peacekeepers assigned to guard the prime minister were also killed. In Kigali, Hutu soldiers and militias, notably the Interahamwe, began to hunt down and systematically kill Tutsis. This was the beginning of the genocide and the resumption of the civil war. On April 8 Jean Kambanda was appointed prime minister of an interim government made up solely of Hutus loyal to the president. On April 11 Belgium began to withdraw its peacekeepers. Four days later the UN Security

Council ordered the withdrawal of the international force, reducing the number of troops from 2,500 to 270. General Marcel Gatsinzi, who had been appointed chief of staff of the Rwandan army on April 7 and who publicly stated his opposition to the massacre of civilians on April 12, was dismissed. Starting on April 19, the Tutsi genocide began to spread to the entire territory under government control. On July 4 the RPF seized control of the capital. By July 17 the Rwandan armed forces had been defeated. After more than three months of uninterrupted killing, soldiers and militiamen began to flee Rwanda taking with them in just a few days nearly two million Rwandans, who congregated in huge refugee camps on Rwanda's borders, particularly in Zaire (now the Democratic Republic of Congo). The RPF victory brought an end to the genocide of the Tutsis. On July 19 a national coalition government was formed, led by a Hutu who had escaped the massacres and who had been appointed to this position under the Arusha Peace Accords. General Paul Kagame, the RPF commander and Rwanda's new strongman, was named vice president and minister of defense.

The International Tribunal

On November 8, 1994, the UN Security Council established the International Criminal Tribunal for Rwanda (ICTR) to try the primary perpetrators of the crimes committed in Rwanda in 1994. Its prosecutor, Richard Goldstone from South Africa, was also the prosecutor of the International Criminal Tribunal for the former Yugoslavia (ICTY), which had been set up a year and a half earlier in The Hague. In February 1995, Arusha, Tanzania, was chosen as the seat of the ICTR. The Office of the Prosecutor was based in Kigali and headed up by a deputy prosecutor, while the prosecutor and the appeals chamber were based in The Hague. In May the UN General Assembly elected six trial judges for the ICTR, and the first investigators arrived in Rwanda. In November the first indictment was prepared.

Court of Remorse

The ad hoc tribunals for Bosnia and Rwanda are an excellent idea. The International Criminal Court is also an excellent idea. But implementation is very important; it can ruin a great idea.

Judge Lennart Aspegren, interview,
April 16, 1998

Prologue

Standing over six feet five inches tall, Laïty Kama had a bird's-eye view of the world, yet seemed to falter a little as he looked down over it. In court, he would sometimes rest his head on his right hand, so long and slender that it covered his entire forehead. In this weary posture, the Senegalese judge would mumble or stiffen his face in a gloomy, sullen pout. When he did crack a smile, as wide as an ocean sky, his small round eyes would light up. At fifty-six years old, Laïty Kama had risen through the ranks of the public prosecutor's office in Senegal to become the prosecutor at the Dakar court of appeal. Now, he was one of six judges elected by the United Nations General Assembly to sit at the ICTR, which was tasked with punishing the main perpetrators of the crimes committed in the hills of Rwanda in 1994, and he had been chosen by his peers to preside over this tribunal.

On May 30, 1996, two other judges were seated beside him in court. To his right was Lennart Aspegren, a sixty-five-year-old Swedish judge with expertise in public administration and governance. To his left was fifty-five-year-old Navanethem Pillay, who had made a name for herself as a lawyer under apartheid. She had just been appointed to sit on the South African Supreme Court when her name was proposed to the UN as a judge for the tribunal set up in the northern Tanzanian town of Arusha. Kama's authoritative manner during the hearing was somewhat brusque.

"Mr. Akayesu, how do you plead—guilty or not guilty?" he asked in a deep, gruff voice.

"Not guilty, Mr. President."[1]

Jean-Paul Akayesu had been arrested seven months earlier while seeking refuge in Zambia. He had just been transferred to Arusha along with two fellow countrymen, Clément Kayishema and Georges Rutaganda. These men were the first accused to be brought before the international tribunal. They were middle aged—in their forties or nearly so—though their weary faces bore witness to their two years in exile. All three were from Rwanda's largest ethnic community, the Hutus. All three were suspected of helping to organize the genocide of Rwanda's main minority group, the Tutsis.

Rather tall and slender, Jean-Paul Akayesu was light skinned with delicate features and almond-shaped, almost slanted eyes. He was the exact opposite of the stereotypical image of the stocky, pudgy Hutu. He was fast becoming the judicial symbol of an ideology that had led Rwandans to exterminate fellow Rwandans on the basis of such irrational stereotypes. And yet his appearance betrayed these simplistic ideas. He seemed to have acquired this newfound notoriety as the emblem of Hutu ideology despite his non-Hutu appearance.

Akayesu was also the least likely of the three suspects. Up until July 1994, he was only a *bourgmestre* (the equivalent of a "mayor" in the vocabulary inherited from Belgian colonization) of a small commune in central Rwanda. Three months earlier, when the massacres started in Rwanda's capital in April 1994, this well-liked teacher and novice politician, with no history of extremism, allegedly did an about-face, turning against the Tutsi population in his commune and orchestrating their extermination—approximately two thousand killed, according to the Office of the Prosecutor, which indicted him.

The impression one gets of a man suspected of murder makes you realize the power of prejudice. Suddenly it seems difficult to see him as anything but guilty. But Jean-Paul Akayesu, indirectly accused of two thousand murders, defied expectation. At first glance, he could instill a shadow of a doubt.

Not Clément Kayishema. This former prefect of the Kibuye region in western Rwanda had hunched shoulders and a slightly stooped back that made him look guilty in spite of himself. There was a rare intensity in his round, deep-set eyes, and he had an incandescent, mechanical gaze that caused people to look away instinctively. Accused of having directly or indirectly caused the death of tens of thousands of people, Clément Kayishema did not challenge the public opinion's preconceptions. He magnified them. He also pleaded not guilty.

The third man, shabbily dressed in a faded green jacket, looked intimidated. Yet on paper, Georges Rutaganda had the highest profile of the three. In April 1994 he was one of two vice presidents of the main militia group, the Interahamwe, whose name came to symbolize the terror and cruelty of the extremist Hutu forces that massacred several hundred thousand of their fellow Tutsi countrymen and women in just three months, between April and July 1994.

The word "genocide" was coined by a Polish Jew in 1944. In 1994 Rwandans invented a term for the exterminators: "genocidaires." It was not a French word (the correct term in French would have been *génocideurs*), but it soon came to be. It had already entered English usage; a language lacking a word of its own readily accepts one of foreign origin. To name is a victim's privilege. In 1994 the Interahamwe in Rwanda were *genocidaires* par excellence, and Georges Rutaganda was one of their five national leaders. He was thirty-five at the time. "I plead not guilty," he replied in his turn, in a soft, respectful voice.

The brief hearing of Jean-Paul Akayesu, Clément Kayishema, and Georges Rutaganda was somewhat of an adventure. It was not held in a real courtroom. The ICTR didn't have one yet. Instead, a makeshift room had been hastily set up. In the offices of President Kama and his colleagues, it was not unusual to see a pail on the floor in some incongruous spot, on account of the leaks in the ceiling. But no matter: all that international justice needed at this point was a couple of tables, a few dozen chairs, one or two interpreters, and a squad of security guards. Form was not yet important. The passion of the participants and their determination to uphold the dignity of these proceedings, at least until the hearing was over, swept away all concern for appearances. Everyone wondered: How long would it take the tribunal to accomplish its task, which objectives would be met, which obstacles overcome, how many individuals would be targeted, on the basis of what strategy and at what cost? What would this tribunal bring for Rwanda? Everyone had ideas, variously grandiose, minimal, punitive, reconciliatory, dissuasive, and, above all, contradictory. No one knew for sure. But everyone was certain of one thing: justice must be done.

This was not yet the beginning of the trial. Rather, it was a routine procedure, the initial appearance—the first formal contact between the accused and those responsible for trying them. The trial on the merits would begin four months later according to the announcement made in court. All the same, this hearing in Arusha had a unique symbolic importance. It was the first tangible, memorable, and convincing manifestation of the desire expressed by the world a year and a half earlier to ensure justice for the Tutsis of Rwanda. In two days, these three handcuffed men had given a face to the unspeakable, offered retribution for human civilization, and provided an outlet for eight hundred thousand victims and redemption for the community of nations.

It was no ordinary experiment. In 1945 the victors of World War II tried two dozen high-ranking Nazi leaders in one year at the Nuremberg trials, while the Japanese leaders, who had also been defeated, were tried in Tokyo. But forty years of the Cold War put a damper on the plans to create an international criminal justice system. The idea of holding leaders accountable for their crimes did not resurface until the beginning of the 1990s. A decisive step was taken in 1993, when the UN Security Council voted to establish an international tribunal to try the perpetrators of the crimes that were being committed in the Balkans. This tribunal was named the International Criminal Tribunal for the former Yugoslavia (ICTY) and was based in The Hague, in the Netherlands. One year later, the confetti-sized central African country of Rwanda sank into a state of ultraviolence. Though the violence lasted only three months, it resulted in the greatest human massacre ever seen in such a short period of time. The international community reacted decisively: within two weeks it left the country, withdrew 2,500 UN troops who had been stationed there, and abandoned the Rwandans to the hands of the militias. Then, in November 1994, five months after the terror ended, it attempted to repent by creating a replica of the ICTY for Rwanda—the ICTR. "Honor is lost but once," later wrote Rwandan priest and journalist André Sibomana.[2]

Nestled at the foot of a 14,980-foot imploded volcano that is covered by a thin layer of snow in January, Arusha stands out as an oasis. An island of banana plantations and old-growth forests of ficus, acacia, and flamboyant trees surrounded by vast, arid, or sandy plains, the city sits on the edge of the gigantic geological fracture that divides eastern Africa, chisels its great lakes, and carves out the Eastern Rift Valley. In the mid-1990s Arusha was shaking off two decades of Tanzanian-style socialism that had unified the country and prevented it from drifting into totalitarianism and war, but had nevertheless been an economic failure. Dusty and decrepit, it looked like a city straight out of the Wild West. It was a large village that foreigners merely passed through on their way to see animal paradises or to conquer Mount Kilimanjaro. Safari tourism was booming, and two other main, and more discrete, industries sustained the city's economy. Miners had struck "blue" gold with tanzanite, a semiprecious stone prized by Western jewelers, while the floral industry flew thousands of roses out of Arusha each week to supply Holland's flower markets.

Arusha was the perfect choice for the UN tribunal. It was a city that needed time to adjust. But that's not why it was chosen. Any city in Rwanda itself had been ruled out to guarantee the tribunal's safety and independence. Zaire was eliminated from the list because it was both a logistical nightmare and a political ally of the toppled Rwandan government responsible for the Tutsi massacre. Uganda, bordering Rwanda to the north, was ruled out because on the opposite end of the spectrum, it was allied with the Rwandan rebel movement—which had won the war and scattered the *genocidaires*, but had also committed serious crimes. To the south, Burundi, divided along the same ethnic lines, was in the throes of its own civil war. To the east, Kenya was equipped with modern means of communication and was the regional economic, diplomatic, and media hub. In addition, its capital, Nairobi, was already home to an impressive UN compound. But the Kenyan president, suspecting the ICTR of partiality and bias, vehemently refused to allow the tribunal in his country. That left only one option: calm, stable, and relatively middle-of-the-road Tanzania.

"A community—an enclave geographically and socially—of the many and varied people crowded into the enclave and following a semicolonial life-style while they wrestled with the professional and personal problems that pressed upon them."[3] Arusha at the end of the 1990s? No, Nuremberg in 1945 as depicted by one of the American prosecutors, Telford Taylor.

Arusha the isolated, Arusha the boring. The international jurists who moved there to set up the tribunal complained constantly. The link between Nuremberg and Arusha cannot be easily denied, except perhaps in the symbolism. Before serving as a venue for Nazi trials, Nuremberg had been the scene of major Hitlerian gatherings and the Third Reich's show of force and its imposition of anti-Semitic laws. Arusha, on the other hand, was the political symbol of that which was betrayed in Rwanda in 1994. It was here that the warring Rwandan parties had signed a peace agreement in 1993, eight months before the genocide began. The Arusha Accords symbolized the end of the civil war that had begun in 1990, as well as the promise of power-sharing among the country's main political groups, and especially among the political elite of the two communities engulfed in a violent clash, the Hutus and the Tutsis. Arusha was a symbol of peace, and the UN tribunal was an attempt to restore it in the eyes of its creators.

Fourteen years after the first hearing in May 1996, the ICTR still exists, but it does not look the same. Beads of water from the gutters no longer form on the ceilings of the judges' offices. A thousand people work there, and the tribunal has a steady, annual budget of approximately $140 million, more than triple what it was receiving in periodic installments at the beginning of the trials. It has four modern courtrooms equipped with digital cameras, flat-panel displays, and infrared microphones where abstruse and laborious proceedings are conducted with a fastidious respect for form, robes, and decorum.

At the time of this writing, the tribunal has arrested seventy-seven individuals in countries all over Africa, in Europe, and in North America. Eleven more suspects remain at large. Jean-Paul Akayesu, Clément Kayishema, Georges Rutaganda, and more than forty others have stood trial. The principle of international justice, still in its infancy at the time of these three men's initial appearance, has triumphed. Since then, 110 countries have agreed to be subject to the authority of the International Criminal Court, the ICC, which was established in The Hague in 2002, not for a single country for a specific period of time but permanently. Now legal professionals from the world over are regularly tasked with investigating, prosecuting, and defending men, and in some cases women, suspected of having committed crimes against humanity in various corners of the world. Most often, these places are on the African continent. The first official cases brought before the ICC relate to crimes committed in Uganda, the Democratic Republic of Congo, Sudan, and the Central African Republic. Behind this new generation of men and women with their mandate to render justice, the memory of a pioneering and promising undertaking—the tribunal in Arusha—stretches out like the shadow of a fading sun.

To recount the trial of these men accused of the genocide of Tutsis in Rwanda is to retell three histories that intermingle and collide with one another: History with a capital *H*, the history of Rwanda, which provides the backdrop and the foundation; individual history, the history of each person accused of the "crime of all crimes," which knits the story together; and the history of justice, of a new kind of international tribunal in search of its own existence and legitimacy. The story that follows is woven from the convergence of these inextricable histories. It is the story of a tribunal—the ICTR—that was supposed to be the heir of the Nuremberg trials without being a form of victors' justice. A tribunal that, in trial after trial, would render an unexpected form of justice to a community of nations seeking to regain its lost honor—justice out of remorse.

1

The Addis Ababa
Departure Lounge

> In trying to mend fences or succumbing to blackmail—depending on
> whom you talk to—the tribunal recently acquiesced to allow a major fig-
> ure of the genocide to be tried by the national courts of Rwanda (and ex-
> ecuted), rather than before the tribunal. By not invoking its "primary" ju-
> risdiction, the tribunal may have lost the opportunity to have this alleged
> architect "flip," and perhaps help make cases where tangible proof is slim.
>
> Michael Karnavas, attorney, *The Champion*,
> May 1997

Little is known about the life Froduald Karamira led in Bom-
bay, India, and even less about his deportation from the
country on June 4, 1996. Rwandan intelligence agents acted efficiently and
discretely, leaving no trace behind. The work of true professionals. The operation was conducted in utmost secrecy. It was more like a covert operation to
extract a secret agent than the mere deportation of a criminal. When Karamira
boarded the Ethiopian Airlines plane for Rwanda, no one had gotten wind of
it—a remarkable feat within the Rwandan community, where information
generally travels faster than an airplane.

Suddenly, the operation went awry. Just a few seconds of inattentiveness in
the transit lounge during the layover in Addis Ababa, and Karamira escaped.
Not for long, of course. The Ethiopian police arrested him right away, but he
had nonetheless managed to extricate himself from the hands of those who
wanted to try him for his role in the 1994 genocide. The secret of his transfer
was revealed. The press reported that this major suspect in the Rwandan massacre was being held in a prison in Ethiopia's capital. In turn, the news reached

Richard Goldstone, the South African prosecutor of the ICTR in Arusha. He immediately asked the authorities in Addis Ababa to hand over the Rwandan leader in their custody. In Rwanda's capital, Kigali, anger and frustration ran high. The Rwandan government had narrowly missed the opportunity to get its hands on a person it considered to be among the top twenty perpetrators of the Tutsi genocide.

The ICTR had gotten off to a rocky start. In July 1994 those who had immediately called on the international community to help render justice were the same ones who, after a hard-fought struggle, had just seized power in Kigali amid the ruins and mass graves left by the *genocidaires*. Yet when the UN established the tribunal in November, Rwanda was the only state to vote against it. This court was not what it had requested.

The new Rwandan government at the time comprised two main factions: the Rwandan Patriotic Front (RPF), an armed, Tutsi-dominated rebel group that had just driven the ex-government forces out of the country and ended the genocide; and a handful of survivors from the Hutu democratic movement who had managed to escape the killers who had ruthlessly hunted them down because of their refusal to support the genocide. These survivors and the victorious RPF both shared the desire to bring the perpetrators of these crimes to justice, but they never considered delegating this responsibility to someone else, much less to the international community that had abandoned Rwanda rather than protect the civilian population. In requesting an international tribunal to prosecute and try the perpetrators of the genocide, the new Rwandan government was envisioning the establishment of a court in Kigali where Rwandans would be involved and the death penalty would be applied. Instead, the UN Security Council chose to set up the tribunal outside the country and, in order to guarantee its impartiality, barred Rwandans from having any judicial responsibility. It also decided that this tribunal should try all crimes committed in 1994, including those perpetrated by the RPF. Relations between Rwanda and the tribunal were tumultuous from the outset. One of the Rwandans' points of contention was that the maximum sentence the ICTR can impose is life in prison. When the tribunal was created, the Rwandan ambassador to the UN, Manzi Bakuramutsa, commented dryly that a tribunal "as inefficient [as this] will serve only to appease the conscience of the international community, since it will not meet the expectations of the Rwandan people."[1]

One year later, Rwanda's national coalition government collapsed. The key Hutu figures who were part of it (and who had placed some hope in the international tribunal) either left or were expelled from the government. The RPF—the war's only true victor—solidified its power. It deeply despised the

UN and was determined to pursue its own efforts to render justice. To this end, the RPF took action on two fronts. Within the country, tens of thousands of Rwandans suspected of having taken part in the genocide were thrown into prison. Out of a population of over 7 million, up to 140,000 people were imprisoned, according to the Red Cross. Outside its borders, Rwanda began locating the former leaders in exile and preparing international arrest warrants against them. Given the chance, it did not hesitate to resort to kidnapping, such as in the case of the former minister of justice who went missing in Zambia, where she had sought refuge, only to reappear in the Kigali central prison at the beginning of 1997.

Determined to act, and relying on its own investigations, the Rwandan government took new initiatives at the beginning of 1996. In March it asked Cameroon to arrest and extradite nineteen high-ranking dignitaries from the former regime. Twelve of them were arrested immediately. Among them was Colonel Théoneste Bagosora, the man described as the main mastermind behind the genocide. The arrests were a resounding success for the Rwandan government. However, the legal battle for extradition was far from being won. For political, legal, or humanitarian reasons, most countries were reluctant to extradite anyone to Rwanda, and many were openly opposed to it. Cameroon, therefore, was the first true test case.

However, no sooner had the arrests been made in Yaoundé than the ICTR prosecutor decided to exercise his rights. Richard Goldstone exerted the international tribunal's primacy over national courts. He informed the Cameroonian authorities that the suspects were all persons of interest to him. In the eyes of Kigali, which had initiated the arrests, this act was impertinent at best, and at worst, an outright insult. At the beginning of May, Goldstone formally indicted four of the twelve detainees in Cameroon, including Colonel Bagosora. They therefore managed to avoid extradition to Rwanda, which was bitterly angry and felt that the UN tribunal was merely reaping the fruits of its labor.

Froduald Karamira is considered to be the inventor of "Hutu Power." Behind this powerful slogan were the tenets of the ideology that had led to the extermination of Tutsis. This Rwandan politician single-handedly symbolized the rallying force behind this criminal operation and its pathology. Karamira was born a Tutsi before deciding to become a Hutu. He was one of the architects of the Rwandan democratic opposition that formed in 1990, before becoming a zealous ally of the most hard-core elements of the Habyarimana regime, which had been in place since 1973. His political path is an open window to Rwandan ambiguity, the tangled web of contradictions in which justice has been called upon to find the truth. In April 1994, at forty-six years old, Froduald Karamira did not hold a high-ranking position, but he played a pivotal, behind-the-scenes role in setting up the government that would lead the country during the genocide. As a key player in Rwandan politics in the 1990s, he was clearly one of the most wanted persons for the crimes that were committed in Rwanda. Up until June 4, 1996, the only great mystery about him was his whereabouts.

Richard Goldstone was flabbergasted when he learned of Karamira's arrest in the Ethiopian capital. Given Karamira's importance, Goldstone immediately seized the case. But this time the Rwandans felt he had gone too far. Unlike the case of the suspects in Cameroon, Rwanda had a real chance to secure Karamira's extradition this time, given that Ethiopia was a political ally. The strongman of the Rwandan judicial system, Gerald Gahima, was urgently dispatched to Addis Ababa to ensure that this suspect was handed over to his country. Before leaving, he told the press, "We are the ones spending our time and money to catch these people, but each time we obtain their arrest, the tribunal steps onto the scene to take them. It is unacceptable."[2]

The message was personally delivered to prosecutor Goldstone. "I got a huge protest from Kigali. Had I known that Karamira had been sent from India to Ethiopia at their instance, I wouldn't have sent a letter to Ethiopia without consulting them. I didn't know. It had been withheld from me. Had I known, it would have almost been a fraud on them to have gone behind their back and use their sleuthing work . . . especially immediately after the Bagosora incident, and grab Karamira," he told American researcher Victor Peskin a few years later.[3]

At the time, the prosecutor was not quite so transparent. He wrote to Belgian lawyer Johan Scheers (who had told him not to let Rwanda try Karamira) that, despite evidence to the contrary, he "had not been informed that any criminal proceedings had been initiated against Mr. Froduald Karamira before any of the national courts in question."[4] In reality, when he wrote this letter, on July 10, the ICTR prosecutor had already given in to pressure from the Rwandan government. On July 20 Karamira was back at the Addis Ababa airport. His layover in Ethiopia had lasted six weeks. His final destination would be Kigali, not Arusha.

By that time, barely a year since the tribunal's first investigators had set up shop in the Rwandan capital, relations between Rwanda and the ICTR were more strained than ever. The Office of the Prosecutor (OTP), based in Kigali for the purposes of its investigations, was particularly vulnerable. At the end of January 1996, three tribunal investigators were assaulted by soldiers. The Rwandan authorities declared the UN peacekeepers to be useless and unwanted. In March they were forced to leave the country. With their departure, the prosecutor's office lost the bulk of its security and logistical support. Extremist Hutus exiled in neighboring Zaire continued to wage guerilla warfare. According to estimates, more than two hundred genocide survivors were killed in attacks in 1996. Moreover, Tutsi survivor associations harshly criticized the exhumations of bodies by the tribunal's forensics experts. They protested vehemently in the capital. At the end of April the ICTR registrar announced that the OTP would not exhume any more mass graves. The atmosphere was highly charged following Goldstone's interference in the case of the suspects arrested in Cameroon, including Théoneste Bagosora.

"Once I put down my foot on Bagosora it made it even more difficult to insist on Karamira," explained Goldstone in 2003. "It would have clearly been another souring of the relationship. It would have been seen justifiably by [the Rwandans] as a breach of faith from somebody that they've learned to trust."[5]

According to some rumors, the Rwandan government was much more direct. Allegedly, it coldly told the prosecutor that if he insisted on the Karamira case, the security of ICTR personnel would no longer be guaranteed, and that, in short, the ICTR would have to pack up and leave. There has never been evidence of this threat being so clearly stated. Masters of intimidation, Rwandans do not always need to be so blunt. "We didn't even make threats. We had a tug of war. Justice Goldstone for some reason decided to defer to us. . . . I think he did it out of the spirit of cooperation because [we] have to work with each other. Any [one] knows that cooperation takes give and take," Gerald Gahima explained in a cryptic tone in 2002.[6] "Politically, I don't think I had any options," emphasized Goldstone. "It would have been the end of our relationship and the end of cooperation."[7]

Such are the ties that bind. The international tribunal could not operate without the cooperation of Rwandan authorities, particularly because it would not have access to witnesses in Rwanda. In the Karamira case, however, the Rwandans not only imposed a two-way cooperation with the UN tribunal, but they also limited the prosecutor's choices for his prosecution policy. Rwandans are experts when it comes to power relationships, and they knew that someone who has given in once will give in again.

Jean-Paul Akayesu's trial opened in Arusha on January 9, 1997, seven months after his initial appearance. It was the ICTR's first trial. Eager to prove that it was still one step ahead of the tribunal, Rwanda had begun its own trials two weeks earlier in Kigali. Then on January 14 it began the trial of Froduald Karamira—a much bigger fish than the *bourgmestre* on trial in Arusha. The Karamira trial was broadcast live on national radio. It did not take long. After a minor false start, a two-week postponement, three days of hearings, and two weeks of deliberations, the defendant was found guilty and sentenced to death.

During the six weeks in 1996 in which Karamira's fate hung in the balance in Addis Ababa, those who wanted to prevent his return to Rwanda at all costs tried to convince Goldstone that this key player could also be a key witness. "I thought this was more convincing to them than saying I think it is immoral to extradite someone to somewhere where he won't have a fair trial," explained Filip Reyntjens, a Belgian researcher and expert on Rwanda, who was among those trying to sway the ICTR prosecutor.[8] Karamira had long been a source of valuable information for Reyntjens. Among other information, Karamira had given him the names of some of the commanders of the Interahamwe, the Hutu militia group whose vice president, Georges Rutaganda, was also on trial in Arusha. One of the names Karamira disclosed was that of the infamous Colonel Bagosora, the ICTR's highest-ranking defendant.

After Karamira was convicted, investigators from the OTP went to see him in the Kigali prison. They attempted to convince him to testify against the other defendants in Arusha. Karamira imposed conditions, including a retrial before the ICTR. This was possible under the tribunal's rules. However, according to an investigator involved in the negotiation, this demand was "unacceptable" in the eyes of the Rwandan authorities.

In February 1998, one year after Karamira was sentenced to death, lawyers for Interahamwe leader Georges Rutaganda also sought to call Karamira as a witness. They wanted him to explain what he knew about how the militia leadership operated. The prosecutor objected. In March, judges Kama, Pillay, and Aspegren denied the motion filed by Rutaganda's lawyers, citing two arguments in support of their decision. On the one hand, the defense had not proven that Karamira was willing to testify. On the other hand, it had not been established that he had exhausted all avenues of appeal in Rwanda. Politically speaking, it was a comfortable argument. It enabled the ICTR to avoid confrontation with the Rwandan government. Legally speaking, and in terms of the quest for truth, it lacked both finesse and courage.

In reality, Froduald Karamira never showed the slightest hint of remorse. He always maintained an air of defiance before his judges in Rwanda. When his lawyer urged him to ask for forgiveness, he replied simply, "If my death can be a source of peace in Rwanda, I accept death." On April 24, 1998, he was shot to death along with twenty-one other convicts before tens of thousands of Rwandans who had gathered at the stadium in Nyamirambo, the Kigali neighborhood where Karamira had lived. These were the only court-ordered executions following the genocide.

2

The Eagle Eye

People were slipping brown-paper envelopes under my door alleging fraud and conspiracy. It was a mess.

Louise Arbour, prosecutor, in *The Lion, the Fox and the Eagle*

Richard Goldstone had to be replaced. After three years of dealing with all the start-up problems as the first prosecutor of the tribunals for the former Yugoslavia and Rwanda, he was stepping down. Names of candidates began to circulate. Among them was Louise Arbour, a forty-eight-year-old judge in Ottawa. Arbour was a discreet person totally unknown in advocacy and political circles. Consequently, everyone started digging up her past.

It was a disaster. In Canada, she had turned women's groups against her by declaring unconstitutional a law precluding use of a rape victim's sexual past as a means of defense. Worse still, after being appointed to the Ontario appeals court, she and a majority of her fellow judges upheld the acquittal of a Hungarian man accused of war crimes, solely on the grounds that this was not a prosecutable offense under Canadian law. To top it all off, Judge Arbour also granted prisoners the right to vote. This clearly worried representatives of the nongovernmental organization (NGO) community, which was rallying behind the UN tribunals. They felt it was urgent to sound the alarm. "A flurry of faxes to New York explained why Arbour was an enemy of human rights and unworthy of the position. American agencies reacted quickly with a campaign to stop the appointment. The Working Group on Human Rights of Women sent out a fax, asking anyone who cared to tell the powers that be to hold off on the Arbour appointment," recounted Canadian journalist Carol Off.[1]

Madeleine Albright was the new U.S. secretary of state but had been the U.S. ambassador to the UN back when the Rwandan tribunal was established. After she expressed concern about Arbour's candidacy, the Canadian ambassador to the UN arranged a private meeting between the two. The closed-door session lasted only fifteen minutes, but when she left, Arbour, a jurist who was more rigorous than rebellious, had the support of the world's leading power. "The complaints about Arbour kept coming in, but Albright was prepared to ignore them. In fact, it was precisely because Arbour had no history of activism that she was attractive to Albright. Arbour represented no cause. She might actually win unanimous approval by the Security Council."[2]

Louise Arbour took up her post as prosecutor on October 1, 1996. "But from the moment Arbour arrived, she suspected that the UN was not interested in war crimes trials at all. It was interested in the *appearance* of war crimes trials," wrote Off. "Louise Arbour went to Africa to take stock of what she had inherited in the fall of 1996. She was overwhelmed. She had thought her job was to investigate a travesty of war, but she found she had a travesty of bureaucracy."[3]

The OTP in Kigali lacked strategy, discipline, and coherence. In fact, the entire tribunal administration, the so-called Registry, was in serious crisis. New York assured Arbour that this was not going to last. Change came a few months later in the form of an investigative report by the UN Office of Internal Oversight Services. The report noted that "in the Tribunal's Registry not a single administrative area [finance, procurement, personnel, security and general services] functioned effectively," and concluded that "key administrators in the Registry and Office of the Prosecutor did not effectively fulfil their responsibilities."[4] In the euphemistic language of the UN, it read like satire.

On the basis of this report, the UN took measures that were extremely rare for this international organization: the registrar and the deputy prosecutor were both forced to resign. Kofi Annan had just been appointed UN secretary-general with the backing of the United States on the promise of reforming an institution drowning under the weight of bureaucratic waste and incompetence. Annan saw this as an opportunity to reassure those who had put him in charge of the administration that had produced him. For Arbour, meanwhile, it was an opportunity to reorganize her office.

The Rwandan government, for its part, did not wait for the report to be published before lambasting the tribunal. Gerald Gahima promptly stated, "It would be preferable to dissolve the ICTR completely and to use the money for rehabilitation programs such as aid for the widows and orphans in our country." Or else, he said, the tribunal should be transferred to Kigali and have its own prosecutor who was not shared with the ICTY. "The government would like to see Mrs. Louise Arbour dismissed from her duties, or if not, that she be placed in charge of the former Yugoslavia only," he concluded dryly.[5]

Arbour experienced some of her most difficult months. When she traveled to Rwanda, she was greeted by demonstrations of survivors demanding her resignation. The tension mounted when she failed to announce any new indictments, which could have calmed the situation. She weathered the storm, tried in vain to explain her approach, and continued working in utmost secrecy.

From the moment she arrived, Arbour had a very clear sense of her task: to prosecute a very limited number of individuals, those who bore the greatest responsibility for the genocide. In Arusha she decided not to drop any of the cases she had inherited from her predecessor, including some that involved relatively low-level players. But from that point on, she would focus on national-level authorities or on the highest-ranking leaders at the local level.

In May 1997 Bernard Muna, her new deputy from Cameroon, took over the reins at the Kigali office. At the end of May a strategic meeting of all the key players at the OTP was held in Dar es Salaam, the economic capital of Tanzania. On July 16, two minibuses filled with two dozen members of the prosecution team left Arusha for Kenya's capital, Nairobi, where they met up with Muna and his closest assistants. At dawn on July 18 this team of approximately thirty ICTR staff with the assistance of thirty-six Kenyan police officers launched Operation Naki (for "Nairobi-Kigali"). Up to that point, the UN tribunal had always seemed to show up late, reaping the rewards of others' work. This time, it wanted to strike hard and strike alone. In one morning, seven Rwandans were arrested in Kenya on its orders, and two others were arrested in the days and weeks that followed. Six people managed to slip through the tribunal's hands in this major dragnet, but among those arrested were Jean Kambanda, head of the government during the genocide, along with one minister, two high-ranking officers of the ex-Rwandan forces, and the most famous journalist from the extremist press. It was a resounding success. Ten months after her arrival, Louise Arbour—the "eagle," as Carol Off calls her—could savor the initial results of her secret work.

But was it really secret? Not to everyone. Two days before Operation Naki, the strongman of Rwanda's new government, General Paul Kagame, the former military leader of the Rwandan Patriotic Front who was now vice president and minister of defense, made a surprise visit to Nairobi. It was his first trip to this country since his troops' victory three years earlier. Bernard Muna dismissed this happenstance, saying, "It was pure coincidence." But coincidences were hardly this Rwandan strategist's style. One observer of these subtle comings and goings preferred to explain them with an Arab proverb: "If you go to my enemy, I'll be there first." Whether directly or indirectly, the

Rwandan government showed the ICTR that it was sticking to it like a leech — and that it was remarkably well informed about the tribunal's activities.

However, it also became clear in 1997 that there were limits to Rwanda's ability to act. Although Rwandan authorities had managed to forcibly secure the extradition of Froduald Karamira, they realized that they would not have the same success with the suspects they had had arrested in Cameroon in March 1996. Indeed, the court in Yaoundé denied Rwanda's extradition request on February 21, 1997. Those who were not snatched up by the ICTR were immediately released. The international tribunal could legitimately claim that without it, the former regime's most powerful leaders (all living in exile) would escape justice.

On a political level, the existence and efforts of the UN tribunal proved to be more effective than any other instrument. As soon as former Rwandan leaders in their precarious places of refuge started to feel the threat of prosecution before the ICTR, they disappeared from the political scene. This was not the fruit of a carefully thought-out strategy by the UN at the time of the tribunal's creation. Rather, it was the result of the subtle but powerful symbolic force of justice. By turning these men and women into potential suspects or worse, criminals on the run (even if only virtually so), the tribunal reduced them to silence, even in cases when it did not actually arrest them.

Beyond its duty to prosecute and try alleged perpetrators, the ICTR's heavy mandate included nothing less than the restoration of peace in the region. The burden was overwhelming. In this improbable context, however, there was one area where it quickly became clear that the tribunal could have an influential impact. Indirectly yet decisively, the tribunal was helping to eradicate the supporters of Hutu Power from the political scene and public space. Of course, the tribunal could not completely eliminate this ideology, but it did neutralize its spokespersons. In 1995 one of the most famous Hutu Power ideologists, Jean-Bosco Barayagwiza, wrote while living in exile in Cameroon (still believing he was safe at the time): "Sooner or later, all the protagonists in the ethnic-political conflict in Rwanda will be forced to have a dialogue."[6] Perhaps. But thanks in part to the tribunal, he would not be included.

By the end of 1997 Louise Arbour was starting to reap the first fruits of her labor. Although the UN had been declared financially bankrupt, its member states granted the ICTR a 40 percent budget increase. Arbour saw this as "a remarkable vote of confidence."[7] The tribunal had proven that it was capable of having high-profile suspects arrested. Established a year and a half after its counterpart in The Hague, disparaged for its disorganization, pitied as the "poor cousin" of international justice, the ICTR seemed to be making out all right. In the eyes of Arbour, the Rwanda tribunal's prospects were looking better than those of the tribunal for the former Yugoslavia. It was now up to the court to demonstrate its ability to try the suspects she was prosecuting.

This was Arbour's chief task. Having redefined the prosecution strategy, she turned her attention toward making it more legally cohesive. This project fully bore her mark and that of her closest collaborators. It represented a year's worth of work and articulated the theory that her office had established, that is, the Rwandan genocide was the result of a conspiracy and the trials of the alleged perpetrators should be based on this argument of a major, joint criminal enterprise. In 1945 the Allies initiated the process of bringing Nazi leaders to justice with a major trial of twenty-one leaders in Nuremberg, all accused of having plotted against peace. At the beginning of March 1998, after months of work, Louise Arbour presented a massive indictment that grouped twenty-eight defendants around one person, Théoneste Bagosora. This massive trial was her legal project, her vision for history. Three weeks later, her effort ended in a procedural impasse before the judge in charge of confirming the indictment. The court denied her request for a joint trial on legal as well as logistical grounds (many at the court were dreading the organization it would require). There would be no big trial. It was the greatest setback for this previously unknown prosecutor who had managed to give the position renewed luster. Arusha would be no Nuremberg—not in spirit, not in symbolic force, and certainly not in speed.

3

At the First Judgment

ASPEGREN: Is the natural tendency to obey or to oppose?
AKAYESU: To obey.

questioning of Jean-Paul Akayesu by Judge Lennart Aspegren,
March 13, 1998

Suddenly, in a matter of days, the judicial machine finally creaked into motion. Jean-Paul Akayesu's trial had started fourteen months earlier, and, as Judge Laïty Kama, president of the tribunal, had persuaded himself, "a trial is conducted in order to be concluded." Twenty-eight witnesses came to testify against the former *bourgmestre* of Taba, and twelve testified on behalf of the defense. There was no material evidence. Events in this small commune in central Rwanda from April to June 1994 were reconstructed solely on the basis of witness testimony.

There is nothing more abundant than human testimony. There is also nothing more fragile and more easily influenced. Thus, as this first case was coming to a close before the international tribunal, a legitimate doubt still remained about what really happened to Akayesu during those weeks of terror. It had been established that he was part of the moderate opposition to the Habyarimana regime. It had been established that in the two weeks following the beginning of the massacres on April 6, 1994, the *bourgmestre* had valiantly protected his district from the militia attacks with the help of only eight commune police officers.

Everything changed after April 18. On that day, the government organized a major meeting of all the local authorities (*bourgmestres* and *préfets*). Up till then, some regions had been spared from the massacres. But the day after this meeting, the genocide began to spread to the remaining pockets of the country where the local officials had been resisting. According to the prosecutor, Jean-Paul Akayesu did a complete about-face after attending the meeting, joined the killers' cause, and oversaw the genocide of his fellow Tutsi countrymen and women. The defense argued that following this fateful day, Interahamwe militias took power in Taba under the command of their local leader, Silas Kubwimana. From that point on, Akayesu was allegedly no more than a mere bystander, trying to save his own life and the lives of others whenever he could. How could he have done more with only eight police officers, argued his lawyer, when Roméo Dallaire, the Canadian general who commanded approximately 2,500 UN forces, had testified on the stand that even he had been incapable of fighting the "force of evil"?

Akayesu's moment of truth came on March 12–13, 1998. The former *bourgmestre* had asked to testify last in his trial, as did nearly all his fellow detainees after him. With virtually no direction from his lawyer, he had ample time to tell his story. His account was lively, dense, and rambling, as though he could no longer contain himself after two years of confinement in his cell. First, he spoke of the period from 1991 to 1993, when the multiparty system spread rapidly, exacerbating the crisis. He described the deteriorating and violent relations between the opposition parties and the presidential party. From a legal point of view, the testimony had no value. In terms of the political context at the time, it was enlightening.

Originally a school principal, Jean-Paul Akayesu became *bourgmestre* in April 1993—a post to which, he said, he had never aspired. One year later, on the morning of April 7, 1994, he learned that the president of the Rwandan Republic was dead. The evening before, Juvénal Habyarimana's airplane had been shot down by missiles upon its descent into Kigali. There were no survivors. The assassination of the head of state, a Hutu who had been in power for twenty-one years, was to be the event that triggered the genocide of the Tutsis. Starting at dawn the next day, the killings began in the capital, where numerous roadblocks were set up and manned by soldiers, militiamen, simple civilians, or a combination of the three. At these barriers, Tutsis were singled out based on identification cards or for the random crime of merely looking like a Tutsi and were summarily executed. "A roadblock is a small pile of stones in the middle of the road and a big pile of bodies on the side of the road," wrote André Sibomana, a well-known Rwandan human rights activist, in a glacial tone.[1]

"In such a situation, you have to see what needs to be done," testified Akayesu, whose commune was a half hour's drive west of the capital. "All the police officers were gathered at the commune office, waiting for instructions. I immediately wrote a letter to the commune counselors asking them to do absolutely everything in their power to ensure the safety of people and property. I asked that there not be any roadblocks. We knew what was happening at the road-blocks. We had to avoid them at all cost." Starting on April 8, a large number of refugees began pouring into Taba from Kigali and the surrounding com-munes where the killings had already begun. The situation was becoming dan-gerous, and the *bourgmestre* organized security patrols. When the first Intera-hamwe attacks occurred, people stood firm behind Akayesu and managed to drive them back. Several militiamen were killed, and six were placed in the commune jail. Akayesu tried unsuccessfully to meet with the *préfet* in order to obtain police reinforcements. "Normally, when an event like this occurs, the *bourgmestre* should receive instructions from the *préfet*. The *préfet* never wrote any letter instructing us what to do. The force of evil that we were fighting was growing increasingly stronger."

On April 18 Akayesu was summoned by radio to the meeting organized by the new interim government set up after the attack on the president. "We en-tered the room in a very formal manner. The prime minister was sitting at the front of the room. He asked each *bourgmestre* to report on the situation in his commune. I was the last one to speak. Rather than cut to the chase and discuss the security problems, we skirted around the issue. I requested three gen-darmes. Nothing more!" exclaimed Akayesu before the judges. In response, he continued, they gave him "the same old song and dance": the gendarmes were already busy at the front because fighting between the government forces and the RPF rebels had resumed as of April 7. "Nothing came of the meeting. It ended and we left," explained Akayesu.

"Was mention made of killing Tutsis?" asked his lawyer.

"No, no, no. Honestly, there was never any mention of killing Tutsis. Never."

"What happened after April 18?"

"I returned to Taba that evening. I was tired. I went to the commune office to rest in the corridor. That was not the first time [I had done so] because I was a wanted person at the time. Around four o'clock in the morning, someone knocked on the door and I opened it. It was the treasurer. He told me: 'There's a problem at my house.'"

A little later that same morning, Akayesu went to a neighbor-hood in his commune called Gishyeshye. Between one hundred and two hun-dred people were gathered there. "The Interahamwe started to shout. They were saying that the RPF-Inkotanyi [soldiers, primarily Tutsi, from the armed rebellion] had infiltrated," recounted Akayesu. His treasurer, who was married to a Tutsi and was being threatened, begged him to come search his home in order to convince the militias that he was innocent. "I took two Interahamwe with me. I searched. We did not find so much as a stick inside. No sign of a weapon. Nothing, nothing, nothing. The Interahamwe were not at all happy." Another Tutsi neighbor asked him to do the same thing. The *bourgmestre* explained that he had wanted to use these examples to calm the people down, but the Interahamwe spoke up. One of them brandished a list of names and titles.

"Read it!" he ordered the *bourgmestre*.

"No, I will not read it," replied Akayesu.

"Aha, you see! We told you that you were an RPF supporter. And now, we're telling you that there are RPF people here and you don't want to understand. Aren't these people on the list here RPF?" threatened the militiaman.

Akayesu stated that he then told the people that they had to "be wary of these types of documents."

He returned to the commune office, where the scene was already horrifying. "It was awful. The Interahamwe had come and had already started killing refugees, many of whom were women, children, and feeble men. They were killing just about everywhere. Who were they killing? Tutsis. I walked around a little. I said, 'Watch out! The gendarmes are going to be arriving.' The situation was becoming extremely dangerous, and I had been putting up a resistance for a long time. There was also my family [to think of]. I thought about giving it all up and running away."

In an uninterrupted flow of words, Jean-Paul Akayesu covered three weeks' worth of events in April 1994 in under an hour. He then recalled another event occurring at the beginning of May that many of the prosecution witnesses had reported. "I received a letter from the *préfet* telling me to hold meetings to keep the people calm. The letter also talked about self-defense and how to fight against the enemy," he continued. He said that he, Cyrille Ruvugama, a member of parliament from his district, and Silas Kubwimana, the head militiaman, had been chosen to hold these public meetings. The first meeting was held on May 5 or 6 near the commune office. "As *bourgmestre*, I called the meeting to order. I explained the *préfet* and the prime minister's decision and that we had to be in charge of civil self-defense and live with our neighbors in peace. Then it was Silas's turn. He set everything in motion. He said that when we talk about the enemy, we were talking about Tutsis and that we had to get rid of the enemy." The atmosphere in the courtroom grew tense, as if the room were starting to swell with the murmur of the survivors. Akayesu tried to explain his actions. "I was doing my job. I read the letter."

But he couldn't linger on this. He had so much to tell. On May 15 the government forces, which were retreating from the RPF advance, set up their command in the *bourgmestre*'s commune. It was clear that Akayesu still had respect for their commanding officer as he explained what life was like at the colonel's side. He retrieved entire conversations from his memory. "I had become like a child at home. I saw all the high-ranking officers come and go. I lived [with the colonel] on very friendly terms. There was also a major who was a first-rate man. I wasn't supposed to do anything to disappoint the colonel. One evening, he gave me a military jacket. Of course, there was Silas, who was causing a fury throughout the rest of the commune, but he could no longer venture over to the commune office." He explained that from that point on, he was armed with an FAL (Fusil Automatique Léger) rifle. He still had so much to say. He started talking nonstop again for an hour and fifteen minutes. During the rare moments of silence, Judge Kama seized the opportunity to interrupt the monologue.

"It has been said that you changed starting on April 19 . . ."

"I tell you and I swear it—to say that Akayesu changed on this date, is more than a sin."

"One witness was surprised you were not killed by the Interahamwe. What do you think of that?"

"Indeed, everyone was wondering the same thing. One can see that I almost was. It was clear that the colonel and the gendarmes helped me enormously and saved me. Silas tried to plot against the colonel. It did not work. I would not wish it upon anyone to have to live through these events. You have to look at the context. At what point in time should I have tried to make my escape? Up to April 18, the police and the people had been holding out. We had managed to defeat all the forces coming in from the outside. Anyone who resigned [his post] had to provide a reason. It was not at all a solution. I had to fight to the end, to do something. To resign and flee would not have resolved anything."

The day had been long, an effort to retrace a lifetime in a couple of hours. The court adjourned and would resume again the following day.

At thirty-six years old, Pierre-Richard Prosper was a young, ambitious, and effective prosecutor. Born to Haitian parents who had emigrated to the United States at the end of the 1950s, he was the ultimate embodiment of the American dream. Thanks to his Caribbean background, he had a working knowledge of French, which he used to his advantage at the officially bilingual tribunal. Above all, however, he was a successful product of U.S. law schools—confident, polished, and pragmatic. He was not as inspired as some of the great lawyers, but he was a good litigator—clear, concise, and meticulous. He joined the OTP in Kigali in May 1996, just before Jean-Paul Akayesu's initial appearance in Arusha. From then on, his job was to bring the charges against the former mayor of Taba. With only about ten years of professional experience, Prosper was not initially intended to play the leading role in this case. However, when Louise Arbour took over the prosecutor's office in October 1996 and discovered that chaos reigned yet the beginning of the trial was fast approaching, she quickly looked around to see whom she could count on. The senior trial attorney on the Akayesu case did not instill much confidence in her so she asked the young American prosecutor to take over. For Prosper, the Akayesu case was minor only in appearance. In his eyes, this case evoked nothing less than "human frailty, people across the lines, betrayal, and the history of Rwanda."[2] A year and a half later, on March 13, 1998, the day after Akayesu's flood of testimony, Prosper had just a few hours to flawlessly substantiate all his evidence, while trying to obtain the most devastating confession of all: an accidental one.

The confrontation was tense at first and looked as though it could get bogged down. Then the prosecutor and judges turned their cross-examination questions to the public meetings held in Taba at the beginning of May 1994 where Akayesu had read the government memo on civil defense. Judge Kama questioned the defendant:

"How many meetings were held where you read this letter aimed at establishing civil defense?"

"I believe I held six meetings."

"Let us take the context into account. The massacres were starting to become widespread. Tutsis were being killed because the Interahamwe were inventing lists and saying that they were passing information to the Inkotanyi. In such a context, don't you think that a speech about creating self-defense groups to fight the enemy would be likely to encourage the massacres?"

"I do not think so, given how the letter was written."

"I can see that you do not share this position, but in such a context, don't you think that this type of message resembles a call to action?" continued Judge Kama.

"I do not think so."

Prosper interjected, "You stand up and say, 'Fight the enemy.' Silas Kubwimana then stands up and says, 'Fight the enemy, the Tutsis.' In this situation, don't you think the people would conclude that they should fight the enemy, that is to say, the Tutsis?" he retorted.

"I was very clear with the text. I am sure that the people got my message. I am certain that the people who were there could not have cared less about Silas."

"You continued to run around with Silas, holding these meetings. You did not distance yourself from him, did you?" replied Prosper.

"I had to circulate the message. And this message was not at all bad. I am certain that people understood me a thousand times better than Silas."

"What was the order in which you, Silas, and Ruvugama spoke?"

"I opened the meeting on civil defense and pacification. I read the document, and I pleaded on behalf of certain people. Silas spoke next, then Ruvugama."

The prosecutor took advantage of his offensive position and shifted his line of questioning. He came back to the meeting in the Gishyeshye neighborhood on April 19, the day that Taba fell prey to the killings. That morning, several witnesses came to say that the *bourgmestre* had publicly read out a list of people who had been denounced as being enemy accomplices.

"Was it said that certain people were Inkotanyi accomplices and that they had to be flushed out?"

"No. We said that some families were housing RPF soldiers."

"Was there a list, names given?"

"No."

It was 4:05 p.m. For two days, Jean-Paul Akayesu had been defending himself alone before his judges, largely left to his own by his lawyers. Under the prosecutor's constant barrage of questions, tension had inexorably begun to fill the courtroom, as slowly and silently as sand in an hourglass. There was no other sound. Every word rang out in the courtroom and hung in the air, where it was scrutinized, pondered, contemplated, analyzed, and dissected before being accepted or rejected. In two hours, the trial would be over. Every sentence seemed to help shape and carve the verdict. The prosecutor would insist; the defendant would get ruffled, trying to correct his answers. And then everything started to fall apart.

"Go back to that. I will tell you who was on the list. No one read the names on the list. Only one name was given, that of Ephrem Karangwa. I didn't read it," said Akayesu, apparently becoming confused.

"Did you summarize it?" the prosecutor demanded.

"I used language that I can explain here. Since I had the list, I read it without raising my voice, do you see what I mean . . ."

Akayesu had tried to deny the existence of a list. He was now explaining that he read out several names before the people, including that of Ephrem Karangwa, a Tutsi detective with the criminal investigation department (IPJ) in Taba, who would later become *bourgmestre* after the genocide and who accused Akayesu of having ordered the murder of his three brothers.

"And what about Rukundukuvuga?" interjected the prosecutor, in reference to another victim.

"He was on the list, but I did not read it."

"Did the people read your mind?"

"I did not come with the list. Someone tossed it to me. I caught it in my hands." The defendant was evasive, in distress.

"Saying that they were RPF accomplices was tantamount to handing out a death sentence, was it not?"

Akayesu tried to dodge the question. Prosper repeated it.

"By saying they were RPF accomplices, that meant death, didn't it?"

"Of course," the defendant muttered.

Truth is a physical sensation. First, the body stiffens, paralyzed. There's a hot flash, anger, hatred, a desire for vengeance. Then a great sense of weariness sweeps through, providing relief in this strange, sobering moment, as though all feelings were dying away.

Prosper relaxed his grip on his prey, asked a series of questions about the commune office, then went for the jugular.

"There were intellectuals on the list, right?"

"Indeed, on the list there was the IPJ from Runda, Karangwa, Rukundu-kuvuga, and another teacher," Akayesu now admitted.

"What role did Silas Kubwimana play during this period?"

"He was in charge of all the killings. He was all-powerful. He was the commune *bourgmestre*."

"You never said that Kubwimana was all-powerful," snapped the prosecutor, referring to the interrogations of the defendant when he was arrested. "Is this a new defense? Or were you hand in glove with Silas?"

The defendant didn't say anything. Judge Pillay took over.

"You said that you distanced yourself from him. So when did you join forces with him?" she asked.

"It was at those meetings, starting May 5–7, but it did not last."

"And when was he in your home?"

"He was the one who came. And it was exactly at the beginning of May. The boss came by my house and told me, 'Come on, we're going to the office.'"

"In the English interpretation, I heard 'boss,'" interposed the South African judge, taken aback by the fact that Akayesu had called the militia leader his boss. "Did I hear correctly?"

"That's what I said."

"When did he become your boss?"

"I used that word to illustrate what he was doing. He was the boss [at that time]," replied the defendant, whose voice had faded to an almost imperceptible whisper.

"Wouldn't that have been the time to pack up your bags and go?" added Judge Kama.

"Yes, in a normal situation. But to resign, there would have been consequences . . ."

On September 2, 1998, the first genocide judgment ever rendered by an international tribunal was handed down. Jean-Paul Akayesu was found guilty of genocide, incitement to commit genocide, and crimes against humanity, including rape by virtue of being a superior responsible for the acts of his subordinates. International tribunals are often crippled by "precedents," "groundbreaking" definitions, and "decisive" steps. Nevertheless, these should have a permanent place in history, even if such precedents are rather big shoes for a small-time mayor of a small Rwandan commune to fill. The tribunal recognized that Akayesu did not hold a very high position within Rwanda's governmental hierarchy and that his influence and power over the outcome of the events in 1994 were in keeping with his rank at the time, in other words, minimal, even negligible. Moreover, the judges acknowledged that for nearly two weeks he tried to prevent the massacres in Taba and that the massacres would have started sooner had it not been for his efforts to stop them.

What exactly was punished by this first genocide ruling, awaited ever since the signing of the convention on the prevention of genocide in 1948? According to Prosper, the Akayesu case was "a story of betrayal," a story at the level of ordinary people. In fact, it was not so much a great criminal conspiracy set in motion through the actions of the former *bourgmestre* as the impromptu execution, so to speak, of a genocide legitimized by the interim government on the national level starting on April 18 and implemented in a disciplined manner by a local authority who clearly lacked criminal intent at the start. Did he do it out of fear? Cowardice? Excitement? Political ambition? Maybe a little bit of everything in a man who believed above all that "one had to follow the orders of one's superiors without question."

A month after he was convicted, during his final pleading before the court, which, in the words of Judge Kama was "from the heart," Akayesu spoke of his "compelling need" to ask forgiveness from the Rwandan people for not "having been able" to protect those he governed. He was sentenced to life in prison at the age of forty-five. In the streets of Arusha, his name had taken on a generic meaning. Whenever the convoy of UN vehicles transporting prisoners came through town with their flashing lights and sirens, people would say, "There goes an akayesu."

As for Prosper, he had a sense of mission accomplished. A week after the verdict, he went to the Taba commune office early in the morning so as to avoid any media coverage, which his superiors jealously denied him. He spent an hour and a half, one on one, explaining this three-hundred-page historic decision to Ephrem Karangwa, the survivor from the list that Akayesu had read in April 1994 who later became *bourgmestre* of Taba following the genocide. Prosper had been working at the tribunal for over two years, and he had already made plans to return to the United States immediately after the verdict. Basking in the glory of his legal success, he became the hero of human rights activists, made the front page of the *New York Times*, and received numerous invitations. Prior to leaving Arusha, he revealed in confidence his true aspiration: to go into politics and, ideally, to one day become a senator.

Still in an embryonic stage just four years earlier, international justice was already on the verge of becoming an enduring component of diplomacy. No one understood this better than the U.S. government. Washington had been the driving force behind the establishment of the UN tribunals for the former Yugoslavia and for Rwanda. In August 1997 the United States created the position of ambassador-at-large for war crimes issues and appointed David Scheffer to fill the post. The Clinton administration, whose moral authority had been tarnished after its nonintervention in Rwanda in 1994 and its belated engagement in Bosnia, wanted to set a new standard in the fight for human rights: the ability to prosecute perpetrators of mass crimes. In July 1998, 120 countries reached an agreement on the creation of the ICC designed to take over the role of the tribunals for Rwanda and the former Yugoslavia, which were deemed to be too ad hoc. Yet even though everyone looked to the United States to promote and strengthen the efforts to encourage this fledgling system of international justice, the United States was actually one of a handful of democratic nations that opposed the permanent court. The U.S. government took a critical view of the experiment with the two UN tribunals. In particular, it highlighted the profound disconnect between these courts and the societies for which they had been urgently created. The people in the former Yugoslavia or in Rwanda did not see much of the proceedings taking place five hundred miles away. The trials in Arusha were certainly not helping to develop even the slightest hint of rule of law in the land of a thousand hills. Given this glaring deficit, which lessons learned were being applied to the statutes and organization of the new ICC? At first glance, none. Thus, in short, the Democratic administration in the United States was advocating for a "renationalization" of international justice, so that societies affected by these crimes could take ownership in the international community's effort to promote and implement justice. The United States also had a second, less justifiable reason to oppose the ICC: it did not want its own citizens, soldiers, or leaders to run the risk of being brought before a supranational court. Thus, the United States, which had been a decisive and vital force in the emergence of international justice at the beginning of the 1990s, was one of only seven nations to oppose the Rome Statute, which established the ICC on July 17, 1998.[3]

Pierre-Richard Prosper harbored secret political ambitions but did not have a known party affiliation. So what? Or perhaps, so much the better. Upon his return to the United States, the elegant Haitian American lawyer became Ambassador Scheffer's deputy. Now the former young prosecutor from the Akayesu case, negotiating on behalf of the State Department from a position of power, was returning to Arusha to discuss one on one with his former bosses and judges the necessary reforms his government expected from the UN tribunal. Clearly in his prime, he was learning the ropes of judicial diplomacy and began to tackle the issues involving the former Yugoslavia, Cambodia, and Sierra Leone. He had spent two years training in the shadow of Ambassador Scheffer when, in December 2000, the U.S. Supreme Court installed George W. Bush in the White House, in a five to four vote.

While the outgoing administration had reservations about the ICC and how it was supposed to operate, the incoming administration was completely hostile to it. Just before leaving office, Bill Clinton signed the Rome Statute on behalf of his country, knowing full well that Congress would not ratify it. In an abrupt turnabout, Ambassador Scheffer hoped to be appointed as a judge at the tribunal for the former Yugoslavia, not showing much concern for the appearance of judicial independence in the process. His hopes were soon dashed, however. No sooner had the new administration taken office than it took his name off the list of candidates. Many thought that the fate of his entire staff at the State Department was a foregone conclusion. They would all have to go. However, the new U.S. secretary of state, Colin Powell, was in favor of keeping them on board, especially since he had discovered a man there, namely, Pierre-Richard Prosper, who was particularly well poised to take on the ambassador position now that he had revealed his affiliation with the Republican Party.

Six months later, in the pallid heat of July 2001, the former prosecutor-turned-discreet-servant of a Democrat administration was officially appointed ambassador-at-large for war crimes issues in a conservative government that claimed it was uninterested in the affairs of the world. Less than two months later, Al Qaeda terrorists attacked New York and Washington. The world was drastically changed and so was Prosper's job. Soon he would be deciding the fate of hundreds of prisoners taken by the U.S. army in Afghanistan. The former prosecutor was well versed in the Geneva Conventions, which had formed part of the basis of the charges against the mayor of Taba and his codefendants at the ICTR. Yet suddenly, they no longer applied, at least not to these "illegal enemy combatants," as his government had decided to label the approximately 650 men it confined at Guantanamo Bay, a portion of the Cuban island turned into a "no rights zone." Human rights organizations harshly criticized the illegal nature of these detentions, denouncing the numerous violations they involved and their radical departure from not only the principles of international law but also the fundamental rights enshrined in the U.S. Constitution. Even the International Committee of the Red Cross, which normally takes great care not to violate the neutrality its charter imposes, was disturbed. Prosper was now defending the government most openly hostile to the ICC and the democracy most heavily criticized for the liberties it was taking with the law. Like a faithful servant, he defended, justified, sometimes balked, but always endorsed the policy defined by his superiors. The Bush administration envisaged trying the Guantanamo detainees before military commissions. It would be a classic version of victor's justice for the former leaders of the Saddam Hussein regime. Henceforth, whenever the prosecutor-turned-diplomat made official trips to Arusha, his moral authority was reduced to that of a sponsor.

4

Lines of Defense

To defend the right of a defendant to a fair trial is to fight for an international justice that will not become the laughingstock of its critics the very next day.

Jean-Marie Biju-Duval, lawyer for Ferdinand Nahimana,
March 2004

Besides convicting the *bourgmestre* of Taba, the Akayesu judgment also removed a fundamental obstacle by providing clear and definitive legal recognition of the crime committed against the Tutsis in Rwanda. It constituted a judicial record of the 1994 genocide of the Rwandan Tutsis, giving the "crime of all crimes" against this segment of the Rwandan population the reality and binding force of *res judicata*.

This recognition was a crucial part of the ICTR's work, one of its raisons d'être. Prior to the September 1998 judgment, numerous reports, books, and articles had clearly defined the highly specific nature of the crime against the Tutsis in Rwanda. According to a large segment of international public opinion and the vast majority of UN member states, this was the third recognized genocide of the century, following the Armenian genocide in 1915 and the genocide of Jews and Gypsies at the beginning of the 1940s. The Akayesu judgment legally defined the crime of all crimes committed in Rwanda and gave it the universal value of a verdict rendered by an international tribunal. This is precisely what some had hoped to prevent.

Shortly after the ICTR issued its first indictments, a handful of lawyers met at a hotel in Nairobi at the beginning of July 1996. The meeting was organized by Luc de Temmerman, a Belgian lawyer who had been in charge of the affairs of part of Rwanda's presidential family since the beginning of the 1990s. He had an insider's connection with the former regime's elites who had been ousted and were now scattered to the four corners of Africa and Europe. For a year and a half, he had been making the rounds from Cameroon to Belgium gathering powers of attorney from former dignitaries likely to run into trouble with the UN tribunal for Rwanda. He had collected at least 150 duly signed powers of attorney placing him in charge of their defense should they face prosecution.

De Temmerman liked to flaunt a mix of obscure financial interests and fiendish political convictions. Intriguing and paradoxical, he claimed that he often paid for cases out of his own pocket but barely concealed the fact that he was actually making money. He zealously trumpeted the "Hutu cause" but quietly favored the classic, anti-immigration ideology near and dear to the European extreme right. However, there was one thing that he claimed unequivocally: loyalty to his friends and his commitments. Whether in Canada, France, or Côte d'Ivoire, he worked tirelessly to mobilize colleagues on behalf of his Rwandan clients, some of whom, such as militia leader Georges Rutaganda, were being prosecuted by the ICTR.

The goal of de Temmerman's meeting in Nairobi was to establish a defense strategy. He was marshalling the help of his colleagues not for the sake of the law but rather for a political fight. To him, the courtroom was just another forum to advance the "Hutu cause" and ensure that Rwandan history was written according to this view. And while he was the key driver in organizing the meeting in the summer of 1996, it was financed by a movement called Rassemblement pour le retour des réfugiés et de la démocratie au Rwanda (Party for the Return of Refugees and Democracy to Rwanda), a group that had become the primary vehicle for reorganizing the Hutu elites in exile. De Temmerman unveiled his strategic objective for a shared and dedicated defense (including plans to pay a substantial commission from the legal fees back to "the cause") to the handful of lawyers in attendance. The key goal of this joint defense approach was to negate the genocide of the Tutsis.

De Temmerman was not a specialist in criminal law, and he knew it. He was not interested in the details of case files, charges, and procedures. He was happy to delegate the day-to-day management of the trials to others. His role was to coordinate and supervise this common political defense. Just before the trials opened, he made sure that everyone was marching to the same beat. "Upon my formal appointment in the Akayesu case, de Temmerman cautioned me that I was not representing Akayesu, but 'the Hutu nation' and 'the cause.' I was instructed that a genocide had not occurred, that it was simply Tutsi propaganda; but if a genocide had taken place, the Tutsis were responsible for exterminating the Hutus—something that should be proved by exhuming the mass graves," recounted Michael Karnavas, the American lawyer who briefly represented Akayesu before quickly being dismissed after the tribunal learned that he had also applied for a position with the prosecutor's office.[1]

From the outset, this common defense strategy that de Temmerman was pushing set most of his colleagues on edge. First, lawyers normally are fiercely independent. Second, many of them were concerned above all about protecting the interests of their clients. To them, the "Hutu cause" was both foreign and devoid of interest. Finally, the harsh reality of the legal proceedings quickly set in. The defendants who now stood to lose their freedom before the tribunal were worried about the consequences of de Temmerman's approach. Georges Rutaganda's trial began in March 1997, with de Temmerman as his lawyer. Five months later, Rutaganda asked that de Temmerman be taken off the case and replaced by a young Canadian woman who had been plugging away every day in a more mundane manner, trying to counter the prosecution's evidence. Faithful to his promises, the Belgian lawyer stepped down. "The client wants a strategy that is all polite. For me, giving up is out of the question. But I understand that it is different for him. I am renouncing the fight, but whatever happens, my client runs the risk of this turning against him. I think that it is a mistake to continue in this way. It is impossible to determine the truth due to the defense's inability to verify what the prosecution witnesses are saying. For me, it's about putting an end to all the drama. It is a question not of delaying the trial but of delaying the injustices it promises. Right now, there is nothing objective about this justice. This has to stop. Taking a hard-line approach means filing a motion every ten minutes in order to prevent the prosecutor from continuing."[2]

With de Temmerman's departure, the hard line was ruled out for good. But a year later, after Akayesu was convicted, there was renewed support for the political approach that the Belgian lawyer had promoted. Inside the prison walls, the verdict had the effect of a cold shower. Akayesu immediately dismissed his lawyers and petitioned to have Canadian lawyer John Philpot defend him before the appeals chamber.

Philpot represented an ideological trend entirely different from that of de Temmerman, who, moreover, considered Philpot to be a "leftist" and an "opportunist," commenting: "The difference between him and me is that I do not contest the ICTR."[3] Philpot was among those who believed that the long-standing fight against U.S. imperialism had been transposed to Rwanda after 1994. Furthermore, he defined his approach as "anticolonialist." Several militants from this nebulous group, fed by the South American revolutions and largely dominated by Canadians, came to join the ranks of the defense in Arusha. According to them, the tribunal, in short, was the product of a U.S.

conspiracy to cover its crimes and those of its allies in Rwanda, namely, the RPF. According to Philpot, immunity "is reserved for the United States' powerful allies, while unjust punishment is the fate of oppressed peoples who rise up against Western-sponsored hegemony."[4]

Though they were from opposing political cultures, de Temmerman and Philpot nevertheless agreed on one point: denying the genocide. The Canadian lawyer did not learn of Rwanda's history until after 1994. But he was already presenting a general and definitive analysis of what had happened there. "The plane was brought down. Within two hours the RPF had been activated. People defended themselves. The population resisted. There was a total societal breakdown. It was a war for political power. Excesses were committed on all sides. The government did not know what to do. It tried to maintain some semblance of power. The theory that the government planned the genocide is illogical. The government was weak. It had no interest in shooting down the plane. There is no proof of a plan. The so-called genocide is an excuse to keep the RPF in power. There were mass killings on both sides. I do not think that the government committed crimes against humanity. But the RPF did. It is too easy to accept the genocide theory. Why did the United Nations and the United States withdraw? Because they wanted the RPF to take power."[5]

Thus, the revisionist theories and outright denial of the genocide never left Arusha altogether. In fact, beginning in 2002 some of the "expert witnesses" called by a few of the defense teams tried to revive them. However, these arguments never really resonated with the judges at the international tribunal.

There is hardly a more unpopular job than defending a person accused of genocide. Being the lawyer of a *genocidaire*, even if only presumed, inevitably means being suspected of supporting the *genocidaires* or being their moral accomplice. The persistence of tasteless, revisionist thinking promoted this unfortunate presumption, which permeated the ranks of the defense, even though de Temmerman and Philpot had long been considered the exceptions. But this was not the only factor that caused relations between the tribunal and the defense lawyers to be turbulent, distrustful, and, perhaps even worse, contemptuous.

The defense was blatantly ignored when the UN tribunal was created. The ICTR included a registry, judges, and an office of the prosecutor, but the tribunal's architects never considered the defense to be a full-fledged section of this judicial institution. The only thought given to the defense was limited to the standard proclamation of the need to ensure "a fair trial." To guarantee this, defense lawyers were, in short, a necessary evil. Jean-Marie Biju-Duval, a talented Parisian lawyer totally unfamiliar with the "Hutu cause," was one of the people de Temmerman invited to his infamous meeting in Nairobi in 1996. A solitary man who avoided the media, he was among those who quickly dismissed de Temmerman's plans for a political defense and discredited the negation rhetoric. However, by the time his client's trial opened in Arusha four years later, Biju-Duval had become highly suspect of the tribunal's impartiality. One day, upon leaving the courtroom, he declared with a half smile that his case was like a "Coubertin trial." Baron Pierre de Coubertin, he recalled, had defined the Olympic spirit as follows: "Participation is what matters."

The defense lawyers were never really part of the "family." In fact, the tribunal's behavior toward them was often condescending and petty. During their plenary meeting in June 1998, the judges were both quick and eager to stipulate that these troublemakers have a minimum of ten years of professional experience before being allowed to defend cases before the ICTR. They were very careful not to apply this same criterion to the prosecutors or themselves. For their part, the defense lawyers never grew tired of complaining about their fees, their office, or their photocopier. And yet in this environment of ingratitude and pusillanimity, it was the work of these lawyers that helped improve the quality of some of the trials, in certain cases giving them, if not dignity, at least a basic concern for seriousness. Often, it was their investigations that forced everyone to try to look beyond appearances and prejudices, with greater humility.

The defense lawyers at the ICTR would always be as heterogeneous as they were individual, exactly the opposite of what Luc de Temmerman had dreamed of. Up to the very end, there would always be a mix of those who were greedy and those who had integrity, the mediocre and the inspired, the nitpickers and the parsimonious, the pompous and the first-rate cross-examiners, the brilliant litigants and the boring, the fierce proponents of a Manichean and conspiratorial explanation of history and the thinkers intrigued by its tragic dimension.

The accusations or suspicions of trying to deny the genocide never vanished entirely. But eight years after the trials began, Biju-Duval had an even more unsettling concern: that paradoxically the greatest risk of trivializing the genocide would come from the mediocrity of the judgments, their lack of legal rigor, and their clear bias. Alison Des Forges, an American historian and human rights activist called to testify for the prosecution on numerous occasions, highlighted the crucial need for quality judgments. "The question of credibility is of enormous importance. Not just in the short term—how the accused feels about his condemnation or how his supporters accept it or reject it—but in the future. We know that there are people who deny the Holocaust and there are people who deny the Rwandan genocide. If the evidence has not been solid, if the trial has not seemed to be fair, a certain number of people will reject that conviction and will use it to prove that these trials represent victors' justice or even worse are part of a larger plot."[6] Following the end of his client's trial in 2004, Biju-Duval expressed a more general and persistent concern: that the failure to ensure fair, rigorous, and impartial trials could, in the end, "allow judicial methods and behaviors that to [him] seem contradictory to the rules of justice, to take root under the naive or cynical commendation of public opinion."[7] The six years that followed the Akayesu judgment demonstrated why his concern was well founded.

5

The Fool's Game

In pleading guilty, [Jean Kambanda] recognized and confirmed not only that there had indeed been a genocide in Rwanda in 1994, but that this crime had been organized and planned at the highest political and military levels.

Judge Laïty Kama, press conference,
May 20, 1999

Jean Kambanda was thirty-eight years old when a military escort showed up at his house in the Kacyiru neighborhood on April 8, 1994. Bodies already littered the streets of Kigali, and fighting was again raging between the government forces and the RPF rebels. His hour had come. The soldiers had come looking for him to head a so-called interim government. The Rwandan government was leaderless. President Habyarimana had been killed two days earlier when his plane was shot down by missile fire from unknown assailants. The following morning, the next two people in line to assume power pursuant to the law—the prime minister and the president of the Constitutional Court—were assassinated by members of the presidential guard, along with several ministers known for their opposition to the Hutu extremists.[1]

Kambanda was the director of the Union des banques populaires (Union of People's Banks) in Rwanda and an ambitious politician. He had aspired to become the head of government less than a year earlier. Now, for a hundred or so days, he would come to symbolize the Hutu extremists' rise to power. However, the sinister reputation he earned from leading the government that oversaw the genocide was somewhat misleading. Even in the eyes of those who criticized him for being an opportunistic and zealous servant of the ideology that led to the death of hundreds of thousands of Tutsis, Jean Kambanda never held any real power. This situation was relatively common in Rwanda, where job titles did not always correspond to the reality of power. Kambanda's main utility was that he gave this government concocted by extremist forces the appearance of representativeness (he was from the south, whereas the government had been in the hands of Hutus from the north for twenty-some years) and the illusion that the country was complying with the peace agreements that called for power sharing among the various parties (he was a member of the main opposition party). In short, Kambanda was a pawn, a willing puppet.

Three months later, the Rwandan armed forces collapsed, as did the interim government. Kambanda's position, remarkable but tenuous from the start, had just been dissolved. He was now the deposed prime minister of a banished and permanently disgraced government, living as a refugee in eastern Congo.

What to do? Right away, he thought he should conduct a survey among the refugee population to determine who they believed was behind the "Rwandan tragedy, both on the government side and the RPF side." He wanted to counter what he considered to be propaganda from the country's new leaders, who were trying "to make the whole world believe that in Rwanda there were Tutsi angels or victims represented by the RPF, on the one hand, and Hutu devils or executioners, on the other hand, and that the interim government that [he] led was the standard bearer of the latter." However, when the UN Security Council on November 8, 1994, created an international tribunal to prosecute the alleged perpetrators of the crimes in Rwanda, Jean Kambanda had no illusions: he would inevitably be among them.

He was already thinking ahead to his fate. In June 1995 he contacted Johan Scheers, a lawyer in Brussels who had been a regular visitor to Rwanda since the beginning of the 1990s and was well known among Rwandan elites. He asked Scheers to defend him before the ICTR. He also contemplated filing a suit against the RPF with the tribunal. Above all, he began reflecting personally on what had happened in his country the year before. In February 1996 he even considered addressing the tribunal directly. But, he wrote, the concerns of his entourage, his living conditions, and death threats dissuaded him from doing so. Armed tension at the Rwandan-Congolese border was mounting. In August 1996 Kambanda fled to Kenya like many other leaders of the former regime.

In April 1997 he was living in a converted garage that he rented in a Nairobi suburb. As he continued to write his testimony, he was alerted on at least two occasions that the tribunal was preparing a wave of arrests and that he was to be one of the prime targets. In order to escape, he would have to leave Kenya before the end of June. But after three years of living in exile and secrecy, he wanted to explain himself. He decided not to flee. At dawn on July

18, 1997, he was arrested and immediately transferred to the UN detention facility in Arusha.

Kambanda still enjoyed special treatment. While the other suspects arrested that same day were transported over land, the ex–prime minister was taken by plane. Needless to say, this had nothing to do with his former position. In reality, the prosecution team already knew that they had mutual interests with the former Rwandan leader and that they therefore needed to have some time together with him, alone. At 12:20 p.m., the plane landed at the Arusha airport, located right next to the international prison. As soon as the famous prisoner descended the four steps of the single-engine plane, he was immediately escorted to a vehicle with tinted windows that then sped off in the opposite direction of the detention facility. The operation had been carried out quickly and efficiently. However, rumors had begun to spread even more rapidly. In the halls of the tribunal, word was already out that Kambanda allegedly would be brought to testify in other trials. He was oddly referred to as the "defendant-witness."

For nine long months, from August 1997 to April 1998, Jean Kambanda spent most of his time at a secret location—a huge house in Dodoma, approximately three hundred miles south of Arusha. One of the two Canadian investigators in charge of guarding the prestigious prisoner and who conducted his interrogation referred to the house as the "Royal Palace." The place was indeed quite comfortable. Kambanda now had several code names: "Tango 2" over the radio network, or the more offensive "Kitu," which means "the thing" in Swahili. He was keenly aware of how much attention he was receiving from the prosecutor's office. He was a somewhat fussy man who had a high opinion of himself, and he shamelessly described the three short weeks he spent at the Arusha detention facility in August as being torture.

In exchange for his cooperation, the former prime minister demanded three guarantees: to be able to have Scheers defend him as soon as he so requested, to obtain protection for his family, and to have the tribunal's support in "exposing the various parties to blame for the Rwandan drama," that is, the RPF in particular, according to him. Prosecutor Louise Arbour and her deputy, Bernard Muna, gave him their word, but on one firm condition: before talking about the others, the accused first had to acknowledge his and his government's responsibility in the genocide.

Week after week, interview after interview was held, and eighty-nine hours of testimony were recorded. But months went by and Jean Kambanda still had not appeared before the judges to answer to the charges against him. Amnesty International started to express concern. It was time for the international tribunal to start paying a little more attention to form. Kambanda should have been brought before a judge shortly after being indicted (within two or three days). He had been officially indicted three months after his arrest, and several weeks had already passed since then. The tribunal was gradually beginning to acquire bad habits, which would later be costly. For the time being, the top priority was finding a lawyer to represent the Dodoma recluse. On March 5, 1998, the tribunal registry informed Kambanda that it would appoint a lawyer to defend him. Naturally, he asked for Johan Scheers. The tribunal denied his request on the pretext that the Brussels-based lawyer had allegedly been the subject of disciplinary sanctions by the ICTR back when he was defending Jean-Paul Akayesu. This was not true, and it was perhaps at this point that a downward spiral began. Two years later, it would turn what was meant to be one of the ICTR's major accomplishments for justice and for history into a fiasco.

The confession of Rwanda's former prime minister promised to be the tribunal's moment of glory. No one could resist taking credit for part of this success. The thirst for power was whetted, and egos were revived. The registrar jealously guarded his powers. He held the purse strings, and he was the one in charge of appointing lawyers. The tribunal's spineless and oversensitive administration (the UN is a kingdom for petty tyrants and the obsequious) wanted to keep at bay anyone it considered to be an unruly killjoy. So did Judge Kama, who was outraged at the letter Scheers wrote saying that he felt his legitimacy as a defense lawyer had already been established. Were they worried that Scheers was going to rain on their parade? He did not seem to be someone who was easy to manage. Straightaway he indicated his intent to challenge the legality of the proceedings in this case. That threatened to spoil the party. The prosecutor's office informed Kambanda that he could either accept or refuse the dismissal of his lawyer. But if he refused, the deal with the prosecution would be off. There was considerable pressure on this man who was totally isolated and trapped in a process on which the rest of his life was riding.

Fortunately, deputy prosecutor Bernard Muna had a solution. And that solution was named Oliver Michael Inglis. A native of Saint Lucia, Inglis was the legal advisor to Muna's father, who among other things had been the president of Cameroon's National Assembly for almost twenty years. "Bernard," as Inglis called him, could always count on this longtime family friend. The timing was convenient because time was running out to resolve the problem caused by the refusal to allow Scheers to defend the case. Kambanda was asked to accept Inglis as his lawyer. It did not matter that he was a personal friend of the prosecutor, or that he did not speak a word of French, or that he knew nothing about the case. "Bernard" would be there to help him. Kambanda did not budge. Still, on April 9, 1998, Inglis showed up in Dodoma.

The tribunal offices smelled of fresh paint and new carpet. A long line of furniture was piling up in the hallways and the canteen. In four days, UN secretary-general Kofi Annan would honor the ICTR with a visit. Everyone had to look his best, even if it meant giving into the temptation to put up a facade. An annoyed Judge Aspegren refused to be part of this charade. He would not accept his new furniture until after he had shown the head of the UN his "real" office. However, everyone made sure to show up looking dignified for the hearing on May 1 at least. This long-awaited day of Kambanda's initial appearance before the judges was a rainy one, accentuating the gray of the Arusha conference center that housed the ICTR. It was International Workers' Day. In Rwanda in 1994, "to work" was a euphemism that meant "to massacre." It was as if this double meaning was a sign of the confession to come. The public gallery was packed. Camera flashes rippled throughout the room. All the tribunal's top brass were there. In an extremely rare showing, the registrar himself read out the indictment, an excruciating twenty-five minutes that left the defendant stony faced. If, as French journalist Albert Londres once wrote, "one must look into a person's eyes to see the mood of his soul," Jean Kambanda's eyes were impenetrable. Dressed in a dark suit with his eyes hidden behind a large pair of glasses with outmoded frames, he looked calm and focused.

"I will now ask you to plead guilty or not guilty on each count, with the understanding that if you do not enter a plea, you will be considered to have pleaded not guilty," Judge Kama informed Kambanda. The first count was genocide. "On this first count, do you plead guilty or not guilty, Mr. Kambanda?" There was a brief silence. "I plead guilty, Mr. President," announced the accused. The courtroom froze, as though in a state of weightlessness. Six times, in an increasingly blank voice, the former leader uttered these words, muffled and fleeting like a landslide. Then, three times Judge Kama put him to the test.

"You are pleading guilty. The tribunal would like to know if your guilty plea was voluntary. Did you do so freely? Was there any pressure or were there any threats or promises to make you enter this plea?"

"Mr. President, in deciding to plead guilty, I did so knowingly and voluntarily. No one forced me to do it."

"The tribunal would like to clarify one more point. Do you fully understand the nature of the charges against you and do you fully understand the consequences of your guilty plea?"

"Mr. President, I understand the nature of the charges against me and I know the consequences."

"Is your plea unequivocal? Are you aware that consequently, you may not put forward any other defense to contradict [it]? Are you aware of that?"

"My guilty plea is unequivocal, Mr. President. I am aware of that."

After the court had officially declared him guilty of genocide, Kambanda stood motionless for an instant, then resolutely strode out of the courtroom without looking at anyone. That same evening, he was flown to a prison in The Hague, the lone and still-silent witness to a "tragicomic situation" in which, as he later wrote, "officials from the Registry and the office of the prosecutor fought over who would get to 'supervise' me during the transfer to the Netherlands." Four months passed before Kitu, the thing, returned to face his judges, who now had to determine his sentence. It would also be the opportunity, officials insisted, for this repentant accused to give his big public explanation.

Oliver Michael Inglis had changed his lawyer's robe. The one he had worn on May 1 was in tatters. He chose one for the day of the sentencing, September 3, that made him look a little more dignified. He portrayed his client as a man who was merely a pawn of history, now haunted by remorse. But Judge Pillay wanted to know more. What was this "manifesto for peace and reconciliation" that the accused had written and that Inglis had referred to in his written brief? What was the former prime minister's sense of reconciliation in his country and the role that he could play in it? The South African judge was hoping to get some answers. At a minimum, she was expecting an explanation. There was nothing from Inglis, who appalled the court by seeking a two-year sentence, and nothing from the accused either. At 11:10 a.m. the next day, Jean Kambanda's fate was sealed. He was sentenced to life in prison. The judges unanimously noted that the defendant had not explained his voluntary participation in the genocide, shown any remorse, or expressed any regrets or compassion for the victims. After the hearing was over, Inglis said his client was in a state of shock and felt as though he had been "betrayed." One week later, Inglis was dismissed.

The right to remain silent is a fundamental principle in protecting the rights of the accused. Those who would later follow the former prime minister in the path to confession would come to understand that on the contrary, a confession, even when used as a tactic, is accompanied by the duty to speak out. Jean Kambanda *should have* spoken up during this missed opportunity. So why did he choose to remain silent?

The fool's game in this case was, quite simply, dissembled. Before his confession in April, Kambanda had yielded to the decision to dismiss his Belgian lawyer, Johan Scheers. Bernard Muna had advised him to prepare a document intended for the public, explaining his position. With disturbing honesty, the "penitent" Kambanda thus wrote his first manifesto, "The Truth of the Rwandan Tragedy." However, it primarily consisted in clarifying the truth of others: the army; the Hutus from the north; the president's party, the MRND; the RPF rebellion; the UN mission; the Belgians; the Arusha Peace Agreement; and the international community. Cloaked in his identity as a Hutu and a man of the south, Kambanda essentially saw history through the lens of the two destructive splits in Rwandan politics: the ethnic divide between Hutus and Tutsis, and the regional antagonism between the north and the central-southern part of the country. He clearly had no idea just how deep was the abyss that he had irretrievably fallen into in April 1994. He assumed no criminal responsibility, only "political" responsibility.

Muna found the document unacceptable. However, the thought of limiting the prosecution's success with the former head of government's imminent public confession was just as unacceptable. Therefore, he promised Kambanda that his written statement would be sent confidentially to the judges only. Two years later, the prosecution office discreetly admitted that the document was never forwarded. This begged the question, as one of Kambanda's ardent defenders asked, of whether the text was concealed from the judges "because it contradicted the confession and made it equivocal."[2]

Kambanda's speech, the one everyone had been expecting to hear in 1998, did exist. It was a thirty-six-page document divided into twelve chapters, titled *Le Manifeste de la vérité sur "l'apocalypse" au Rwanda en 1994* (Manifesto of the Truth about the "Apocalypse" in Rwanda in 1994). Recognition of the Tutsi genocide—the central issue in the historic confession on May 1, 1998—was indeed there. However, it was muddled in the guarded and cautious language surrounding it. "Some Hutus armed with army rifles, grenades, or traditional weapons such as clubs, machetes, spears, bows and arrows, swords, and other sticks attacked the homes of Tutsis and chased them out of their places of refuge at commune and prefecture offices, schools, churches, and stadiums in order to exterminate them. I confirm that the objective was to exterminate them, insofar as they were killing men, women, and children indiscriminately. If the international community feels that, legally speaking, the acts I just described constitute genocide, then there was a genocide of the Tutsis during the period from April to July 1994, when I was prime minister," wrote Kambanda. His acknowledgment that Hutu opponents were killed followed the same vague reasoning: "If the international community feels that, legally speaking, . . . then . . ."

Kambanda was especially eager to condemn the RPF army, which "massacred hundreds of thousands of Hutu civilians." In the dialectic of Rwandan politics, arithmetic and semantics go hand in hand. Depending on which figures people use to estimate the number of deaths, they end up taking an ideological position, sometimes without even realizing it. The 1990s defied the possibilities for calculation so much so that the math seemed to transcend the realm of reason. The elites, with help and inspiration from abroad, enthusiastically joined in this national jousting match, which consisted in comparing the number of victims and trying to outdo the other side at best, or at worst, ending up agreeing that it was a zero-sum game. How many Hutus died? How many Tutsis died? How many in Rwanda? How many in Congo? Killed by whom? For what reason? No one knew, or no longer knew, and the dizzying array of figures, which had become meaningless by virtue of their sheer enormity, allowed for all manner of exaggeration, confusion, and alteration. "Algebra is like a thinking machine," said French philosopher Alain. "You turn the crank and you effortlessly obtain a result that would otherwise require infinite effort if obtained by process of thought." Jean Kambanda was turning the crank by the hundreds of thousands.

From his vague and general accusations, the idea finally emerged that everyone was just as guilty and that in any case, he was less guilty than many others. It should be understood, Kambanda explained, that it was simply a matter of "the eternal struggle for power between the Hutus and Tutsis in Rwanda." He did, nevertheless, remember that this speech was supposed to support his guilty plea and did admit to having some responsibility. He acknowledged that his government's orders did not give the *préfets* the authority to remove the roadblocks that the militias had set up everywhere in order to identify, rob, and murder Tutsis. He admitted that by institutionalizing the civil defense program, his government actually strengthened the militia tenfold. He also acknowledged that by replacing the *préfets*, *sous-préfets*, and *bourgmestres* who had been trying to resist the killers on April 18—the infamous day after which Jean-Paul Akayesu stopped protecting the people in his commune and joined forces with the militia—his government enabled the spread of the massacres to the regions of the country that had been spared up till then.

However, this claim of responsibility was timorous, confused, and extremely involuntary, to say the least. "When the people realized that these groups [of killers] were acting with complete impunity, even with open support from local authorities in some cases, they concluded that these acts of killing were supported from above, as they said at the time," Kambanda explained. And since no one showed "any real desire to give orders to stop these massacres, the population's premonition was confirmed and the spread of the massacres became inevitable."

Thus, Kambanda's confession was in no way an act of humility. In his speech that was never read, the former leader still passes himself off as a political thinker. He sees himself as being not on the stand but rather on the grandstand, contemplating the future of Rwanda in a doctoral sort of way. It is difficult to imagine what feelings this keynote speech would have provoked if it had been delivered before the court. He came close to imagining himself involved in new negotiations with yesterday's enemy, under the aegis of the international community, of course. It did not even seem incongruous to him to describe in detail what the agenda of such negotiations would have been. For after all, "the understandable grief of the Tutsi genocide survivors would not be appeased at any rate by blindly imprisoning Hutus en masse, confusing criminals with innocent people, solely for the purpose of clearing one's conscience." He did not realize that he himself had become a convicted criminal.

Kambanda viewed recognition of the genocide as merely a necessary step to placing himself on the new, post-1994 political scene, failing to see that he had been forever banned from it. In fact, he himself had called this acknowledgment "the only guarantee to put an end to all suspicion between the two ethnic groups." A simple guarantee for a simple suspicion—one would like to think the problem was his lack of mastery of the French language. But the linguistic malaise only became worse. "The Hutus," who, four years after the genocide, were still waging a bloody guerilla war from neighboring Congo, "must understand that there is no glory in attacking genocide survivors, women, children, and the elderly, that such acts will only meet with reprobation from the rest of the world, and that in the end, this is not the most appropriate path to a lasting solution to the Rwandan conflict." "Glory," "reprobation," and "appropriate" path—such was the dubious vocabulary of repentance. Why then, and on what basis, did this man decide to plead guilty? "Solely for the political responsibility of the interim government I headed, and [I] loudly and clearly proclaim my innocence as an individual, who, on the contrary, did everything possible, despite being powerless, as everyone knew, to spare his people from the worst."

Kambanda was certain that he had a defensible case. Thus, after being sentenced to life in prison, he sought to have the appeals court invalidate the entire trial before the lower court. In a 120-page document, he finally said what he really thought about the crimes for which he had been tried. There were no surprises. He had merely been a "scapegoat for a tragic situation over which [he had] absolutely no control, as such." No control over the civil defense forces who manned the roadblocks. No control over the distribution of arms. No control over his own government. "My objective must be clearly understood. It is a matter of putting 'the church back in the middle of the village' so that everyone who was directly or indirectly involved in this apocalypse, whether Rwandan or non-Rwandan, can assume his or her own responsibility." Two years after his "confession," Jean Kambanda was now systematically denying all the specific crimes to which he had nevertheless pled guilty.

This was the true sense of Kambanda's reasoning, never expressed publicly, but silently recorded in the judicial archives. The misunderstanding was huge and burdensome, but it was useful for some. Indeed, the former prime minister's confession still serves as a trophy for the UN tribunal. For a long time, it also featured prominently in the prosecution strategy in many of the cases, especially those against the other political leaders and members of government tried in Arusha.

Convicted once and for all, totally alienated from the prosecutor's office, Kambanda lost his place at the modern prison in The Hague. In December 2001 he found himself in a prison in Bamako, Mali. With temperatures of 104 degrees Fahrenheit by day and 91 degrees in the coolest part of the night, and his wife and children living as refugees in the United States, he was nearing rock bottom. "For people from the mountains, Bamako is like an oven, death over a slow fire," pointed out one of his Belgian friends, Alain de Brouwer.[3] Thus, in the fall of 2002, when the prosecution, worried about how solid its evidence was in the upcoming trials, recontacted the secluded desert prisoner, it was first and foremost a chance for Kambanda to get out of this hole. After eleven months of incarceration in the Sahel, he found himself back in the Netherlands, in the Scheveningen prison. Negotiations resumed, this time in the presence of the lawyer of his choice, Johan Scheers. But they never amounted to anything. At the end of June 2003 he was returned to Mali without another word.

In the days after Kambanda was sentenced to life in prison in 1998, the few members of the prosecution team who had worked directly on the case readily admitted their discomfort with the way the case had been handled. Off-the-record conversations revealed a mixture of embarrassment, shame, anger, and sarcasm, not to mention deep, moral vexation after reading the documents that Kambanda had written while in detention.

"Although you are guilty, you have just given me a reason to extend my hand to you. I will never forget your gesture and I promise you that I will do everything in my power to help you appease your conscience, starting by showing my gratitude here," wrote Yolande Mukagasana in a letter she sent to the former head of the interim government—a man whom she had "every reason to hate to the end of [her] days"—following his confession on May 1, 1998. This genocide survivor, who had lost her husband, three children, and a large part of her family, was not the only one who had felt a big breath of hope that day. But it was a fool's game.

Kambanda called his case "obscure" and emphasized the real turpitudes in it. However, his explanations force us to ask ourselves an entirely different question: was his "confession" really a confession? Those who had hoped to see it as a great moment of remorse and a form of moral redemption might just as well have spared themselves the trouble. Had the trial been "deliberately rigged from the start," as Kambanda claimed? Most likely not. But almost nothing remains of the promise of this trial and of that which prompted Yolande Mukagasana and others to write with hope to the most famous "repentant" criminal in the history of international justice. Jean Kambanda's statement to the investigators was never made public. His recognition of the crimes was, at a minimum, severely weakened by his ambiguity and, at worst, erased by his failed attempt to revoke it. By saving itself from having to hold a trial, thanks to the deal struck by the prosecutor and the accused, the tribunal also created an illusion of justice. In no longer serving the interest of truth, it allowed the interests of the institution to dominate. And yet, whether it was naïve or not, the expectations and hope surrounding Kambanda's confession had been based on this contribution to truth. As Canadian law professor William Schabas put it, the confession was supposed to be "another nail in the coffin of revisionists and those who deny the existence of genocide."[4] More likely than not, for both Kambanda and the tribunal's senior officials, it will continue to be a silent illustration of the vanity of men.

The Fool's Game

6

Counting Up
the Interahamwe

The Interahamwe were innumerable, like sand on the beach.
witness W., Kayishema/Ruzindana trial,
October 6, 1997

Jean Kambanda's intuition was not always wrong. He was not mistaken, for example, about the role that a certain Dieudonné Niyitegeka played in the July 1997 roundup that led to the arrest of the former prime minister and several other Rwandan leaders in Kenya. Indeed, this man, he wrote, "purportedly served as an informant to identify the homes of the various people arrested during this operation. Then the same office of the prosecutor allegedly concealed his escape to West Africa and later, his immigration to Canada."

It is entirely normal for a prosecutor to infiltrate the milieus he is investigating. The names of those who served as informants to the OTP were an open secret in the suburbs of Nairobi, where the Rwandan exile community was concentrated and where the spectacular arrests of 1997 had occurred. However, it was the not-so-ordinary identity of these informants that really raised Kambanda's hackles. "Rather than bring these people before the tribunal to account for themselves, this office [of the prosecutor] uses people like Dieudonné Niyitegeka, the official treasurer of the Interahamwe, an organization that the whole world accuses of being the main perpetrator of the massacres and the genocide in Rwanda, to track down Hutu political leaders and soldiers," protested Kambanda.

One name will forever be identified with the violence and genocidal terror in Rwanda: Interahamwe. Pointless debates still continue as to the exact translation of this Kinyarwandan term: "those who advance together," "those who attack together," or "those who have a common goal." More relevant quarrels persist over the evolution of this youth wing of President Habyarimana's party created in November 1991 as it progressively morphed into a militia and ended up spearheading the genocide in April 1994. From that point onward, "all militias and anyone who manned the roadblocks were called Interahamwe," as Belgian expert witness Filip Reyntjens explained on the witness stand. Shortly after the ICTR got under way, there was no doubt that the leaders of the Interahamwe were, in principle, one of the prosecution's priority targets. Yet in most cases, they wound up being its best helpers.

In April 1994 the Interahamwe's national committee comprised five people: Robert Kajuga, president; Phénéas Ruhumuliza, first vice president; Georges Rutaganda, second vice president; Dieudonné Niyitegeka, treasurer; and Eugène Mbarushimana, general secretary. In addition to this core group were six subcommittee chairmen, including Ephrem Nkezabera and Joseph Serugendo.

When the ICTR investigators began their work, it had already been established that Kajuga was dead. Georges Rutaganda quickly became the subject of a targeted investigation into the crimes committed in Rwanda's capital. He was known to be living in Zambia. An indictment was issued against him in February 1996. Three months later, he was one of the first accused to be transferred to Arusha. As for the others? For ten years, there was no news—nothing that was public at any rate.

In taking the reins of a prosecutor's office that was deeply confused about its strategies, Louise Arbour immediately understood that in order to investigate this type of crime, she had to infiltrate the group's core and persuade some of the perpetrators to "flip." Just as Italian anti-Mafia judges used the testimony of a few *pentiti* to convict the Cosa Nostra godfathers, the prosecution team felt that the only way to obtain solid evidence of the genocide conspiracy was through a few perpetrators-turned-informants. Those who wound up playing this role with great enthusiasm and a clear interest were the Interahamwe leaders.

In November 1996 the Rwandan government published an initial list of two thousand main genocide suspects. This list contained errors and had been seriously manipulated. It was highly controversial. However, no one was surprised to find the names of the six members of the Interahamwe's national leadership. Two of them, Dieudonné Niyitegeka and Phénéas Ruhumuliza, were already refugees in Kenya by then. Now that they had become suspects on the run, they turned informant for the international tribunal's OTP. Niyitegeka was the kingpin of this network of informants.[1] The former treasurer of the reviled Interahamwe was now its chief "snitch." He helped place a few other ex-militiamen into the paid service of the UN tribunal, and he himself cost some thirty thousand dollars, according to the prosecutor's office. The major accomplishment of these converted ex-militias was Operation Naki, the much-vaunted wave of arrests in Kenya in July 1997. This was the ICTR's first resounding success, and it helped put the tribunal back in the saddle after being destabilized six months earlier by the conclusions of the UN internal oversight report condemning its serious operational problems.

Following this masterstroke operation, it was time to "exfiltrate" those who had made it possible. The group of informers ended up in West Africa, except Dieudonné Niyitegeka, who received special treatment. He was given refuge in Canada, where he lived under the protection of Canadian police, pursuant to an agreement obtained by Louise Arbour.

He denied any involvement in the genocide, and the prosecution investigators believed he was telling the truth. They said they did not find any evidence linking him to the massacres. Anything is possible: in the Rwanda of 1994, appearances could not be trusted, even when they overwhelmingly went against someone as in Niyitegeka's case. Moreover, no one seemed to care about his whereabouts, and the investigators with the prosecutor's office were content to go along with the secret cooperation, obviously a necessary criterion for an effective informer. Hidden away in the shadows, the former treasurer fulfilled his role of discreetly helping to convict others. Twenty-six hours of interviews were recorded, in which he talked about the 1990s, when he knew so many key players. These confidential transcripts are housed at the tribunal's registry. Niyitegeka had every reason to be happy with his lot. While his friend Phénéas Ruhumuliza died of a disease in Côte d'Ivoire, he was able to make himself forgotten and to obtain special protection from the tribunal. International justice was grateful to him for what his collaboration helped accomplish. How could it not be? He could now hope to live a tranquil life. Granted, it would be far from the land of a thousand hills and under a new identity, but he would have one substantial privilege: freedom.

The years went by. At the beginning of 2001, the ICTR had just begun a major trial of three of Rwanda's top media personalities, and it was in a rare state of chaos. With unreliable witnesses, messed-up sound archives, and an inept strategy, the flagship trial involving the infamous Radio-Télévision des mille collines (RTLM) and the *Kangura* newspaper—the propaganda machines referred to as the "hate media"—was on the verge of becoming a farce. The number one priority was to save the trial. In an attempt by the prosecution to salvage whatever it could, the handful of "insiders" who had been collaborating with them for several years were called in to the rescue. Dieudonné Niyitegeka, whose recorded interviews were lying dormant in the archives, would have to come out of his North American hiding place. The prosecutor promised the judges that if they admitted this former Interahamwe leader's belated deposition, it could take the place of at least eighteen other witnesses. But like any other tempting offer, this one came with a price. There were specific conditions, and they were quite unusual.

The prosecutor requested that the witness be allowed to testify anonymously via videoconference without the accused being present. The judges agreed to only the first two conditions. But that was enough to make a mockery of a fundamental principle of justice: the right to a public trial. This had already become a widespread phenomenon at the ICTR. Like leaving a beautiful piece of woodwork to be slowly eaten away by worms, month by month, year by year, anonymous testimony and closed-door hearings were becoming the norm rather than the exception. In Niyitegeka's case, the anonymity was meaningless. On the one hand, he was not the one who had initially requested it, as would normally be the case. The prosecutor had. On the other hand, every Rwandan, or anyone who had the slightest interest in knowing at any rate, already knew the identity of this major witness. Moreover, as if to add to the illusion of anonymity, both he and the judges made references to his former position during his testimony. As a result, another key principle of justice ended up being perverted in the process: witness protection.

In Rwanda, witnesses did not testify anonymously before the national courts, which were also trying tens of thousands of people suspected of involvement in the genocide. In Belgium, where Rwandans were tried on four occasions in 2001, 2005, 2006, and 2009, the witnesses from Rwanda also testified openly using their true identity. In Arusha, on the contrary, almost all of the witnesses testified anonymously behind a curtain. The initial concern for their security was noble. However, the reality was quite the opposite. In Rwanda, precisely where the alleged risk was, everyone knew who went to Arusha to testify. Except for their time in Tanzania, the protection given to witnesses was illusory. This was not the tribunal's fault. The Rwandan authorities always claimed that the safety of witnesses, just like that of any other citizen, fell under their jurisdiction. Moreover, they always made it impossible for witnesses to remain anonymous due to the administrative procedures required to get them out of the country. Consequently, an unpleasant result of this anonymity and the systematic, closed-door hearings at the international tribunal was that they nullified the very reason for a public trial: to ensure that justice is transparent and that those who testify are also held accountable to society, which is another way to ensure the truthfulness of their testimony.

Protection is not synonymous with anonymity. If there was one person whom the UN tribunal truly protected, it was Dieudonné Niyitegeka. His identity was changed. He was under the close supervision of a special witness protection program in Canada, which meant that even the ICTR prosecutor could not contact him without the authorization of Canadian authorities. During his videoconference testimony, it was normal for his face to be concealed. However, it was absurd and pointless to not say who he was. And that was not the only deviation: 40 percent of his testimony was given behind closed doors. "Public access is less important than the speed of the trial. It is not the primary concern," declared Norwegian judge Erik Mose, then vice president of the ICTR, during the hearing. In a media trial that took ten years from the time the accused were arrested to the ruling by the appeals chamber, the comment was a bit too much.

As if this shadow theater were not opaque enough, the prosecutor's office could not find any of the twenty-six original cassette recordings of the statements Niyitegeka gave between 1997 and 1999. What is more, in looking for them, the prosecutor found other cassette recordings dating back to 2000 that had not been transcribed and were missing the names of the investigators who conducted the interview. The prosecution's integrity was in shreds after this performance, but Niyitegeka made out all right. Being an informed informant, he placed a condition on his testimony: a promise in writing from the chief prosecutor that he would not be prosecuted. The letter was signed on February 5, 2002, less than two weeks before he testified.

"My conscience is clear. I know that I did not participate in the genocide," Niyitegeka told the court. On the defense side, British lawyer Diana Ellis wanted to be sure.

"In the weeks following April 6, you regularly associated with people who confided in you that they were killers, did you not? You ran around with them, you lived with them, you drank beer with them. They were friends, weren't they?" she questioned.

"I continued to run around with these people. But the whole time I was with these individuals, I never saw them kill," he replied.

"If you disapproved of the killings, why did you agree to continue associating with them on a daily basis?"

"The period after April 6 was dangerous. I could not say anything. If you so much as opposed them, you would die."

Does this sound a little like the defense that Jean-Paul Akayesu had tried to advance?

Despite the tribunal's increasingly numerous measures to shroud the proceedings in opacity, some of the facades nevertheless crumbled over the years. Although Niyitegeka escaped prosecution, his closest associate, Ephrem Nkezabera, had no choice but to accept it.[2] In June 2004, Belgian police arrested this former chairman of the Interahamwe's economic and financial affairs subcommittee in utmost secrecy. One month later the ICTR prosecutor explained that he had asked the Belgian authorities to locate the suspect and bring him to trial. Rumors quickly began to circulate that Nkezabera had confessed. The camouflage was well designed, but it did not fool everyone. In reality, after having been granted a tenuous immunity in exchange for the service he had rendered to the prosecution as an informant, Nkezabera became caught up in the prosecutor's problems in the trial of the former regime's senior military and political leaders. The prosecution needed him as a witness, and for that to happen, the former Interahamwe official would have to stand trial first. Belgium was only acting as a respectable subcontractor in the matter.

The former Interahamwe leader, who was a manager of one of Rwanda's major banks in 1994, denied having killed anyone but did admit that two people were killed in front of him by individuals in his direct entourage. He admitted to having encouraged the militias at the roadblocks on April 8 and 9 and to having distributed weapons on April 11 and 12. Forty hours of testimony were recorded. For the ICTR prosecutor, he was a substantial witness in some of the major trials. For Nkezabera, at fifty-three years old, there was one advantage to being tried in Belgium: unlike the tribunal in Arusha, the former colonial power offered some guarantees for parole once he had served half his sentence. At the same time, Nkezabera made sure to sign an agreement with the ICTR prosecutor stipulating that his family would be transported to a third country and that he would be protected once he was released.

Thus, through a twisted, winding path, the fate of the former militia's murky network became clear. Of the five national leaders, two were dead, one had been sentenced in Arusha to life in prison, and another continued to serve as a prosecution witness. The only one who managed to escape it all was the former secretary general, Eugène Mbarushimana. On April 12, 1994, less than a week after the massacre had started, he was among those who were evacuated from Kigali aboard a French plane. Thus, there was not sufficient evidence against him. In the years that followed, he was in contact with the investigators on a regular basis, but he never really collaborated. Being the son-in-law of the wealthy businessman Félicien Kabuga, the ICTR's most wanted fugitive since 1997 for whom the United States offered a reward of up to five million dollars, he refused to serve as bait or a handsomely paid dragnet.

Of the six subcommittee chairs who rounded out the militia's national leadership, one died in the first few days of April 1994, and the fate of two others is unknown. A fourth was arrested in May 2004 in the United States, where he was being held for making false statements to the immigration services. Rwanda was seeking his extradition, and the ICTR's office of the prosecutor held damning evidence against him. The only one left was Joseph Serugendo, who, along with Ephrem Nkezabera, was always said to be of great interest to the international tribunal. Indeed, both men served as a link between the militia and RTLM radio. In addition to being the second highest financial officer of the Interahamwe, Nkezabera was also in charge of RTLM, SA's finances. Serugendo, chairman of the Interahamwe's nicely named "Research and Development" subcommittee, was also the extremist radio station's chief technical editor. So how did this person who was so important and was clearly on the minds of the investigators working on the media case from 1995 to 1998 end up dropping off the prosecution's radar screen for several years? It is a mystery. It is not for lack of knowing where he was hiding. His friend Dieudonné Niyitegeka had told investigators of his whereabouts back in March 1997. Yet he was not contacted at his place of refuge in Gabon until September 16, 2005, when he was finally indicted and arrested. (Ill at the time, Serugendo pleaded guilty to a surprisingly light charge, was sentenced to six years, and died in prison in August 2006, without ever giving public testimony of what he knew.) On November 30, 2009, Nkezabera was found guilty by a Belgian court and was sentenced to thirty years in prison. Suffering from cancer, he did not attend his trial.

Out of the eleven national leaders of the killers who came to symbolize the effort to exterminate Tutsis, three were dead, two had vanished, three others were entirely or partially spared by justice, and three had been tried, albeit quite belatedly. The efforts to prosecute the Interahamwe leadership seem, therefore, to have been motivated by interest more than duty.

At the beginning of June 1998, operation Kiwest (Kigali-West Africa), the code name of a second massive wave of arrests, was conducted under the ICTR's orders in several West African countries. Among those arrested was Omar Serushago, one of the five Interahamwe leaders in Gisenyi province in northwest Rwanda.[3] At thirty-seven years old, this father of six children was one of only two local militia leaders to be tried before the tribunal. When brought before a judge in Arusha one month after being incarcerated, he corrected the official version of his arrest, saying that he had "turned himself in" to the Ivorian authorities. Omar Serushago had, in fact, been one of the prosecution's collaborators since 1997. He served as an informant just like his superiors Dieudonné Niyitegeka and Ephrem Nkezabera. He was forced to come out into the open for the same reason that Nkezabera was imprisoned six years later: the prosecutor needed him as a witness against several key accused. Serushago had admitted to the direct murder of four people and the indirect murder of thirty-three others, so in order for him to be presented as a witness with a minimum of decency and credibility, he first had to stand trial for his crimes.

Having gotten burned on the Kambanda affair, the prosecution paid much closer attention to form in the Serushago case. This militiaman did not hold the same importance as the former head of government. He did not provoke the same power struggles or rouse the same sense of pride among the tribunal's top brass. The case file was placed in the hands of sensible people. It was handled wisely and effectively. The dignified Tanzanian lawyer Mohamed Ismail put up a good show in defending the interests of this repentant militiaman. On December 14, 1998, the tribunal ended its best year since its creation by recording a second guilty plea, which, incidentally, was only a partial one. After pleading guilty to four charges, Omar Serushago did not agree to the fifth count against him: rape. He was accused not of directly committing sexual violence himself but of allowing his men to do so. In his eyes, that was going a bit too far. He had already admitted to participating in genocide, directly or indirectly committing dozens of murders, and engaging in acts of extermination or torture, but he refused to be held responsible for the rapes that his subordinates may have committed. Such is the sensitivity of a *genocidaire*.

The prosecutor did not hesitate. He withdrew the accusation, leaving room for a mutually acceptable agreement between the two parties. Less than two months later, Mohamed Ismail scored a second victory: whereas the prosecutor was seeking a twenty-five-year sentence, the judges ordered fifteen years in prison. Omar Serushago, who was better advised than Jean Kambanda, had understood the critical nuance between confession and remorse. When invited by the judges (the very same who had sentenced the former head of the interim government to life in prison) to express himself on the stand before receiving his sentence, he read aloud for several long minutes from a text in which he asked forgiveness from the Rwandans and "especially [from] the members of the Tutsi ethnic group, among whom [he] created victims, and who are [his] brothers."[4] As he held up a copy of the Koran written in Arabic in one hand and a copy of the Bible in Swahili in the other, his voice choked with emotion. For a few moments, a peculiar honesty emerged from the incongruity of his words. Oddly enough, he appeared to be asking his judges to give him a "lighter sentence," to keep him under house arrest so he could serve out his sentence near his family, or even to give him a residence where he would "have sufficient security" upon his release.

No matter what the crime, the sentence is always too heavy in the eyes of the convicted. For Omar Serushago, who was found guilty of genocide, fifteen years "was unacceptable." So out of professional duty, his lawyer appealed, arguing that under Rwandan law, to which the ICTR could refer in sentencing matters, his client would have gotten a seven- to eleven-year sentence. The task of cutting this proposed debate short fell to Judge Shahabuddeen. The elderly, implacably courteous justice from Guyana generally slipped the rope around his interlocutor's neck with the suave tone of a person holding a fireside chat with individuals from a long line of nobility. This time, after numerous attempts to find some semblance of intellectual stimulation in the legal dilemma that was being raised, he went right for the jugular.

"If Rwandan organic law were set aside, would you say that fifteen years is too much for someone who committed three crimes against humanity and one crime of genocide?" he asked in a caustic tone.

"I would hesitate to respond," admitted Ismail softly.

The judges were not so hesitant. Fifteen years it was.

7

The White Man's Grave

I realized that the Rwandan detainees were not all my friends. So I thought about the reasons why I was in prison. Instead of showing solidarity among us, which could have helped us defend ourselves, they would insult me and throw me my food. I realized I was not one of them. Gradually, I came to realize that I had taken part in a genocide. The only solution was to face up to the problem and, therefore, to plead guilty.

Georges Ruggiu,
March 1, 2002

On a December day in Kigali in 1993, as he was walking downtown, Georges Ruggiu chanced to encounter the presidential motorcade. Being a respectful man and an ardent admirer of the Rwandan president, he saluted. The car stopped, and Georges Ruggiu was invited to step into the vehicle carrying President Juvénal Habyarimana himself. That same evening, the president's office issued instructions to have the young Belgian hired to work at RTLM. The following day, he was called in to meet with the station's founder, Ferdinand Nahimana. On January 6, 1994, he was recruited as a journalist after being interviewed as a mere formality. For most—or perhaps, for those to whom it happens—being stopped by a head of state while hitchhiking is either a privilege reserved for a beautiful actress, the sign of a lucky day, or the result of being mistaken for someone else. For Georges Ruggiu, it was the beginning of all his problems.[1]

RTLM was already well known in the streets of Kigali. Its music programming was decisively modern and brought in good ratings. But above all, its political orientation, which consisted of all-out resistance to the Arusha Accords, made the station the talk of the town and the democrats' worst fear. A puppet of the anti-Belgian and anti-RPF discourse that characterized the station,

Ruggiu did not immediately become a star of the airwaves. He started at the bottom rung of the editorial ladder. With no training in journalism and no experience in radio broadcasting, he was placed under the supervision of the head of the French-language division. For the most part, he hosted a five-minute talk show around 9:30 p.m., either alone or with a guest. Often, the editor in chief was his discussion partner. The two men addressed each other informally during the show and chatted as though they were in a friendly, enlightened Parisian lounge. "Monsieur Georges," as Rwandans took to calling him, used a tone intended to sound doctoral and serious. Speaking in a calm voice, he punctuated his analyses with statements that were suddenly authoritative.

Around this time, at the beginning of 1994, the political climate in Rwanda began to deteriorate seriously. Acts of violence, attacks, and murders were on the rise. Starting in mid-March, Ruggiu began receiving firm instructions from the station manager: adopt a more hard-line discourse and draw parallels between Rwanda's current political situation and the one during the 1959 revolution, when the Hutu majority took power, ending Belgian colonization and the Tutsi royal domination, at the cost of anti-Tutsi pogroms. The neophyte radio host became increasingly keyed up. He talked about the "bloody, feudal monarchists in the RPF" and warned the Belgians and the UN force to watch their step. Otherwise, "the fight against a colonialist-inspired Tutsi occupation army [would] be ruthless."

On April 7, 1994, Ruggiu read the official press release over the radio in French announcing the death of President Habyarimana. In the days that followed, he worked at the radio station on a regular basis. On the way to his house in the Kicukiro neighborhood, he saw a large number of houses that had been razed and roadblocks set up to inspect and identify Tutsis before eliminating them. On April 9 his colleagues informed him that a price had allegedly been put on his head and that the Belgians were contemplating killing him. He first went into hiding at the station's headquarters. Later, he stayed with the Rwandan armed forces at the Kigali camp, "in the fridge," as he called it. Around that time, between April 12 and 14, he took part in an organized tour of the streets of Kigali that had been arranged for Rwandan journalists. Ruggiu saw "mutilated bodies with their thoraxes still quivering about, struggling to get air." In one neighborhood, he counted "up to 129 bodies of women who all appeared to be Tutsi." At the end of this personal tour into the depths of hell, Georges Ruggiu could no longer plead ignorance. He took the irretrievable plunge into a life of crime.

He left the camp with the help of a driver who also served as his bodyguard. Soon after, he started wearing a khaki uniform, with a Spanish Star 9mm pistol attached to his belt. The military authorities put him up at the

Diplomates hotel. His station manager was clear: he had to make a choice. If he quit his job, he would lose all protection. The radio broadcasts, both in Kinyarwanda and in French, had to take on an even harsher tone because the station had now entered the war, the manager insisted. After the RPF tried unsuccessfully to bomb the station on April 17, RTLM went into hiding. Kantano, the station's most famous program host, who succeeded in using humor to incite people to kill their fellow Tutsis, ironically described their place of work as an "armored vehicle." In reality, RTLM never had a mobile station and was not set up inside one of the Rwandan army's tanks, as it was asserted for quite some time. That was a myth. Up until July 4, it was simply broadcasting from its basement.

There are all sorts of coded ways to incite people to massacre. This phenomenon is not specific to Rwanda. The use of metaphors or euphemisms is common practice when it comes to getting the masses to kill en masse. Trivializing the crime makes executing it more commonplace and breaks down the taboo. Starting around March, RTLM journalists received firm and specific instructions that whenever they spoke of the RPF, the object of their obsessive hatred, they were to use only the expression *inyenzi*, which meant "cockroach." The word "Tutsi" was also supposed to be replaced with *inyenzi*, that is, an "annoying domestic animal that is harmful to the population," as Ruggiu explained. After April 6, when used on the radio, it signified "a person to be killed." When Ruggiu urged the people to take charge of civil defense, he also used the expression "go to work," which, as he knew, meant "go out and kill."

Thus, Ruggiu the "journalist" actively took part in the dirty work over the airwaves of "Radio-Télé La Mort" [Death Radio-TV], as it was dubbed. In mid-May, his bosses ordered him to crank the killing machine up another notch. They said his programs had grown "too soft," even though Ruggiu had been broadcasting "wanted notices." This consisted of giving the names of individuals over the airwaves and, whenever possible, the model and color of their vehicle or their license plate number, the routes they used, and the people they traveled with, all based on information provided by the army or militias. Wanted persons were then located and eliminated by the Interahamwe, who had their ears glued to their radios.

Sometimes, Ruggiu's appeals were more generic. During the first week of the genocide, when he claimed he had been informed of a large-scale RPF infiltration in Gikondo, the neighborhood where his editor in chief lived, he broadcast a warning over the airwaves. His boss later told him that several people, including women and children, had been killed that evening as a result of his appeal on RTLM.

"Monsieur Georges" also had his personal whipping boys, such as Faustin Twagiramungu, the (Hutu) prime minister designate of the transition government to be formed under the Arusha Accords. He warned over the radio that the "popular masses were lying in wait for him in order to settle a few scores." Twagiramungu, who later questioned the mental stability of his radio persecutor, escaped the killers by seeking refuge with the UN forces. Many others were not so fortunate. Starting the day after the attack on Habyarimana, Ruggiu drew up a list of names of the various political figures who were being threatened and hung it up at the RTLM offices. It was a practical tool. "The names on this list were crossed off as people disappeared." For approximately a month, both the Interahamwe and soldiers who came by the RTLM office could freely consult this list. RTLM was not only a media outlet. It was a meeting place where one could obtain information about the killers' successes and the contracts that remained to be executed.

And then, of course, there were the Belgians, the despised compatriots of the young radio broadcaster. He didn't shout, "To each his own Belgian!" as it had been written, but on several occasions, he blamed the Belgian contingent of the UN for the death of Habyarimana. He declared that the president's plane had been shot down with Belgian missiles and that Belgium was responsible for the Tutsi oppression of the Hutus. On April 7, ten Belgian peacekeepers were massacred at the Kigali camp, the very same place where Georges Ruggiu would seek temporary refuge "in the fridge" a few days later.

For three months Ruggiu congratulated, encouraged, preached to, advised, and thanked these "valiant civilian combatants" in the militia who had to "work" with the army and the government to defend the country. And when the very same people were driven out in July 1994 and fled en masse to neighboring Zaire, the Belgian broadcaster from RTLM stuck with them until the very end, like a fungus on a dead branch.

Georges Ruggiu went to Zaire, Tanzania, back to Zaire again, and finally to Kenya—the peaceful country of refuge for leaders of Rwanda's former regime. He knew he was wanted, by the Belgians for sure and most likely by the international tribunal as well. He had a South African passport, frequently changed his address, and lived under the bizarre alias of Trevor MacCusker to evade Interpol agents. He also wrote a pamphlet titled *Dans la tourmente rwandaise* (In the Rwandan Turmoil). It was a second-rate epistle that smacked of negationism and fortunately was printed only for private circulation. The Hutu cause no longer published except clandestinely, and its apologists, when they were not being incarcerated, kept a low profile. It was time for the Belgian broadcaster to embrace a new vision of the world. So Georges Ruggiu became Omar Ruggiu.

The person who initiated him into Islam, the one he considered to be his godfather and who oversaw his conversion to his new faith, was his good friend Musa Kazungu. He stayed at Kazungu's house in a neighborhood primarily inhabited by Somalis. Now every morning, Georges Omar Ruggiu would apply kohl to his eyelids, say his prayers, and don a djellaba and a kaffiyeh. He learned verses from the Koran inside out and thought seriously about going to live in Afghanistan (of all places), via Pakistan. To that end, Kazungu gave him six hundred dollars, the origin of which Ruggiu claimed not to know. That was in 1997—Arusha almost could have had its thunder stolen by Guantanamo. Then on July 23 at 2:55 a.m., near a mosque in the large Kenyan coastal town of Mombasa, Georges Henri Yvon Joseph Ruggiu, a.k.a. Omar, was arrested. At forty years old, he was the twentieth detainee at the ICTR. It was probably the best thing that had happened to him in four years.

If Belgian comics writer Hergé had seen Mohamed Aouini and Jean-Louis Gilissen walking toward him with their backs to the sun, he would have thought he had finally met Thomson and Thompson from his *Tintin* strip in person. You never saw one without the other. They were always chatting. They had the same walk, the same honest handshake with their bodies leaning forward slightly to convey sincerity, matching smiles, and identical mustaches. They had met at a conference in Arusha two years earlier. When Aouini found himself appointed to defend Georges Ruggiu, he immediately called his friend Gilissen to assist him. The former RTLM broadcaster had chosen the Tunisian attorney to defend him because he wanted a Muslim lawyer. Gilissen happened to be an equally good fit as he was originally from Belgium, from the same region as the accused. Discreet, hard-working, and modest, the two lawyers formed a defense team of rare harmony. They worked this case like a potter at his wheel—patient, steady, and cautious. "It's a human story," they never grew tired of saying. Astute and ever friendly, they knew how to put a conciliatory spin on their relationships with the prosecutor, the tribunal, and their client. There was really only one topic that angered the Tunisian lawyer: the issue of human rights in his country. He was a party man, a loyal supporter of President Ben Ali. Normally warm, friendly, and generous, Aouini would tense up and bristle in an instant if the regime was criticized. Back home, he was an active and uncompromising supporter of the government in place. On the contrary, in Arusha, where the political situation in Tunisia was moot, he could be Amnesty International's most convincing activist. Just like democracies that have no qualms about forgetting their values outside their own borders, he knew how to apply them everywhere except at home.

Jean-Louis Gilissen had a youthful look. He shared with his Tunisian colleague and friend an unmistakable human sensitivity. A good listener who always gave the person he was talking to the impression that he found him or her to be perceptive, he was a man of moderation and conciliation. However, there was one thing that could make him suddenly go red in the face, become agitated, and perhaps even fly off the handle: dishonesty, even mild.

Under the guidance of these two men, it was time for Ruggiu to return to reality. It started with a clothing makeover. When he arrived in Arusha, Georges Omar Ruggiu was wearing a white djellaba and brown sandals. His face was covered by a denim jacket, and he was clutching a copy of the Koran in his hands. Three weeks later, his face was still hidden under a black and white kaffiyeh. After three months, he had traded the black kaffiyeh for a yellow one; his head was still covered, but his face was not. Six months later, he was wearing an elegant, North-African style charcoal gray suit, with a fez as a discreet sign of his religious convictions.

At the UN detention facility, Ruggiu discovered a prison reproduction of the power relationships that he had seen in Rwanda under the interim government. The detainees organized internal meetings, which helped maintain psychological control of the group. However, Ruggiu quickly felt excluded. Plus, there was that devil Hassan Ngeze. Georges Ruggiu did not like this "colleague" at all. Ngeze was the most famous journalist from the Hutu extremist print media, and it so happened that he was also the brother-in-law of Ruggiu's good friend Musa Kazungu. Ngeze—"a big guy who makes a lot of noise but is empty on the inside," in Ruggiu's estimation—took infinite pleasure in harassing Ruggiu and making fun of him. In the months following their arrest, they were kept in the same wing of the detention facility, along with four other suspects. Ngeze's cell was in the middle of six jail cells. Ruggiu's was at one of the far ends. The prison guards instructed them not to have any contact with each other. But Ngeze paid no attention. "Hassan Ngeze would systematically come and sit in front of my cell, shouting, making noise, and laughing," and "that really hurt me," recalled the former RTLM broadcaster, sounding somewhat childish. He had many grievances with his tormentor, and he never really seemed to see how ridiculous the situation was. There was the ball scene, for example. During a soccer game, the ball came rolling through the little garden that Ruggiu maintained in front of his cell. In his mind, this was not an accident but was, in fact, the doing of his Rwandan torturer. That was the incident. "I insulted him because he had annoyed me, and I treated him like an animal. I felt that sometimes he acted like one. He knew that I was very sensitive to noise and that I was growing a garden in front of my door. He and some others tried to destroy this garden. He also made a lot of noise. So I got irritated," said Ruggiu, a man who could fly off into a fit of anger and rage, before calming down just as abruptly. By the end of June 1998, he could not take it anymore and asked to be moved to a different wing of the prison.

"Don't think this means he is about to come clean," Ruggiu's lawyer Mr. Aouini was quick to assert. The fact that his client had been separated from his fellow inmates was due to the oppressive climate in the prison, where Ruggiu was treated like an *inyenzi-muzungu*, the "white cockroach." But the mirror was starting to shatter. Ruggiu was already saying he had been manipulated. Soon he would recognize the reality of what happened in 1994 but, in short, would plead ignorance. Then, around the month of October, when the jacarandas are in full bloom against the backdrop of the spring sky in northern Tanzania, Ruggiu was joined in his isolated quarter by Sylvain Nsabimana. The former *préfet* of the southern region of Rwanda had been doing some thinking himself. He did not feel guilty, but he also did not want to show solidarity with his comrades. Everyone has his own burden to bear, seemed to be his attitude. He brought with him a copy of the book that the detainees in Arusha had collectively written a year earlier in an attempt to explain the events of 1994 to their lawyers. Georges Ruggiu had cosigned it. But times had changed. The Belgian had reached a new stage in life. "I am expressing my utter disagreement with the content of this document," he wrote to his lawyers. The divorce between him and his former friends was final.

At the beginning of 1999, Ruggiu changed residences again, supposedly due to construction work at the detention facility. For approximately two months, he was incarcerated in a villa in Arusha, in a bizarre cohabitation of four accused who, on the contrary, really should have been separated. They included Georges Ruggiu, still in his reflective phase; Sylvain Nsabimana, the loner; Omar Serushago, the confessed killer and informant for the prosecutor; and Pauline Nyiramasuhuko, a former minister who did not display the slightest intention of admitting to any of the things with which she was being charged. The UN bureaucracy has proven to have boundless imagination when it tries hard enough. It would also have other occasions to demonstrate its assiduity in this respect. Nevertheless, this was a period of relative tranquility for the Belgian detainee, who now had a plot of land far from Hassan Ngeze where he could garden. Those who enjoy pulling weeds know the calming effect gardening has on the soul. His thinking grew more mature. "We do not often talk with Ruggiu. We say hello and that is all. He became a good Muslim. I think that he is ready," confided Omar Serushago. The time had come. For its part, the prosecution had not been sitting idle. The initial indictment against the Belgian from RTLM had been the tribunal's most succinct. Three short pages supporting "only" two charges: direct and public incitement to commit genocide and crimes against humanity for persecution. Now the prosecution was preparing a new indictment against him, and it was an entirely different story. The crimes being charged were more specific and the evidence more developed. The result: if the judges confirmed this indictment, Georges Ruggiu would have four new counts against him, not the least of which were conspiracy to commit genocide, complicity in genocide, and crimes against humanity for murder and extermination. If he was found guilty, he would have a life sentence hanging over his head.

This heavy threat was about to materialize when, in April 1999, Ruggiu agreed to be questioned in connection with an Italian investigation into shipments of antipersonnel mines to Rwanda during the genocide from a factory in the Puglia region in eastern Italy. Two members of the ICTR prosecutor's office attended the interviews. Even though Ruggiu's revelations about the shipment did not amount to much, this was an opportunity for the prosecution to see that he could be of interest.

That same month, Aouini and Gilissen obtained authorization from their client, who in the meantime had been taken back to the central detention facility, to enter into negotiations with the prosecutor's office. Mohamed Othman was in charge of the negotiations on the prosecution side. This Tanzanian, whose straightforward, consensus-seeking approach earned him criticism for not being authoritative enough, handled the matter with finesse and psychology. His clear but flexible position helped convince Ruggiu to confess, while at the same time, the other detainees were starting to push Ruggiu over the edge. In mid-June, when his fellow detainees prevented him from accessing the communal telephone, Ruggiu reached his breaking point and shattered all the windows in one of the prison hallways. His lawyers rushed to Arusha. The next day, the prosecutor gave them a list of discussion points. On Monday, June 28, in a room set up near the detention facility entrance, the first tripartite meeting between the accused, his lawyers, and the prosecutor was held. For five hours, Ruggiu calmly engaged in a lengthy monologue. His confession had begun. The prosecutor agreed not to file a new indictment against him. "It was a difficult week, but things started moving," the two inseparable defense attorneys explained discretely.

Following several long months of interviews and negotiations, Ruggiu acknowledged that the media, particularly RTLM, "was one of the key instruments used by the extremists to mobilize the people and incite them to massacre Tutsis and political opponents." He admitted that the journalists, management, and editorial staff at RTLM bore "a real and full share of the responsibility" for the genocide.

On May 15, 2000, after nearly three years of incarceration, Georges Ruggiu pled guilty before judges Pillay, Aspegren, and Kama. He was the third defendant in two years to confess before the Rwandan tribunal (following Jean Kambanda and Omar Serushago), which was badly in need of such successes to improve its image and its record. The ICTR had been experiencing its bleakest judicial year ever: only one person was on trial even though the court had nine judges and approximately thirty accused in detention. The spectacular completion of the Ruggiu case was, therefore, beneficial. It would also prove to be especially noteworthy in terms of substance.

How is it that Georges Ruggiu, a low-ranking, anonymous, and harmless civil servant with the Belgian social security office in Liège just six months before the start of the mass killings in April 1994 in this far-off, tiny country in central Africa, ended up playing an active role in the extermination of Tutsis in Rwanda? How is it that this social worker, whose former friends described him as generous and concerned about the poorest of the poor, was able to transform himself into a broadcaster for a hate-radio station? Although Jean-Louis Gilissen had neither the ambition nor perhaps the desire to fully understand the whys and hows, this was surely the big question that he hoped to raise at this hearing, taking the court beyond the cold task of trying and convicting Ruggiu.

"Yesterday at the prison, he told us: 'The most important thing is not the sentence. It is that people understand why I am confessing.' If you want to understand his guilt, you have to understand how he got there. If you understand that, you will understand the nature of his guilt," explained Gilissen two days before his closing arguments to the court. "Is the ICTR capable of hearing an individual story?" was the question he posed to the judges at the outset. It was neither incongruous nor impertinent. Largely overlooked in the Kambanda case, this question was given only brief, perfunctory attention in the Serushago case. But for Ruggiu's conscientious defense team, it was vital. It was the central issue on the day of confession.

Georges Ruggiu was born on October 12, 1957, in the small town of Verviers to an Italian immigrant father who became a miner in Belgium and a Belgian mother who was an elementary school teacher. He was seventeen before he acquired Belgian citizenship, without renouncing his Italian nationality. His family relations were rocky and antagonistic and his academic record chaotic. Later, he briefly saw a psychiatrist. For years he served as a teacher, working with mentally disabled children. Then he worked for a Catholic charity called Emmaüs for a year and a half, where he dealt with ex-offenders, illegal immigrant workers, and the homeless. In 1992, after a period of unemployment, he became a civil servant at the family benefits division of a local branch of the national social security office.

Testifying under a pseudonym, shielded from the public eye, a young thirty-year-old woman came to describe this Georges Ruggiu to the court. He was her former coworker and friend at parties, where they would try to solve the world's problems. He was a man "of ordinary appearance," she said, "short, someone who went unnoticed" (Ruggiu is about five feet one). He had an "enormous amount of energy and was very sociable, open, dynamic and generous in his work"—the type of energy, she added, that sometimes more resembled a fit of anger. At work, he was known for his union activity. "He had a need to enforce the rules, to make sure that they were being applied. I never sensed any injustice in what he said. He did not have any prejudices. He tried to be as fair and impartial as possible." He was a real stickler for rules who clashed with the management but obtained benefits for all the employees. The young woman explained that outside of work, she discovered that he had "an even more varied personality" and that he also had a sense of humor. Georges Ruggiu loved to talk and debate. He would argue and reflect and was a good listener. "He was well educated and knowledgeable. In other words, he was intelligent and had good manners."

The young woman's voice was cheerful and light. The slight crack in her voice added to its calming power. Her delivery was smooth, and her vocabulary was precise and expressive. Her almost sweet and innocent smile accentuated the impression of gaiety that she exuded and commanded the court's attention. "Was he a thinker?" interrupted Judge Navanethem Pillay. "Yes, I think so," replied the witness at first. "He was both thoughtful and spontaneous, two contradictory traits," she added, qualifying her response. "Did he think before making a decision?" continued the judge. "He was very spontaneous, very direct. I'm not sure he thought first, but he had the ability to recognize his own mistakes and to modify his future behavior," replied the young woman.

Ruggiu continued his humanitarian pursuits outside work. His world was one of drudgery and anonymous assistance to others. He occasionally worked as an ambulance driver and helped the local Red Cross distribute food or clothing. Among those who benefited from his charity work were many immigrants, especially from Africa and in particular former Belgian colonies including Rwanda. However, those with whom Ruggiu formed friendships came from a very specific background: students from influential families in the regime who were deeply involved in politics. His new friends included the president of the MRND (President Habyarimana's party) chapter in Belgium and his press attaché, a man related to Habyarimana who was directly appointed by Kigali to be a liaison between the president's office and the party in Belgium. "To his great misfortune, all these Rwandans were Hutus from the north who were extremely active in politics. Mr. Ruggiu was in the MRND's den," explained Gilissen.

In the summer of 1992 Ruggiu spent his first vacation in his new friends' country, in the land of a thousand hills. He remembers his arrival in the Rwandan capital like a champion's first time on the winners' podium. At least fifty or so people he didn't know were waiting at the Kigali airport to greet him with a celebrity's welcome. On the very first evening, he was an honored guest at the table of the district court's chief justice—a man who had powerful connections within the Habyarimana regime. Upon his return to Belgium, he began his political activism. When the RPF rebels launched a new offensive in February 1993, Ruggiu did not hesitate. He set himself up as a political commentator and analyst on behalf of a Rwanda he felt he knew and loved already. He wrote and sent letters to the king of Belgium and even to the president of Rwanda. In Liège in the spring of 1993, he met Ferdinand Nahimana, who had come to hold press conferences to defend the regime against the already alarming reports from human rights organizations. In May he was personally invited to meet Juvénal Habyarimana, who was visiting Belgium and whom he had come to greatly admire. A few days later, he met Habyarimana a second time at the Hilton hotel in Brussels, where the president thanked him for his work and for portraying a good image of Rwanda and the MRND in Belgium. Though it seemed somewhat ludicrous, Habyarimana even asked Ruggiu for his valued opinion on several subjects. Shortly thereafter, Ruggiu attended a meeting where there was discussion of plans to set up a new radio station in Rwanda. Like his friends, he bought "shares" in this Radio des mille collines station in the works—two shares for eighty dollars.

Thus, he was already very much an activist when he made his second trip to Rwanda in the summer of 1993. His celebrity there had moved up a notch thanks to his activism. His address book was starting to fill up. He met the MRND secretary-general as well as the chief of staff at the Ministry of Transportation, a close relative of Habyarimana. Along with his political passion, another flame was sparked when he fell in love with a young Rwandan woman on this trip. Upon his return to Belgium, Ruggiu decided to throw caution to the wind and move to Rwanda.

Although Ruggiu had decided to make this big move in order to start a family, a political battle was also clearly in the mix. He needed a commitment, a fight, a cause. "Concerning Rwanda, all he ever talked about was politics. He talked about the political opposition between the government and the RPF. He was clearly in the government's camp and talked about the disinformation on the part of Western media. It was plain to see that he firmly believed in what he was saying," recalled the young woman testifying.

Ruggiu took unpaid leave from his employer and moved to Kigali on November 3, 1993. He applied for a position with the Red Cross in Rwanda but did not get the job. Truth be told, it did not matter. He had known since October that his friend the chief justice had managed to secure him a position, in theory, at the famous new radio station that had started broadcasting in July. Gilissen wished to clarify: "Ruggiu went back in order to establish himself there. That is important. He went not in order to commit genocide but to live there. What was he lacking? He needed to find a job. Ruggiu talked about a wind-power project or opening a restaurant. He didn't have any skills in these areas, but did he have any in radio either? It was nonsense. Ruggiu did not have any experience in radio broadcasting or journalism. But he did not see that as a sign. He rushed headlong into this crazy project and did so like everything else he did, with passion and gusto, even a little excess. He knew that it was not a commercial radio station. He knew that it was a political project. I would challenge anybody to find the slightest criminal aspect in that."

Things were starting to drag a bit. The wonderful promises made by his friends were slow in coming—until that infamous day in December when the presidential motorcade stopped in front of him and took him away.

I discovered Africa through the eyes of Georges," the young woman explained during her testimony. "He shared his passion and his dream. He talked about it with great respect. He had found an adopted family there. Georges was somebody there. People recognized him. They met him at the airport. We were really impressed that someone could be so easily integrated. We found that extraordinary. We thought he was lucky to have found his way. Georges was a good man. He gave without asking in return. He was truly generous. Perhaps he was also someone who was searching for himself and who found importance, respect, and power there that he did not have in our country."

To each his own interpretation. To each his words. Those coming out of the mouth of the young woman with the tender voice flowed into the courtroom like liquid gold. Caught up in a bitter struggle with his Belgian identity, led astray by Hutu Power extremism, and now finding salvation in the religion of the Prophet, Ruggiu's progression was clear: beginning as a man in search of recognition and identity, eager to find his true place in humanity, he would ultimately cut himself off from it.

Understanding is not the same as forgiveness, but it is useful. Georges Ruggiu was probably the only accused in Arusha toward whom a genuine desire to understand him was expressed (for a day at any rate). Was it because he was repenting? That clearly helped. Was it thanks to the work of his lawyers? Without a doubt. Was it because he was white? Paradoxically, it was long thought that his ethnicity was largely going to work against him. In short, because he was European, Ruggiu had even less excuse for having had a hand in the crime. In the absence of any effort to prosecute the foreign powers involved in the Rwandan drama—France and Belgium in particular—it was feared that by default, he ran the risk of having to bear the burden of the infernal trials and tribulations of the white man in Africa, a burden immoderately too heavy for him. Out of precaution, Jean-Louis Gilissen had already prepared his response: "Would membership in a certain ethnic or racial group be an aggravating factor? It is a thought that is perplexing," he observed. To his mind, Georges Ruggiu was of interest to the genocide planners precisely because he was a Westerner. This factor would not aggravate his client's case unless his client had been aware of that fact. But, as he remarked, "this is the cruel irony in Ruggiu's story: he was trying to forget the fact that he was a Westerner." Yet, was it not precisely because he *was* European that it was at once easier, more accessible, to understand this defendant, whose culture and history were suddenly so familiar?

In searching for her own answers, the young woman from the Liège social services remained circumspect. Even so, since 1994, she claimed to have felt the need to find an explanation, even if it meant keeping it simple. "I quickly became convinced that Georges had been manipulated. They played on his sense of social duty and his love for Africa for purposes that he certainly had not dreamed of in Belgium," she assured the court.

"You say that he was capable of making decisions and then you would have us believe that he was manipulated?" asked Judge Pillay.

"I am not trying to make the chamber believe what I am saying. That is not what I am trying to do," replied the young woman with imperturbable gentleness, "but he was nevertheless someone who could be manipulated. I say to myself that it is not possible that he said what was attributed to him in the Belgian press. The only explanation is that he was manipulated, that he was caught in a trap. That's my impression, and it is only my impression."

Mohamed Aouini came to the rescue. "When a storm sets in, it is difficult, when one has Georges Ruggiu's passionate nature, to escape one's own destiny. He made a mistake. You have to bear in mind that the influence was twofold: the indoctrination and the ideological bombardment to which he was subject even before his first trip in 1992. Ruggiu was but a secondary pawn, a minor collaborator who understood almost nothing. The Rwandan drama inevitably had to have altered everyone's perception. Under these conditions, was there any room for free will, with acts that were deliberately intentional? The answer has to be no," he tried to explain without much more success.

At that moment, it was difficult to read anything at all on the face of the short man who all but disappeared behind the closed-circuit television screen placed in front of him. Unlike his Rwandan codefendants, Ruggiu avoided absolutely all eye contact and always kept his head down. When his friend testifying on the stand mentioned his Rwandan girlfriend, he looked broken-hearted for a few seconds but then quickly pulled himself together. As his former colleague's testimony went on, his face softened as if the fanatical RTLM broadcaster was finally fading away before the Georges from the past: Georges the generous. And when the young woman left the courtroom after finishing her testimony, he stared off in the distance, his round blue eyes shrouded in a new emotion, lost on some mysterious horizon. As she had pointed out, he looked "more tired."

Before his client pled guilty, Jean-Louis Gilissen liked to use the well-known saying "The road to hell is paved with good intentions" to explain the story that he had to defend. Judging by the second character-witness testimony filed by the defense, which was handwritten and confidential, Georges Ruggiu's road to hell was also, and above all, paved with fatal attractions. "Georges Ruggiu's personality always seems mysterious to anyone learning his recent history," wrote this man who did not dare to come to Arusha, but who felt a certain sense of responsibility vis-à-vis his Belgian friend. "Indeed, no one understands how a sensible man could put himself in the situation he was in. He dreamed of a better world, which sometimes made him seem like an idealist. Without being naive, he was convinced that with work and perseverance, it was possible to change something in the current unjust system. It was this concern for justice that made him lose his way in Rwanda. In all probability it was in trying to fight for justice for his Rwandan Hutu friends that he got caught up in this Great Lakes quagmire, the stakes of which are still difficult for many to comprehend. The average Belgian who does not fully understand all the issues often tends to support the group (ethnic or regional) that he knows the best. It seems that Georges fell into this trap." This Rwandan, a Hutu and former member of the presidential party, concluded by saying, "Knowing Georges, I am sure that if he had met Rwandan Tutsis, or Hutus opposed to President Habyarimana, he would have acted differently."

Carla del Ponte did not like confessions. The Swiss prosecutor had replaced Louise Arbour eight months earlier in September 1999, at a time when cooperation between the former RTLM broadcaster and her office had already reached an irreversible stage. The day before Ruggiu's public confession, she wanted to meet him. They clearly did not hit if off well. Before the judges, she crushed the person who had promised to collaborate with her, much to everyone's surprise. She tried to depict a man who had gotten too close to the most influential people in the regime. But whether she had not read the file closely enough or she was trying to distort history, she confused "Eugène" Nahimana (MRND press attaché in Belgium) with "Ferdinand" Nahimana (RTLM founder). She thought that, based on the discussions Ruggiu had with President Habyarimana and the fact that Habyarimana had asked his opinion, she could conclude that the accused had become "the president's advisor abroad." She thought this would help the court understand, since it "shows us the individual's importance."

There is no doubt about the crime Georges Ruggiu committed. Tasked with ensuring these acts were punished, del Ponte legitimately emphasized the gravity of the crimes. However, she caused some serious confusion by indicating that she did not believe a single word of what was written in the agreement between her office and the defendant, an agreement that supposedly contained the actual facts as admitted by the parties. "He was fully and completely engaged in the politics, with all the necessary information. Don't try to tell me he was manipulated!" she exclaimed during the hearing. "On April 7 Ruggiu became aware of the true situation. He was aware of the genocide and that there were roadblocks to identify Tutsis in order to eliminate them. And what did our journalist do? He continued his work over the airwaves. He did even more of it. The army gave him the best protection supposedly because the Belgian soldiers were out for his blood. That's straight out of a television movie! Do you think that if the accused Ruggiu was really the person the defense is trying to make him out to be, he would have had this protection? That they would protect foreign journalists like that?"

Was the information that had been gathered and recorded after a year of patient and relatively dispassionate work simply a lure constructed solely for the purpose of practical and procedural interests, as it was in the Kambanda case? Were the dice loaded from the start once again?

"This is what the Ruggiu case is about, a man who understood the significance of what he did very late in the game; it's not a tactical confession," snapped Jean-Louis Gilissen, suddenly going red in the face. Del Ponte persisted: "This is unacceptable! We don't need Ruggiu's agreement. We don't need his confession. We need the truth. It's a matter of applying the law and these are serious crimes." But whose truth was needed?

"Those whom you are trying are not monsters; they are people. For in each and every one of us, there is this porous part, this weakness that could lead any one of us to sink into a life of crime," the lawyer from Liège reminded the court. "There are always bastards, idealists, profiteers, and psychopaths. But there are also honest people who fall on the other side. That's what you have to understand because it is your job to convict. Are we surrounded by deaf people who don't see the difference between Georges Ruggiu and the abominable broadcasts in Kinyarwanda? Mr. Ruggiu is a criminal. His confession is courageous. He is a man who could be reintegrated into the human community. The Ruggiu case is a lesson in modesty and humility for us all, and too bad for those who don't get it."

On June 1, 2000, Georges Ruggiu was sentenced to twelve years in prison. The judges clearly took the defense arguments into account. In the small room adjacent to the courtroom where the defendant and his counsel could consult or rest, Ruggiu looked relaxed. Standing before his lawyers, Aouini and Gilissen, like a Napoleon flanked by two elite soldiers, he regally congratulated himself for the "results of their teamwork," as though he weren't above all deeply indebted to them. Gilissen gasped behind his back before silently shaking his head with the smile of someone who had heard it all. Georges Ruggiu humble? Right![2]

"Are you feeling better now?" he was asked. "Yes, better than before, but still not great. It's a lot to take in after all. Twelve years in prison is a long time," replied the former broadcaster of the wanted notices. Mohamed Aouini hailed the "respectable, humane, and balanced decision." Jean-Louis Gilissen saw it as an appeal to other accused and "a source of hope for the victims that people are coming forward to explain their reality." He would even like to think that "the discourse of a political and obtuse tribunal was no longer entirely credible." For his part, prosecutor Mohamed Othman hoped that the tribunal's clemency would encourage other suspects to admit to their crimes and to cooperate. Less than two months later, at odds with Carla del Ponte, he left the ICTR to take the reins of the international prosecutor's office set up by the UN in East Timor. When it came time to choose a deputy prosecutor in Dili, he called upon Jean-Louis Gilissen to assist him.

The Ruggiu judgment was never appealed, a relative but true sign of its soundness. The matter was justly closed. There would not be a second "Kambanda case." There would also not be another confession for five more years.

8

A Little Murder among Friends

All that is not completely true is not necessarily a complete lie.

protected witness during a closed-door hearing,

2004

The day of his public confession, Georges Ruggiu made a promise to the victims: "I beg them to understand that I am deeply sorry for what happened. There is nothing else I can do but testify, and I am ready to do so in order to make amends." The trial in which his testimony was so highly anticipated was the one that he would have been part of had he continued to deny his involvement in the genocide—the so-called media case. This trial brought together three figures famous in Rwanda at the beginning of the 1990s: Ferdinand Nahimana, founder of RTLM; Jean-Bosco Barayagwiza, member of the radio station's executive committee; and Hassan Ngeze, editor in chief of Hutu Power's leading newspaper, *Kangura*. It opened in October 2000. Sixteen months later, "Monsieur Georges" was called to the witness stand to help rescue a prosecutor's office plagued by serious difficulties. Two other distinguished guests had testified before him: Dieudonné Niyitegeka and Omar Serushago. The barrage fire from the prosecutor's three collaborators promised to be deadly for the defense teams. The resulting collateral damage proved to be even more lethal.

Before testifying as a witness in court, Ruggiu had already made multiple statements, through a book written in exile and hours of interrogation by tribunal investigators between 1997 and 2000. Since he had not had an actual trial, however, he had never really been publicly confronted with his statements. Jean-Marie Biju-Duval, Ferdinand Nahimana's lawyer, happily took advantage of this mountain of materials to undermine Ruggiu's credibility. When he confronted Ruggiu with the numerous contradictions, the former RTLM broadcaster set about refuting the veracity of certain points in his agreement with the OTP, the very same document upon which he had been tried and convicted. "I do not agree with what is written. I signed it, but it doesn't correspond to reality," he said. Sardonically, the lawyer asked if the tribunal's judgment with respect to the repentant Ruggiu was therefore based on lies. "No, it wasn't deliberate. I would call it an error," the convict defended himself.

Ruggiu's constant fidgeting with a ballpoint pen betrayed his underlying nervousness. Never looking directly at the lawyer who was questioning him, he glanced toward the prosecutor's bench after each response, as though seeking approval or support. He became restless, flew off the handle, and lost control of himself, only to regain his composure again. His agitation then gave way to an autistic-like state as he seemed to retreat within himself, giving only cursory yes or no replies and keeping his head down for the remainder of the time, with his lips sometimes moving as he mumbled to himself, betraying his inner torment. "Let's go," he sighed as though in pain when the issue of the contradictions was raised again. "I will end by . . . ," he muttered in a faint, almost inaudible whisper, without finishing his sentence.

As he sat there sulking, he would suddenly become animated while giving a detailed response or in a fresh burst of irritation that was childlike at times. In many cases, Biju-Duval would let him talk because the more Georges Ruggiu talked, the more his tendency to invent stories would resurface. In 1999 he had told investigators that during his last meeting with Ferdinand Nahimana in July 1994, he had "not personally seen him." During the hearing, he retold this story in great detail before defying the science of perception by saying, "I did not see him personally, but I saw him." Laughter erupted in the courtroom. "Mr. Ruggiu, that's a contradiction in terms," smoothly replied defense counsel in a suave tone. "Well, be happy with it!" snapped the irritated witness. "Did you see him, yes or no?" asked counsel. "No, it was reported to me," the former broadcaster finally conceded. Georges Ruggiu's testimony was expected to be a formidable weapon for the prosecutor against other alleged perpetrators of the genocide. When the judges issued their ruling against the three Rwandans in the media trial, they had to throw out his entire testimony. He was not credible.

Dieudonné Niyitegeka had also taken the witness stand shortly before Ruggiu, testifying under unjustifiable anonymity and with the satellite transmission scrambled. The former Interahamwe leader came to testify against

Ferdinand Nahimana and, to a lesser extent, Jean-Bosco Barayagwiza. However, as his testimony proceeded, it proved to be particularly damning . . . for Georges Ruggiu.

Starting the day after the massacres began, the RTLM journalists, who were eager to have correct information as Ruggiu later dared to explain, kept an updated list on a blackboard, where they wrote, crossed off, and added the names of opposition figures who had been, or were supposed to be, assassinated. Niyitegeka told how on April 9, he went to visit his friends at the radio station. Georges Ruggiu was there. "I saw a blackboard with a list of twenty or so people to be killed. The names of people who had already been killed were crossed off. Some of the names had question marks in front of them. Others were 'open,' which meant that these people were still alive," explained the Interahamwe leader. According to Ruggiu, this board served to provide up-to-date information. It had two columns: one with people who were threatened and one with people who were already dead. However, according to Niyitegeka, who specified that it was the Belgian who, chalk in hand, kept the list current, this body-count board was more clearly titled "List of persons to be killed." If what he said was true, that would increase Ruggiu's criminal liability. From that point onward, the defense lawyers were only too pleased, and even made it their duty, to stir things up between these two gentlemen. "Did Ruggiu appear to be in favor of these people being killed?" asked one lawyer. "According to me, yes," replied Niyitegeka.

Niyitegeka's testimony against Ferdinand Nahimana, which the judges accepted as being "generally credible," paled in comparison. One of the crucial questions in the trial of RTLM's founder was whether he continued to control the radio station during the genocide even though he had fled Kigali by April 12.

"He could control the broadcasts being sent by RTLM and make comments when the information was false. He was in charge of this radio station. Therefore, he could ask the journalists not to broadcast erroneous or false information," Niyitegeka assured the court in a somewhat speculative manner. "I believe that Ferdinand Nahimana controlled the radio station until the very end."

"Why do you say that?" Judge Pillay pressed the witness.

"That's my conclusion. If the action committee had taken measures at the very beginning [against some of the things said], their duties would have been fulfilled. But they failed to fulfill them."[1]

"Just like you with the Interahamwe?" lashed out the judge.

"Yes," the former militia leader replied hesitantly.

The secret allegiances, friendships, betrayals, loyalties, and never-ending grudges were all revealed in the Rwandan trials. Undoubtedly, not a single trial took place in Arusha without a buried, but not forgotten, long-standing personal matter between certain witnesses or certain accused slipping in, often unbeknown to the court. It seems nothing should ever be forgotten between Rwandans, even the most trifling issues, and even, if necessary, those that never existed. This poisonous game played by the prosecutor's collaborators turned the prosecution offensive into a dangerous suicide mission or a bloody settling of scores among family.

Omar Serushago, the Interahamwe leader in Gisenyi who confessed and collaborated with the prosecutor's office, came to testify three months before national militia leader Dieudonné Niyitegeka. Squeezed into a grayish brown suit and tie that showed off his muscular back, he gazed steadily at the person against whom most of his testimony was directed: Hassan Ngeze, a big, strapping fellow who was also a native of Gisenyi. A psychological tension hung over the courtroom like that at a major boxing match. Serushago squarely accused his friend Ngeze of having been directly involved in the killings. Anxious to convince the judges, he stated that it was hard for him to recall the number of times he had seen the accused at the execution site "because we were encouraging people to kill Tutsis immediately and to rape." To rape? Hadn't he dismissed the accusation of rapes committed by his subordinates just three years earlier?

Bound by prudence, the judges ended up deciding not to accept Serushago's muddled and changing statements unless they were corroborated by other evidence. Thus, everyone could forget not only that he had incriminated himself, but that he had also implicated Dieudonné Niyitegeka, whom he said he saw again in Gisenyi at the end of June 1994, when Niyitegeka arrived armed and accompanied by an escort in the same helicopter as the Interahamwe president. "He was involved in planning the genocide and in that sense, he also killed," Serushago stated with respect to the prosecutor's star informant, who had managed to avoid prosecution. "Did you hear him say that he wanted to kill Tutsis, because they were Tutsi?" he was asked. "That's correct," he replied.

9

Opening Up Kibuye

We gathered on Muyira Hill—a name now well known to everyone from Kibuye. There were a great many of us. At the beginning, we were still strong and [the attackers] turned back. That was at the beginning of April, after the tenth. I was not wounded until sometime between the end of April and the beginning of May. About a week and a half later, we thought that they had stopped attacking. That was on the thirteenth and fourteenth of May.

witness R., Musema trial,
February 25, 1999

Kibuye is perhaps the most beautiful region in Rwanda. It is also the region where the annihilation of the Tutsis continued the longest, and was the most effective. Before the genocide, it was the most economically neglected prefecture and the only one whose administrative seat was not connected to Kigali by a paved road. After the holocaust, it was the province most often visited by journalists in search of traces of the extermination campaign. But there were none. They were long gone.

In olden days, very few villages were built in the Rwandan countryside. Cut off from the rest of the country by a mountain range offering the most spectacular vistas of the renowned "thousand hills" from which Rwanda derives its poetic name (along with "the country of eternal spring," as it was also called on tourism posters of yesteryear touting its exceptional climate), Kibuye was, and still is, largely rural. Since the end of the war, the new government has implemented an extensive, national "villagization" policy. The logic behind this profound, almost intimate, transformation of Rwandan society was legitimately based on economics. There were also political and security reasons: it is easier to protect a village than a group of scattered houses and also easier to monitor its inhabitants. Prior to this policy, however, there were no villages to speak of, just a few rural communities and the small town of Kibuye next to Lake Kivu.

It is easy to spot a place where an entire village has been razed to the ground. It can stay that way for quite a while in poor countries, where building a house can be the work of a lifetime. But a few scattered houses reduced to dust is harder to detect. Most of the visible traces of the war and destruction quickly evaporated after the genocide. All that remained were the survivors' accounts and the memorials erected after 1994.

Bisesero is the ultimate illustration of this impalpable memory. A large mountainous massif that is sometimes difficult to access, this region was traditionally a place where Tutsis sought refuge during previous pogroms in the 1960s. In April 1994, when the violence flared up in Kibuye prefecture, the Tutsis in that region—the area of the country where they were the most numerous—once again fled to these mountains seeking to escape the hordes of killers. They fought off their attackers by throwing rocks or implementing strategies that were both shrewd and unsuccessfully rash. "Some people were saying we should mix in with the assailants so that they would not recognize us. When we did this type of exercise, it also offered us the advantage of being able to rest, because we were very tired," one witness, who was thirty-three years old at the time of the events, told the court. But in the end, the mountains of Bisesero would become the largest open-air Tutsi grave in Kibuye. "We were attacked on all sides. People were shooting in every direction. We were all trying to find a path to escape this place. Those of us who were the strongest managed to escape. The people who were weak, particularly the elderly, women, and children, perished," recounted another witness, speaking anonymously. "The entire hillside was covered with bodies," recalled another.

In 1998 an impressive commemoration was organized in Bisesero. A memorial was erected where the remains of unburied victims scattered all over the hills and valleys were gathered. There were thousands of victims, tens of thousands, according to the accounts of some 1,500 survivors. It was the largest recognized massacre of the genocide, with an estimated 50,000 people dead. The killings continued nonstop from mid-April to the beginning of July. There was likely not a single day of rest for the militias, local authorities, gendarmes, and simple civilians who led this colossal hunt for *inyenzi*. Nevertheless, some attacks were more wide-scale than others. The biggest and best planned of all, in which the victims were surrounded in three successive waves, and which will remain forever engraved in the memories of those who survived it, was the attack that occurred over the weekend of May 13–14. The epicenter was Muyira Hill. The Bisesero memorial now stands at a slight slant on the hillside opposite Muyira Hill.

At first glance, the reason why the hunted Tutsis chose to retreat to this hill rather than another is not readily apparent. Muyira is not terribly imposing by virtue of having a steep incline or dense vegetation. It is separated from the main road by only a small, straight, shallow valley where a narrow stream flows through the middle of a short tract of easily crossable marshland. It was certainly a good place to graze cattle. But to understand the strategic interest of this hill, one has to go higher up. Muyira's slender summit has a wide base and a gentle slope that affords a remarkable view of the surrounding area, an excellent observation post to monitor the attackers' approach. It provides a bird's-eye view of Lake Kivu, Rwanda's natural border to the west, that gives one the feeling of suddenly being at the edge of the world. Cornered.

Kibuye is an enclave. Serving as the administrative seat of the province, this sleepy little town is wedged at the bottom of the tall mountains, nestled along one of those sumptuous strips of the lake that carve into Kivu's coastline like a liquid, brilliant blue tanzanite at the foot of an alpine quartz. The largest Tutsi executions were concentrated at two sites: Gatwaro stadium, which sits alongside the main road, and the Catholic estate comprising a church and Home St. Jean, which sits on the edge of town, around a few hairpin curves in the road. These places have since been restored to their peaceful or functional appearances. Home St. Jean is a large building constructed from the same stone as the church that sits in front of it under the shade of huge eucalyptus trees. The entire estate, which is occupied by monks, sits on a magnificent peninsula jutting out into the section of the lake that forms Kibuye's inner bay. In the early hours of the morning, when the scent of jasmine floats in the breeze and the fishing boats drift out onto the lake, the area reveals a rare meditative power. Here, as elsewhere, the church managed to appropriate the best spot for itself.

The main nave of the church is a big room soberly furnished with rows of wooden benches. The passion of Christ is painted in pastel pinks, grays, and blues on a concrete wall behind a massive altar. The walls are illuminated by patches of light pouring through the numerous small holes in the corrugated iron roof. An estimated five thousand people lost their lives here on April 17, 1994. The following day, the killers moved on to the stadium, a field next to the road in the center of town.

"We ate the meat from the cows we had brought with us," recalled one of the stadium survivors. "We used grass to cook it. Those who had water were the ones who could get to the hospital. There was a crack in the wall that led there. On the night of the seventeenth, survivors came from the Home St. Jean via the forest. They told us that the others had been killed. We could hear the sound of bullets and bombs. Vehicles were driving along the road with armed people aboard. As they drove by, they shouted at us: 'So, the match hasn't started yet?' They came and surrounded the stadium on all four sides. They started firing. I went down toward the field to join my family. We repelled them using rocks. Many people were struck by bullets or trampled by cows that had been hit by bullets. The attackers were gendarmes, police officers, prison guards, and civilians. They were all armed with either traditional or military weapons." Ten thousand people died in Gatwaro stadium.

It was at these places—Kibuye town and the hills of Bisesero— that the first three investigators for the UN tribunal gathered the first survivor testimonies in May 1995. No other portion of the Rwandan tribunal's mandate would be covered so thoroughly and so continuously than the proceedings against the alleged perpetrators of the Kibuye genocide. The crimes committed in this region formed the basis of the first indictment issued by the ICTR in November 1995. Between 1997 and 2005, ten Rwandans were brought to justice for these massacres. Not a single year would go by without there being a "Kibuye trial" in progress. In total, the court indicted thirteen people for this region alone, making Kibuye, a forgotten area prior to the war, the most reliable and unlimited source of cases for the UN tribunal to investigate.

Two government ministers, one *préfet*, three *bourgmestres*, one pastor, one doctor, one factory manager, one businessman, two town councilors, and one restaurant owner—all that lacked was a military leader, making the panoply of defendants from Kibuye the most diverse and complete ever to be brought before the court. They were all prosecuted for massacres at the stadium, Home St. Jean, the church, or Bisesero, and in some cases, for several of these massacres.

The first to stand trial was the *préfet* and former doctor, Clément Kayishema. It took two years for the three judges to complete the trial of Kayishema and another individual, Obed Ruzindana, who seemed to be both Kayishema's polar opposite and his most natural accomplice.[1] A modest shopkeeper according to his defense lawyer and a prosperous businessman according to the prosecution, Obed Ruzindana was as physically large and dominating as Kayishema was hunched, as though trying to make himself disappear from the scene. His high, prominent cheekbones accentuated the closed look of his small, expressionless eyes, while the *préfet* had piercing eyes that bore into anyone whose gaze he met. The businessman would become animated, fidget, chuckle, or seem lost in the oratorical jousting of the men in robes around him, while the former doctor next to him sat motionless, not missing a beat.

And yet both in court and in the witnesses' testimonies, they came off as having always been the best of accomplices.

On May 21, 1999, they were both found guilty of genocide. This case was not one of betrayal or of a person who suddenly changed, but rather killing as a course of action and cruelty as a modus operandi. Fifty-one witnesses came to the stand to describe in gruesome detail the reality of what the *préfet* had described in a telegram as follows: "For the safety of Bisesero sector, Gishyita commune, the people of the region are determined to comb the area in the context of civil defense." Combing was another euphemistic term for the genocidal undertaking. Persuaded by his lawyer not to subject himself to the risk of questioning by the judges and the prosecutor, Obed Ruzindana, who was thirty-two years old at the time, ended up benefiting from being tried alongside a more prestigious and intelligent defendant. He received a twenty-five-year sentence, whereas Clément Kayishema, who was forty years old at the time, received life in prison.

Alfred Musema was the next person to stand trial for the genocide in Kibuye. The manager of a tea factory in Kibuye prefecture, he claimed to have met with Clément Kayishema at least once during the events. That was on April 30, 1994, less than two weeks after the slaughter at the stadium and the church. He recounted what he saw that day: "Before I even got there, I had heard that there had been astonishing, abominable massacres in the prefecture. Along the lake I saw houses that had been burned and banana groves that had been cut down. Upon arriving [in town], you can see the stadium. The entrance was demolished, and there were red stains on the walls, even though the stadium was brand new. There was an extremely foul, very intense odor, which meant there were bodies decomposing. I passed by the St. Jean church and saw that the windows were broken and a fire had been lit in front of the door. And there was the same odor. That was the image I saw of Kibuye before going to the *préfet*'s office."

"What was his attitude toward you?"

"It's difficult to say. He was uneasy, a little confused, not very comfortable in his role as governor, a little strange."

Sitting in the defendant's seat four years after this encounter, Kayishema was no longer confused, but his perception of the events was still rather bizarre. "There were people who were drinking at bars in a neighborhood in Kibuye. Words were 'thrown,' followed by Hutus making disparaging comments about Tutsis, and Tutsis about Hutus," he added by way of explanation in his Rwandan French. The contrast between the descriptions given by the former *préfet* and the former tea-factory manager was striking. This would not be the only difference between the trials of these two men.

10

Be like the Arab

(Reason to Doubt)

At the end of the defense presentation, the words of a poem by Longfellow came to mind. I thought to myself that the prosecutor should "Be like the Arab / Who in the night / Quietly folds his tent / And as silently steals away." But that is not the case.

Steven Kay, lawyer for Alfred Musema,
June 28, 1999

A trial, especially one that lasts as long as those before the UN tribunals, can be a numbing process. To guarantee their impartiality, the proceedings must take place under the anesthesia of rules of procedure and legal decorum. Form and codes are all-important. The vocabulary is abstruse and disembodied. The dynamics of the legal battle between the parties emphasize this cold distancing of what is really at stake, shifting it to a place shielded from emotion and feeling. The product of the trial—the judgment of an individual—can also, therefore, appear to be technical, as though it were necessary to downplay the toll it takes on a person's life. Paradoxically, in Arusha this effect was multiplied by the social promiscuity of the various parties involved in the trial and by their shared life in the ICTR's little world (whether they rejected it, embraced it, feared it, or longed to be part of it). Over the months and over the years, people became familiar characters in a deceptive play in which they were all simply going willy-nilly about their lives, which in most cases were actually pretty good.

A verdict is the complete opposite. It's short; it's rapid; it's an instant, a word. And everything that preceded it—the warrants, interrogations, motions, replies, investigations, hearings, witnesses, cross-examinations, delays, adjournments, briefs, arguments, closing remarks—is swallowed up. Evaporated. Paperwork. Poof!

Civilized to an extreme, silent and disciplined, never protesting, never provocative, with utmost deference to the court, Alfred Musema allowed the professional confrontation around his "case" to unfold in accordance with the rules. Of course, in the final days of his trial, when prosecutor Jane Adong speculated that he was playing with the court, he reminded her, ever so courteously, "This is about my life; I am not playing around." But like a quick needle prick, this reminder of what was truly at stake was not enough to "un-numb" the proceedings.

On January 27, 2000, everything happened very quickly. Alfred Musema was found guilty of genocide in Bisesero and sentenced to life in prison. On paper, the case differed from preceding ones on two points only: the trial took only one year from start to finish (a record for the tribunal), and in addition to genocide and extermination (the law draws a subtle distinction between the two), the defendant was the first to be convicted of direct rape.[1]

For those who followed this trial, however, the matter was entirely different. It was a case of bad conscience, a murky zone between the illusory certainty of facts and the possibility of a miscarriage of justice. Consequently, the verdict in this case—an instant, a word—was that moment where one had to either abandon one's doubts in favor of the judges' sovereign decision or acknowledge that the judges had emancipated themselves from the law.

Every day for a week during the month of May 1999, the defendant would leave his seat and slowly walk over to take the witness stand with his hands clasped in front of him. Before reaching his spot, Musema would systematically pause for a second to bow obsequiously to the judges, who, for that brief moment, felt they had a duty not to notice anything. Before he sat down, he would always turn and give a discrete little bow to the prosecutors, who made a habit of looking busy in that fleeting instant. For a person accused by twenty-two witnesses of committing the worst crimes imaginable—murder, mass attacks, rape, collective "fumigation," all without interruption for nine weeks (from April 14 to June 22, 1994, more precisely)—Alfred Musema was infuriatingly polite.

On the witness stand, where he always maintained civility, it was clear that underneath the patina of his suave personality was a determined, highly intelligent person. The man was tough. He was sharp and perceptive. His French was precise, even rich. He rarely misused the idiomatic expressions that are so often poetically distorted in Rwandan French. Always focused, his answers were well thought out. He often removed his glasses when he did not need them for reading, revealing a face that was always expressive, though not very charming. He had a readily piercing look that sometimes gave him the false appearance of sarcasm, which unfortunately was reinforced by his slight natural grimace.

Faced with a defendant who was both smooth and tough—the very image that his British lawyer Steven Kay had intended to portray—the prosecutors did not have an easy time. Charles Adeogun-Phillips and Jane Adong were sharing the job of trying to "put him to the question" in its infinitely more civilized version under Anglo-Saxon law: the cross-examination. The judges regularly interjected their contribution in a game of cross fire that was particularly lively given that this case was entirely, or nearly so, based on the defendant's testimony and the documents supporting his version of the facts, namely, his alibi. For Alfred Musema's defense was simple and clear: he was not there. He claimed that except for being at the Gisovu tea factory (where he was the manager) on April 14, 1994, he was never at any of the numerous places where witnesses alleged they saw him in April, May, and June, leading and participating in the attacks on the Tutsis in the Kibuye region.

It took five days for Musema to give an unusually meticulous, day-by-day, almost hour-by-hour accounting of his life from April to July 1994. It was the work of a weaver, masterfully orchestrated by Steven Kay. The accuracy of the defendant's day planner was supported by a mass of materials the likes of which the court had never seen before: dozens of documents, meeting minutes, receipts, and invoices that the defense had found and recovered in Rwanda. Several of these documents contained irregularities, especially the one that was the defense's cornerstone: a travel order issued to Alfred Musema by the interim government containing stamps, dates, and signatures attesting to his visits to various tea factories throughout the country during these crucial months in order to conduct site inventories and to establish the terms for reopening the factories. This mission, which according to the defendant was extended while in progress, covered the period from April 22 to May 31, 1994, that is, the exact same time as the accusations against him. The prosecution tried to exploit certain errors in the dates marked on some of the items in the case file. Based primarily on the interviews with the defendant in 1995 and 1996 by authorities in Switzerland, where proceedings against Musema had begun in 1995 before the UN tribunal took over the case, the duel between the prosecutors and the man on the stand was almost entertaining.

"When you were questioned shortly after the events, five years ago in 1995, you did not recall the facts. Isn't that strange?" asked Charles Adeogun-Phillips.

"There is nothing strange about it. Investigations and research had to be conducted in order to verify the dates," replied the defendant, unruffled.

"You waited to see what the accusations against you were and then you prepared a watertight alibi based on these allegations," asserted Jane Adong in turn, pushing the falsified document theory to an extreme logic.

"I am pleased that you find my alibi to be watertight; it is supported by material evidence," replied Musema, still showing restraint and no animosity.

The prosecution never provided the slightest proof that the documents produced as evidence had been falsified. In reality, this was simply impossible. They had all been found by either the Swiss authorities or the defense lawyers during their respective visits to Rwanda in 1995 and 1999. Most of them had been found in the archives at the Gisovu tea factory. If Musema had really tried to construct such an alibi, would he have taken the risk of leaving the country without bringing these documents with him? It would take an extremely twisted or deliberately dishonest mind to believe that. But some did. The story Musema told the Swiss police was identical to the one described in the documents found during the investigations in Rwanda. None of the documents contradicted his story in substance. What was different however, were the dates that the defendant had recalled from memory in his cell in 1995 and those contained in the documents at the time they were recovered. Having run out of arguments, Adong therefore resigned herself to focusing on the contrast, which, granted, was radical, between the prosecution evidence, based solely on eyewitness testimony, and the exculpatory evidence, supported almost entirely by documents. "Are the witnesses lying, or are you lying?" she finally summarized. Musema replied, "We are dealing with an extremely serious situation. Thousands of people died in Kibuye. I could not allow myself to lie to this court. I was not at Muyira," he stated, citing the name of the infamous hill in the Bisesero massif where thousands of Tutsis perished on May 13 and 14, 1994, and where, according to the statements of several witnesses, the manager of the Gisovu tea factory was among the killers. Backed into a corner, Adong attempted the absurd: "Can you look the judges in the eye and say to their faces that you were not there and that you did not take part in the attacks?" Of course, the question was pointless. "Madame, before both the judges and God, I swear that I was not at Muyira."

Musema did not give them much to work with. As a result, everyone got off topic. Oddly enough, the judges began to criticize this man accused of genocide for the fact that his mission report on the tea factories was poorly written. While that may have been true, it was most likely not an indication of criminal intent. Meanwhile, the prosecutor attempted to find some sort of subterfuge or lie in the fact that when the killings started in the Rwandan capital, the defendant had to climb over the wall of his neighbor's yard to use the telephone "rather than going through the gate."

Musema was both intelligent and cautious. When the prosecutor asked him to state the ethnicity of the people who were massacred in the Kigali neighborhood where he was at the beginning of April, the defendant gave a guarded reply.

"What did they look like?" Adeogun-Phillips tried again.

"Mr. Prosecutor, do not lead me into the trap of making such a misjudgment," he replied, equally politely.

Musema's position vis-à-vis the events in Rwanda in 1994 was entirely unique among the Arusha detainees. With the exception of those who had pleaded guilty of course, he was the first, and he would be the only defendant to recognize from the outset, without any qualms or hesitation, that the Tutsis had been the victims of genocide. Some admitted it at the last minute, when the noose was already around their necks, so to speak. Others propped up their defense on the fact that there were a lot of killings on both sides. From the start, Musema was unambiguous about the fate reserved for the Tutsi community, of which his mother-in-law was a member. For example, he described the behavior of those he saw manning the roadblocks when he left Kigali as follows: "They were scrupulously checking identity cards. They were saying, 'You look like an *inyenzi.*' They were asking for money." Judge Kama asked if one could thereby deduce that they were looking for Tutsis. "The deduction can be made unmistakably," emphasized Musema.

The defendant showed little vulnerability in that respect. Instead, what continued to plague the court was the fact that during those three months of terror, he never demanded any explanation of the killings he witnessed. How could he not ask the soldiers in Kigali why they were killing, the prosecutor questioned? "That is difficult, Mr. Prosecutor. I did not dare do so. When they came to ask us to bury people, it was a group of paracommandos with civilians. We went to the plots and saw the horror. I did not ask the paramilitary forces why these people had been killed."

Even when he arrived at the Gisovu factory on April 14 and discovered that his senior Tutsi assistants had been killed, he asked no questions, certainly not of the *bourgmestre* and the killers who were there.

"I was overcome by fear. I was horrified. I was in shock. I did not ask him. I could not ask for explanations from a *bourgmestre.*"

"But by not asking, did you not give the impression that you were totally fine with their presence at your factory?"

"It was not a matter of being fine with it or not. *Bourgmestres* have the authority to go anywhere they want in their commune."

"You had just seen the bodies of five members of your senior staff. Didn't you feel you had any responsibility? You didn't even deign to ask a single question?"

"I admit it, Mr. Prosecutor. And it was not five people; there were several who had been killed. The *bourgmestre* arrived with an armed IPJ [inspector with the criminal investigation department]. Do you think I should have asked them, 'Are you the ones who killed?' It was not a question of lack of responsibility or consideration toward those people, not at all."

"I find that very difficult to believe. Surely you have an explanation. Didn't you care about them?"

"If it is a normal state of affairs and if I notice a dead person, I go see the IPJ; I call the prosecutor's office and they make a report. But I am telling you that we were no longer in a normal situation. When I arrived, I asked the policemen who were there what had happened. They explained to me that these people had come from Gikongoro and had massacred people. The IPJ, the *bourgmestre*, and the teacher arrived armed. What do you think I should have asked the IPJ to do? Go make a report? The *bourgmestre* told me he was in the process of cleaning up. So what was I supposed to ask him? If I had had the time, I certainly would have asked."

Musema wished to avoid venturing into the territory of accusing those he may have suspected of having committed the crime.

"How could the killers have known they were Tutsis?" asked Judge Aspegren, referring to the factory workers who were killed just before Musema arrived.

"That is one of the factors that reinforces my conviction that it was a genocide. They were killed because of their ethnic group. I have no hesitations about that. If you were to conduct an investigation, you would surely find people who pointed them out."

"Who would have pointed them out?"

"That is difficult to say, Mr. President."

"You did not find out who?"

"No, I did not conduct that investigation. I'm sorry, Mr. President."

"So you do not know anything about the people from the factory who helped the killers?"

"That's correct. I do not have that information. If I tell you what I heard, it is hearsay and I cannot verify it. The *bourgmestre* of Gisovu commune was reportedly at the site. But that is what people told me; I do not know for certain," Musema replied, even though he had also said with respect to this *bourgmestre* (who was indicted by the ICTR but never arrested) that he "was already a man whom I might suspect of complicity with the group of killers."

"Were workers from the factory involved in the attacks on Muyira?" asked prosecutor Jane Adong.

"I do not know of any, Madame. I did not conduct any investigations along those lines. I had no suspicions whatsoever. Based on what I [know], I am not aware of any vehicles being used. But there were times when I was away from the factory. I cannot vouch for the periods when I was not in Gisovu."

Even so, there was one piece of evidence in this respect: a warning to all the factory drivers that Musema himself had signed on June 14, 1994. Their gasoline usage was completely out of the norm: approximately 1,900 liters were used between April 6 and mid-June, whereas the factory did not start operating again until May 9. This was precisely the defense's theory, that because factory vehicles were used for the attacks, the defendant was mistakenly identified as being in Bisesero.

Alfred Musema did not oppose the killers. This was an established fact that he himself admitted. Most, if not all, of the other defendants claimed that they had tried to save someone here or there. Not Musema. He was both the only one to recognize the crime for what it was, without any ambiguity, and the only one who felt no vainglory. "I did not participate or take part in the genocide. I cannot boast of having done anything. Unfortunately for Rwanda and for all of humanity, there was a genocide. Many people could have helped. Some did. Those are the facts. It is bitter for me. I therefore have no reason to boast about having taken such and such action. My job was to run the factory. I never led any gangs of criminals. How do you expect me to have gone and done anything about the killers' actions? I am not a monster. I have my weaknesses. I ask forgiveness for these weaknesses. But I am not a savage. I could have done something, but I didn't. I was afraid. I admit it. Am I to be condemned for this fear or this weakness?"

The son of a farmer, Alfred Musema managed to climb unusually high up the social ladder. He grew up in the northern province of Byumba, where his father ensured the family's self-sufficiency through farming, herding, and itinerant commerce. Although his father had embraced the Anglican faith, his son was raised a Catholic, starting at age six. That was in 1955, the year that Alfred Musema began elementary school. Middle school in Kigali confirmed that he had promise. He was first in his class, something he still states with pride. He would have gladly majored in mathematics and physics, but the scholarship advisor for Belgium counseled him to follow a course of study related to his country's economy instead. So the young man enrolled in the Gembloux School of Agronomic Sciences in Rwanda's former colonial power. Musema was both brilliant and lucky. At twenty-five years old, he was the first college graduate in his family. When he returned to Rwanda, he was an agronomist with a specialization in agricultural engineering. He had also met Claire Kayuku, whom he married in 1975 and with whom he would have three sons. The following year, advancing by leaps and bounds, he was named director general of agricultural engineering and soil conservation at the Ministry of Agriculture. It was a remarkable promotion even though, as Musema pointed out, there were only two other Rwandans in the country at the time who were equally qualified. Up to that point, life was rosy for this man of humble origins.

In 1984 his future started to look bleak for the first time. He and two other director generals at the ministry were suspended. He was appointed manager of the Gisovu tea factory in Kibuye. It was a punishment. He claims not to know the reason for this sanction, but he immediately felt the consequences. Kigali was a much more attractive place on the professional, financial, and family level. Now that he had been exiled to the enclave of Kibuye, a region he did not know, far from his roots and the capital, Alfred Musema felt as though he were "fastened by [his] feet to the Gisovu factory," which sat in the middle of nowhere, several dozen kilometers away from the sleepy town of Kibuye.

The factory had been operating for just under a year when he took over. Its production level was extremely low—around 200 tons for a factory that normally should have been producing 1,200 tons per year. The plantations were also young, dating from 1977. However, the tea that was produced there was high quality. "In 1993 Gisovu was one of Rwanda's top factories and was among the group of high-quality factories on the international level," he pointed out under the expert eye of his British lawyer. But that did not compensate for his family difficulties. After a year, the couple was separated from their children, whom they sent to Kigali. Gisovu has a luscious green carpet of plantations as its horizon and a dense forest as its only way out. Musema had an unquenchable desire to escape his infinite isolation and get his future back. He applied for several positions with the African Development Bank, put in his application at the World Bank, and approached the Agency for Technical Cooperation. "I did not see how I could change my family's future by staying in Gisovu. Living apart from one's children is not a future. I thought that I could secure my future by advancing in the international system," including on the financial level of course. On that point, his audience in the courtroom could sympathize with him.

In February 1994 his wife went to live with the children in Kigali for good. A trip to the Gisenyi region, a funeral in Kigali for the manager of another factory, a trip to the Office of Tea headquarters: starting March 12, Musema delegated management of the factory to his head accountant and then to the plantations manager when the accountant went on vacation, as indicated in the factory records. He claimed he was also friends with the two assistants directly under him, whose abilities he praised. When he returned to the factory on April 14, he learned that these two men had just been killed along with their families. They were Tutsis.

Did Alfred Musema apply ethnic quotas at the factory, in keeping with the Rwandan government's official policy of discrimination at the time, which granted the Tutsi minority access to teaching and government jobs only in proportion to their supposed representation in the population (9 percent according to the government of independent Rwanda, 14 percent according to colonial demographers)? "I showed some disobedience in that respect. The one-party state had a sort of policy of limiting members of the Tutsi ethnic group to 10 percent. At the factory, it was nearly 20 percent, so there was no discrimination," he defended himself naively, adding later on that he was not the only one who disregarded the quota policy. Was ethnicity nevertheless a selection criterion? Musema claimed he did not know the ethnic background of his employees. This was hardly credible, but the fact remained that most of his top managers at the factory were Tutsis.

Musema swore he was never involved in politics. In 1980, when one of his brothers-in-law was suspected of being involved in a plot against Habyarimana, several members of the family were imprisoned, and he was questioned by government security agents. But the only political involvement he acknowledged was in his native region of Byumba, where he was a member of the prefecture committee.

"Were you ever a member of a Hutu Power party?" asked his lawyer Steven Kay.

"Never."

"Did you ever promote extremist group politics vis-à-vis Tutsis?"

"I would never do that, not in the past, present, or future."

Was Musema more politically active than he cared to admit? If so, the prosecutor of this international tribunal tasked with trying high-ranking officials either did not really want to prove it or was unable to do so for lack of any substantial evidence. Only one witness came forward to support this theory, called in at the last minute when the prosecutor felt the case might be slipping through his hands. André Guichaoua, a French expert on Rwanda, observed that after the country transitioned to a multiparty system in 1991, Musema ran unsuccessfully for the *préfet* position in his native region of Byumba. Beyond that, the only proof of any political activity was in a letter written on September 28, 1992, by the then prime minister criticizing the roles that a certain number of key figures, including Alfred Musema, were playing in the antigovernment protests in Kigali staged by Rwandans from Byumba prefecture who had been displaced due to the armed conflict with the RPF rebels. At the time, the RPF rebel advance into northern Rwanda had, in fact, driven tens of thousands of Rwandans from their homes; these refugees then settled further south, particularly around the capital. In his letter, the prime minister objected to government officials leading unauthorized demonstrations against their own employer. That is the only trace of Alfred Musema's political activism.

During his testimony, Guichaoua also explained that during the war of April 1994, tea and coffee production, which was a vital source of income for the interim government, was the object of "extraordinary draconian oversight by the central government." In his opinion, the role of a factory manager at that time was above all to maintain the production infrastructure and export levels. According to him, managers also had an additional mandate of "pacification." So, was their role to maintain the industrial tool or to pacify? And what was meant by pacification, given the ambiguity of this term during the genocide? This appeared to be the crux of the debate in the Musema case. Unbeknown to him, the French expert testifying for the prosecution had just boosted the credibility of the mission order issued to the defendant during the war, which was clearly part of the government's "draconian oversight." Somewhat inadvertently, Guichaoua's testimony touched on what may have been the true issue in the Musema case: industrial support for a criminal regime. But in this respect, like others, Nuremberg was more ambitious than Arusha.

With her simple elegance, delicate appearance, and short hair that did not look overly styled, Claire Kayuku was the first wife of a defendant to testify openly in court. In Rwanda, there are no family names. Everyone has his or her own name, which is generally composed of a Christian or Muslim first name and a second, authentic Rwandan name. Alfred Musema's wife was an exception. She bore the name of her father, Kayuku, a member of the national assembly and a prominent figure in the 1959 social revolution who was assassinated in 1961 by Tutsi combatants waging a guerrilla war against the authorities under Rwanda's first republic. A street in downtown Kigali is named after this martyred hero of the Hutu revolution. It was often said that young Alfred's sudden rise to the top upon his return from Belgium was also partly the result of this seemingly advantageous marriage. But that was merely speculation. And it was certainly not true after the incident of the thwarted plot against Habyarimana in 1980, in which a member of the Kayuku family was suspected of being involved.

The testimony of his wife, whom he had not seen in almost four years at that point, was one of the rare exceptions to Musema's defense strategy, which

Be like the Arab

was based solely on his credibility and the strength of the documents he submitted in support of his alibi. Even so, Claire Kayuku essentially came to confirm the authenticity of some of these documents: three letters that she wrote in 1994 to a Swiss friend who had been evacuated from Rwanda in April and at whose home these letters had been found. In the second half of June 1994, she described the situation to her friends in Europe as follows: "We are now at the Shagasha tea factory [in Cyangugu province in southwest Rwanda]. Alfred is always on the move. He has been shuttling back and forth and serving as a liaison between everyone: in Butare, Gikongoro, and those of us here in Cyangugu. We no longer know who is alive. It's a good thing that Alfred is here, unshakable. Right now he is in Gisenyi. We have dubbed him the Rambo of the family. He was urgently summoned by his minister, but we still don't know why. For the time being, it is impossible to get out. The only possibilities for communication are in Goma. If he [Alfred] is able to contact you, it would be great. Alfred would stay here, at least initially. He does not want to leave." Further on she wrote, "No one in Alfred's family survived. When the RPF came through, everything was decimated. It was terrible. I don't have much news from Gisovu. [We had] a stopover there on May 27–28. Alfred goes there on a regular basis, but I fear the worst."

Claire Kayuku's testimony was brief. When it was over, she asked to say a few words.

"What is it about?" asked Judge Aspegren.

"About my husband," she replied, specifying that she wanted to say something about her spouse's point of view regarding extremism and ethnicity and about his relationships with Tutsis.

"I do not think that will be necessary," declared the judge.

Seven letters were thus submitted as evidence: three from Claire Kayuku, three from Alfred Musema, and one dated June 7 that was sealed to protect the identity of its author. They were documents of striking veracity, but also fragile evidence. For example, none of the envelopes had been saved. "I received several letters during that period, often with European stamps. At that time, I did not see the need to keep the envelopes," explained the Swiss friend with a hint of sarcasm. Hence, there were no postmarks, only the handwritten date on the letters themselves. One of these letters could have tipped the scales in favor of Musema because it was signed by the defendant himself and bore the heading "Butare, May 14, 1999." That was the second day of the massive attack on Muyira Hill. In this letter, he mentioned the "tragic events that have plunged Rwanda into a deep abyss" and wrote, "Since April 6, there has been an unbelievable bloodbath in the country: ethnic unrest, massacres, theft, everything one could possibly imagine, or rather could not even imagine, in terms of human horror." Could Musema have been in the Bisesero massif on May 13, killing, raping, and leading a bloodthirsty horde, as twelve witnesses confirmed, and then have returned to Butare, in the south of the country, written so conscientiously to his Swiss friends, and gone back the same day to massacre people in the hills? Or had this date been mischievously added after the fact?

Steven Kay knew the importance of this deadly weekend in Bisesero in mid-May. Consequently, he also submitted as evidence a receipt from a gas station in Gitarama dated May 14, along with meeting minutes that were found at the factory. These were signed by the personnel director, dated May 19, 1994, and said the following: "The manager reminded us that he has just spent a few days making the rounds but that in the meantime, he has been unable to return because his car broke down, even though he has sent word to have the vehicle repaired." Finally, the defense counsel called his only two protected witnesses, a husband and wife, to the stand. The wife had left Rwanda on May 17, via former Zaire, as her passport attested. She spoke using remarkable French, and she was the one who had written the June 7 letter sent to the same Swiss friend. She wrote at the time, "I received your letter concerning Alfred Musema's family. Unfortunately I do not have any recent news of them. But when I left Rwanda on May 17, they were in Butare at Claire's parents' house." Judge Aspegren asked her to clarify what she meant by "they." She replied, "Alfred, his wife, and the children."

Her husband testified that he had stopped by the family home of his old friend Claire Kayuku as he was fleeing Rwanda via Burundi, for which he also had a stamp in his passport as proof. (For security reasons, the couple had decided to leave the country separately. They returned to Rwanda after the genocide before finally going back into exile.) He said he ran into Alfred Musema there. That was fifteen kilometers from Butare, and it was May 13. But notwithstanding the stamp in his passport, this evidence was once again testimonial.

At the end of the trial, there was only one certainty: doubt. When the doubt was not being fueled by a piece of material evidence supporting the defendant's alibi, it was metastasizing by virtue of the sheer volume and persistence of these documents. The only question now was whether, in the eyes of the judges, this doubt was sufficient to conclude that in the end the prosecutor had not proven Musema's guilt *beyond any reasonable doubt*, in accordance with the famous formula that served as the ultimate threshold for decisions before the international tribunal. On the one hand, survivor witnesses had come forward to confirm that Alfred Musema had taken part in the attacks led to exterminate them on various days in April, May, and June. Several of these testimonies had made it through Kay's cross-examination unscathed and could therefore be admitted and used to support a guilty charge against the former factory manager. On the other hand, there was a body of proof and hard evidence gathered by the defense that, if admitted as a continuum, would have made it impossible for Musema to have committed the alleged crimes, even if he were a major schizophrenic.

After seven months of deliberation, judges Kama, Aspegren, and Pillay accepted the vague memory of survivors over the defendant's flawed alibi. Alfred Musema was found guilty beyond any reasonable doubt. However, this was the first time that the judges differed substantially over the factual conclusions. Only the acts that took place in mid-May in the mountains of Bisesero, particularly on Muyira Hill, resulted in a unanimous conviction. At the heart of the judges' differing opinions on everything else was, of course, the defendant's alibi.

Judges Kama and Aspegren accepted parts of it, but different parts in some cases. The charges against Musema were based on acts spanning a seventy-day period. Based on the reliability of the evidence and the strength of the alibi, Lennart Aspegren ended up convicting the defendant only for the acts during the period between May 7 and 19, 1994, in other words, essentially for the Muyira attack. Laïty Kama accepted the alibi for four attacks led in April, May, and June, but rejected it for two others—one at the end of April and one at the end of May—and for the one in mid-May at Muyira. In their own way, they each took the "reasonable doubt" into consideration. Navanethem Pillay, for her part, chose to avoid it. She "assessed the evidence of alibi presented at trial as a whole, rather than piecemeal, or on a day-by-day basis." According to her, "the defendant was not a credible witness," his testimony had been "riddled with inconsistencies," and she doubted the authenticity of the defense's key document: the infamous mission order. Insofar as Claire Kayuku's testimony did not corroborate her husband's in Judge Pillay's opinion, and the other defense witness was not deemed credible, she "reject[ed] the alibi defence, as it [was] not supported by sufficient evidence to make it even possible to cast reasonable doubt on the other evidence the Chamber [found] to be credible." It was so much easier that way.

The judges' differences did not end there. They also disagreed on the credibility, reliability, and/or the probative value of the prosecution evidence. Several witness testimonies were deemed credible by only two of the three judges, but not always the same two. Granted, that was enough to convict, but was it enough to convince? Behind the seemingly compact appearance of the Musema verdict was a judgment of conflicting geometry. His conviction ended the suspense of the trial, but it did not dispel the doubt. Worse still, one of the tribunal's findings gave rise to a much more serious suspicion, that of partiality.

It was not difficult to gather evidence in Rwanda. "Basically, conducting investigations was not complicated. In Rwanda, everyone knows everything, and everybody knows everybody," one of the investigators on the first team in charge of investigating Kibuye in 1995 candidly explained to the court. Whether one liked it or not, the unfortunate reality was that it was possible to obtain five or more testimonies against one individual without this necessarily being sufficient to ascertain the person's guilt. There were countless cases of Rwandans being falsely accused, whether deliberately or not. Instances of denunciation and false evidence were abundant, but so were witness accounts that were simply erroneous without meaning to be. Such is the fragile nature of human testimony. It is obviously even more fragile in a society in which lying has been elevated to the status of a value; although it would be in very poor taste for an outsider to say so publicly, any Rwandan would readily admit that is the case in Rwanda. "That's how it is; in Rwanda as in Burundi, we are masters of the art of lying, probably more so than any other people. In fact, traditionally, lying is viewed positively: it is a sign of maturity and clear-sightedness. Why? Because it is often the only means of survival. Traditional arms are not enough; people have had to resort to cunning and lies to have a chance of survival," wrote priest and journalist André Sibomana.[2] Logically, the more notorious the suspect, the greater the risk of lying, and notoriety was a given with all those accused by the international tribunal due to publicity surrounding their indictment and arrest.

Thus, the real difficulty was not in finding witnesses but in dealing with the legal consequences of such readily available testimony. Under these circumstances, how was it possible to ensure that the main perpetrators of the genocide did not escape justice simply because there was not enough hard evidence to support the fragile proof of human testimony alone? On the contrary, how could the tribunal continue to try them (both a moral necessity and a legal obligation), while ensuring at best, or at a minimum, that the proceedings were shielded from injustice, doubt, and lies? It would take both courage and the hope of finding a solution to face this twofold challenge. The majority of the tribunal's key players lacked the first. The second was also in short supply, which convinced the few who were courageous to give up in the face of the difficult task.

Establishing individual responsibility years after the events in the "hill trials," as the cases involving genocide in the rural zones may be called, was largely, if not totally, impossible, except of course in cases where the

Be like the Arab

perpetrators confessed. This was already true at the time of Musema's trial only five years after the events. Ten or fifteen years later, the trials of this nature in Arusha were a depressing fiction that everyone went along with like an absurdist play. Yet it was unacceptable and at the very least morally intolerable to say or admit this, given that the ultimate crime had been committed and it ultimately had to be punished. This is why everyone avoided asking the question: at what cost?

Faced with this reality, with the formidable tension between the suspicious abundance of incriminating testimony and the precious, even singular truth that could be found in this evidence, the prosecution should have thought more strategically about how to limit the adverse effects on its investigations. However, they did the exact opposite. Rather than stepping up efforts to cross-check testimonies and expand the search for material evidence (of which there was more than they ever acknowledged), they dropped the ball. Information reported about the various accused no longer seemed to defy the improbable or appeared to be too spectacular. After months, sometimes years, of investigations, no direct proof of murder ever surfaced against this leader or that high-ranking official? No matter. Then, years later, just before a trial was about to start, the perfect proof of guilt, sensational as a gunshot, repugnant as a rape, sinister as a death sentence meted out in private, would emerge at just the right time from a witness who came out of the shadows, both alive and anonymous, convincing, yet unverifiable, as unique and fragile as it would be immoral to fail him or her.

This tension was not new. In the trial of Nazi Adolf Eichmann in 1961, the prosecutor had alleged in vain that the man who had formerly headed the deportation of Jews had personally killed a child in Hungary. In Arusha, unlike Jerusalem, the malaise stemmed from the fact that such allegations were presented not just *in addition to*, but often *for lack of* other evidence, in order to compensate for the investigators' failure to search relentlessly for hard evidence. Was it simply a matter of negligence? Nothing could be less certain. On one of the documents found in the files at the Gisovu factory, there was a mysterious handwritten note, dated October 1996, which was precisely the period when the office of the prosecutor was conducting investigations in Kibuye. "I will not ask any more questions about it," Steven Kay lashed out, insinuating that in reality, the prosecution had inspected the factory's files and then left them there because they did not support its accusations.[3] Two days before Musema's lawyers visited the factory in early 1999, members of the prosecutor's office made a hasty trip there on the sly. In the manager's absence, they were unable to examine any of the factory's records that day, but they left him a note requesting a copy of anything that the defense counsel might take when they visited. This was strange behavior. "We could not conduct an investigation that would have the slightest credibility if we remained blind to all the elements that could either lessen guilt or suggest a defense: no investigator worthy of that name would investigate only incriminating evidence," stated chief prosecutor Louise Arbour at the time when the Musema trial was being held. Credibility, worthiness—these words were both golden and bitter.

For beyond its complexity, beyond the convictions one may have about whether the defendant was guilty, Alfred Musema's trial highlighted the failures in the investigations, the advent of a sordid temptation to go overboard, as if it were imperative that criminal behavior or responsibility be as *physically* horrific as the nature of the crime. The prosecutors were not the only ones to promote this idea. The judges also went along with it.

Anyone who observed the Musema trial knows how astoundingly difficult this case was to try, as discretely evidenced by the disturbingly tangled threads of the judgment. Yet the worst suspicions were not aroused by the decision to find him guilty or not guilty of the attacks against Tutsis in Kibuye. After all, as it stood with all the information produced in this case, there was perhaps just as much to support a verdict of guilty as a verdict of not guilty. Perhaps— but this judgment zone, this mysterious place in the conscience where what lawyers in France call "intimate conviction" and what common law refers to as "beyond any reasonable doubt" takes shape, did not exist for at least one of the charges: rape. Everyone knew, including the judges' own legal assistants, that in *this* trial, it was completely unreasonable to admit the evidence brought against Musema. However, this was one of the few charges on which all three judges unanimously, and in all conscience, convicted him.

Five witnesses came to court alleging acts of sexual violence that the defendant either committed or ordered, including two instances of direct rape. The circumstances in which the testimony of four of these witnesses was admitted had already been the source of some tension. Indeed, their statements had all been taken on the same day, in a hotel in Kibuye one week before the trial opened in Arusha. Suddenly, five years after the events, it appeared that not only had Alfred Musema led the attacks, but he was also a serial rapist. To add to the malaise, the judges confirmed an amendment to the indictment just one day before the prosecutor finished presenting his evidence and after these witnesses had testified, deeming that it "[would] not cause irreparable harm to the defendant."

The judges found that only one of the two direct rape charges was credible. It was supported by a single testimony: that of witness N., a man who was thirty-four years old at the time. The setting was May 13, 1994, on Muyira Hill, during an attack against Tutsi refugees that was considered to be the most massive and deadly of all those that riddled the one hundred days of the genocide. During the various trials related to the crimes committed in Kibuye, dozens of survivors gave detailed descriptions of the manhunt in the hills of Bisesero. In particular, they spoke of the tens of thousands of people who had gathered with their livestock on Muyira Hill. They recalled the hundreds, or perhaps thousands, of assailants singing and calling out for their annihilation. "*Tsemba tsemba tsembe!*" "Let's exterminate them! Let's exterminate them!"

Around 10:00 a.m. on the morning of May 13, when the fury of the attack had been unleashed, witness N. said he saw Alfred Musema and that he was "talking to a police officer named Ruhindura and asking him if a young woman named Nyiramusugi was already dead. Ruhindura told him no. Musema told him that they should bring Nyiramusugi to him before anything else. Finally, Ruhindura caught her around 3:30 p.m. I saw Ruhindura and four others dragging her on the ground, taking her to Musema. Musema had a gun. When they arrived, Musema handed his gun to Ruhindura, then approached the four people who had the girl. They brought her to Musema, stood her up, stretched out her arms, then pushed her down, with her arms crossed. Two men took hold of the young woman's arms; two others spread open her legs. Musema placed himself between her legs and tore her undergarments. After tearing them, he took off his own clothes. He said, 'Tutsi pride ends today.' Then he started to rape her." The witness added, "Musema took one of his arms and wrapped it around the young girl's neck while the four people stepped aside. When Musema had finished, he turned to the police officer and asked him for his gun back." Then the witness concluded his story: "I think she rolled over on her stomach. The four men came over to the girl. They rolled her on to her back and each took a turn raping her. They rolled her toward the valley until I could no longer see them." N. was positive: "It was only these four young people, Ruhindura, and me in the bush." He added that he found the young girl later in the day as night began to fall. She "was wounded all over; you could see scratch marks on her neck; she was covered in blood." He stated that he and three others carried her to his mother's house and later learned from his brother that she had been shot by gendarmes.

It was on the basis of this uncorroborated, miraculously belated testimony, unbelievable in terms of its narrative continuity (the scene took place at several different times during the day, with the same actors, in the horrifying climate of the violence and din of this massive attack on May 13) that Musema was found guilty of rape. With the criterion that a ruling has to be anchored in the notion of "beyond any reasonable doubt" (the words "beyond," "any," and "reasonable" were carefully chosen), justice established a basic precept, just as with the burden of proof or the presumption of innocence. This principle was adopted in order to have safeguards in place against the arbitrary so that everyone can feel confident relying on the judicial system. In this case, when the judges accepted N.'s testimony as being sufficient and credible, Musema was not the only one to suffer from the absence of reasonable doubt. Trust in those tasked with trying him was also shaken.

The convicted Musema was in his cell, waiting for his appeal decision, when one day toward the end of 2000, a fellow detainee handed him the deposition of a protected witness bearing the pseudonym II. This witness, who was recorded in another Kibuye case, affirmed in his written statement that he saw the young woman named Nyiramusugi being raped, on the same day and on this same Muyira Hill, but at midday and by a person named Mika, in all likelihood another person indicted by the ICTR named Mika Muhimana.

On the basis of this discovery, Steven Kay requested that the prosecution disclose all exculpatory evidence that it might have. It would take time, several weeks, said the prosecutor, specifying that there were "thirty thousand documents to be reviewed." Two weeks prior to the hearing before the appeals chamber, Kay received three more witness statements, including one from witness E.B., who was interviewed by prosecution investigators on December 12, 1999, that is, six weeks before the ruling in the Musema case was handed down. This witness also mentioned that Alfred Musema was present in the hills of Bisesero in mid-May. He also talked about the rape of Nyiramusugi. But he gave a third version of the story, different from that told by N. and that of II. According to E.B., the young woman was raped not only by Alfred Musema but also by Aloys Ndimbati, former *bourgmestre* of Gisovu and another notorious suspect whom the ICTR was never able to arrest. So now there were three ICTR defendants all accused of the same rape. And that was not all. According to E.B., Musema raped Nyiramusugi standing up next to a tree. Finally, according to this witness, immediately after the rape, the victim was literally "cut into pieces."

Now, not only could the defense assert that N.'s testimony was unreliable, but it also discretely pointed out the existence of clues about the link between witnesses P., N., and E.B. Witness P. had also testified for the prosecution in the Musema case, but Judge Pillay had found this testimony to be insufficient. P.'s name also appears in the deposition of II, who identifies P. as being Nyiramusugi's brother. E.B. also mentions a link to the young woman, without clearly disclosing it.

Kay never brought up the infamous "informer networks" that other defense lawyers at the ICTR regularly denounced. It was a question of style. Those who were the most vocal critics of these murky networks were also the ones who were most inclined to launch into long political tirades that went well beyond the legal issue at hand. From all appearances, the British lawyer was impervious to political activism, mostly because he was simply not interested in the topic. He was a technician who was just as focused on his case as he was obstinate about ignoring anything not strictly related to its criminal content. This time, however, Kay was most certainly implying that there had been a concerted fabrication of the testimonies.

The London-based lawyer also wished to revisit another testimony given during the trial because he believed that this witness, whose testimony had partly served as the basis for his client's conviction for another massacre at the end of May, had contradicted himself in a new written statement produced after the trial. He allegedly placed the event in a different period and supposedly did not indicate that Musema was present. However, the appeals chamber denied the motion for a new hearing, ruling that the statement did not prove that the conviction was likely ill-founded. The chamber agreed to hear only two witnesses and only on the subject of the rape of Nyiramusugi.

On the basis of these "new facts," which were classified as confidential for the most part, and after having heard these two witnesses testify under the secrecy of a closed-door hearing, the appeals judges found that if all the witness statements had been submitted jointly before a tribunal assessing the facts in a reasonable manner, it would have arrived at the conclusion that there was reasonable doubt as to whether the defendant was guilty of rape. The chamber therefore ruled that the "Trial Chamber's factual and legal findings in relation to the rape of Nyiramusugi are incorrect and occasioned a miscarriage of justice." On November 16, 2001, Musema's rape conviction was overturned.

The appeals chamber's conclusion was just. Everyone knew it, and more importantly, everyone had known it even before these "new facts" were submitted. It was also a risk-free decision because, on the one hand, no one pays much attention to the "antinews" contained in an appeals decision, especially when the bulk of it is kept under seal, and, on the other hand, it did not alter Alfred Musema's life sentence in any way. But there was one thing that this decision failed to do: restore trust in the tribunal.

Closing Up Shop

The odds are good that this tribunal, whose judges were just appointed by the United Nations General Assembly, will be able to pull off its mission, given the expertise of the people who make it up, along with the caliber of the prosecutor who is assisting them.

Jean-Bosco Barayagwiza, *Rwanda: Le sang Hutu est-il rouge?*

Louise Arbour had never been so well received in Rwanda. In 1997 the chief prosecutor had been booed at in the streets of Kigali. Survivors accused her of not wanting to prosecute the perpetrators of the genocide, and the Rwandan government called for her resignation. But in this first week of August 1999, that was all just a bad, distant memory. This time, Arbour was hailed, thanked, and honored. The president of the supreme court, the ministers of justice and foreign affairs, and the prime minister all met with her, as did the man who had really held all the power in Rwanda since 1994, General Paul Kagame, the uncontested leader of the Rwandan Patriotic Front. The chief prosecutor had endured so much humiliation from Rwandans over the past three years that she gladly allowed herself to fall under the spell of this unusual outpouring of warmth and cordiality. Touched, she praised the improvement in relations between the Rwandan authorities and the ICTR and suggested taking a hard look at the possibility of holding some of the tribunal's hearings in Kigali. "I think that there is recognition of the progress that has been made in the past three years and an understanding of the direction to take in the future. I am convinced that the year to come will be one in which the ICTR's successes will likely be remarkable," she promised.[1] This visit to Rwanda was a crowning point for her. It would also be her last. One month later, the Canadian prosecutor stepped down from her position and was replaced by Swiss prosecutor Carla del Ponte.

Beyond her initial emotion, Louise Arbour was not wrong. Relations between the UN tribunal and Rwanda had never been so good. Kigali had even decided to appoint an ambassador to the tribunal. "At the beginning, the Rwandan government criticized the tribunal's results, a criticism that was justified. We now believe that the tribunal has made remarkable progress, even though there are still some areas that need to be fixed. This can be done more appropriately and more rapidly if we work alongside the tribunal," declared the Rwandan diplomat upon being installed in Tanzania.[2]

At the same time, there was renewed optimism following the change in presidency that had just occurred at the tribunal. Navanethem Pillay had succeeded Laïty Kama, giving rise to the hope for revival and the promise of accelerating the pace of trials. This was something that had been the subject of discussion for two years but was threatening to become simply rhetoric, similar to when a big corporation declares that it needs to be a good corporate citizen. The Arusha-based tribunal had a growing number of accused behind bars, but the trials were not making any headway. Alfred Musema's was the only trial to be opened in two years. While Louise Arbour was saying her good-byes to the Rwandans, President Pillay had convened everyone else—judges, prosecutors, and lawyers—for an unprecedented judicial marathon, smack in the middle of August.

The goal was to eliminate the procedural obstacles, deal with them more swiftly and resolutely, and set dates for what was hoped to be a large number of trials sure to be held in the fall. The tribunal administration moved into high gear. Hearings were held at a brisk pace. Ten cases were examined in one week. Obsessed with the sudden desire to move quickly, the judges trampled on certain basic principles of what legal experts like to call an adversarial proceeding, that is, giving the prosecution and the defense the possibility of presenting their arguments on the basis of the same information. Having dawdled for over a year, the judges now decided to move full speed ahead. The judicial machine creaked, groaned, warmed up, began to chug, and then conked out. Efforts to organize major trials as announced failed again. All the top cases on the court's docket that had been in the offing for at least two years were now blocked. Defense lawyers filed a flurry of motions before the appeals chamber.

Based in The Hague, this chamber hears appeals for the tribunals for both the former Yugoslavia and Rwanda. Its work primarily consists of ensuring the legality of the proceedings conducted under the authority of the trial judges. On November 3, 1999, at a time when the Arusha-based tribunal was already feeling paralyzed, the appeals chamber handed down a lengthy decision of about one hundred pages. This ruling did not solve the problem of organizing all the trials before the ICTR, but it did settle one case in a rather dramatic way by ordering the immediate release of one of the most important accused imprisoned in Arusha: Jean-Bosco Barayagwiza.

He was an open person. I was unpleasantly surprised to learn that he was one of the CDR's ideologues. People changed and were inconsistent depending on the interests and opportunities of the moment."[3] This recollection by Lieutenant Colonel Cyiza, former president of Rwanda's court of cassation, was difficult to imagine for someone who had only heard about Jean-Bosco Barayagwiza starting in 1992, when he came onto the scene as one of the founders of the Coalition for the Defense of the Republic (CDR), the leading party of the most hard-core supporters of Hutu Power. From that date onward, not a single major initiative was taken by Hutu extremists in which he did not take part or play an active, if not key, role. First it was the CDR. He did not hold a well-defined position at the national level, but he was clearly its main leader. Then in 1993 it was the infamous Radio-Télévision des mille collines, where, at forty-three years old, he became one of three top executives and managers. The CDR and RTLM were the political and propaganda mouthpieces of the forces that fomented, then executed, the genocide in Rwanda. Barayagwiza was at the center of both organizations, standing openly at the helm. Surely no other Rwandan leader can claim such an ideological pedigree.

Moreover, unlike many, he scarcely concealed his ideas. In 1995, when Barayagwiza was in exile in Cameroon, he published a book with the noxious title *Rwanda: Le sang Hutu est-il rouge?* (Rwanda: Is Hutu Blood Red?). In this book, he develops his analysis in a rather candid way. "In the logic of war, the aggressors are the enemy that every person belonging to the country or group under attack must fight. Collaboration with the enemy is unacceptable treason. Thus, the CDR was right to oppose the Tutsis, as well as Hutus, Twas, and any other enemy collaborator," he wrote. According to Barayagwiza, the Tutsis had "alienated the sympathy of Hutus and even attracted their hatred by massively supporting the crazy and destructive ideal of the RPF." With a sharp and characteristic sense of euphemism, he added that "RTLM was the fruit of an ingenious idea that matured within the 'republican' group," noting that "even the station's adversaries recognized its quality. They were stunned and irritated by its independence and bluntness." His inevitable conclusion: "RTLM and its journalists did not, therefore, commit any crime."[4]

Following the genocide, Barayagwiza was one of the Rwandan government's most wanted. In March 1996 he was among the twelve high-ranking leaders of the former regime arrested in Cameroon at Kigali's request. The first ICTR prosecutor, Richard Goldstone, initially took an interest in him before informing the Cameroonian authorities that he did not intend to prosecute him. On February 21, 1997, the Yaoundé court denied Rwanda's request for extradition. The eight persons who had been kept in detention for a year on the basis of this request were released. But not Barayagwiza. No sooner had he stepped outside the prison walls than he was sent right back. The new prosecutor of the ICTR, Louise Arbour, had dispatched an urgent message to the Cameroonian authorities saying that a new arrest warrant had been issued against the cofounder of the CDR and RTLM.

It took nine months for Barayagwiza to be transferred to Arusha. Several problems arose during this period from February to November 1997. The first snag: the accused complained that he had not been promptly informed of the charges against him. That was debatable. The second snag: the indictment was not issued until eight months after he had been placed in detention for the second time. This did not look good for the prosecutor, but legally speaking, the irregular nature of this delay was also debatable. The third snag: Barayagwiza sent a request to Arusha for a hearing on the illegality of his arrest and detention. That is his lawful right. However, the ICTR judges never heard his motion. That is a fact. He finally arrived in Tanzania on November 19, 1997. By law, he was supposed to come before a judge within a few days. The fourth snag: it was over three months—ninety-six days to be exact—before Barayagwiza had his initial appearance. That is also a fact. He had already spent two years in prison by then. And the fifth and final snag: the prosecutor did not do everything in her power to ensure a speedy trial. This is neither debatable nor a fact; it is a question of bad habits.

The appeals chamber judges were of the opinion that these five strikes against the Barayagwiza case had caused irreparable damage. Law, they reiterated, is a matter of rigor and strict application of clearly defined rules. Otherwise, the system collapses. In this case, there had been multiple violations of the defendant's rights. Thus, on November 3, 1999, they concluded, "Nothing less than the integrity of the Tribunal is at stake in this case. Loss of public confidence in the Tribunal, as a court valuing human rights of all individuals—including those charged with unthinkable crimes—would be among the most serious consequences of allowing the Appellant to stand trial in the face of such violations of his rights. As difficult as this conclusion may be for some to accept, it is the proper role of an independent judiciary to halt this prosecution, so that no further injustice results."

The prosecutor had proposed two solutions to the judges to remedy the procedural irregularities: order that a trial be held quickly or credit the defendant with the number of days in detention already served. The judges retorted that the first was already one of the defendant's basic rights and that the second was inadequate: what would be his reparation in the event he was acquitted? The appeals chamber recognized the gravity of the crimes with which Jean-Bosco Barayagwiza was charged, but it underscored the fact that the fundamental rights of an individual who is presumed innocent until proven guilty had been violated repeatedly. The only appropriate sanction was to release Barayagwiza and dismiss the charges.

That was not all. The judges felt that the prosecutor had shown willful nonfeasance and decided to ban her office from ever reopening a case against Barayagwiza. It was the ultimate punishment. The judges further explained that if they did not apply this measure, Jean-Bosco Barayagwiza "would be re-arrested immediately and his fate would remain unchanged." In fact, his situation would be even worse since the three and a half years of prison time that he had already served could no longer be credited to him. He would therefore be a victim of having exercised his rights. The appeals judges cited a U.S. Supreme Court justice in defense of their decision: "To declare that in the administration of the criminal law the end justifies the means—to declare that the government may commit crimes in order to secure the conviction of a private criminal—would bring terrible retribution. Against that pernicious doctrine this court should resolutely set its face." In the age of Guantanamo, some phrases are enduring.

To heal, prevent, and purify: above all, the ICTR appeals chamber had wanted to sound the alarm. The handling of the Barayagwiza case had been a disaster, but it was also symptomatic of a larger problem. "For some, it's a little depressing; others were not surprised. For me, it was a good kick in the ass," one of the prosecution investigators summed up following the decision.[5] The affair dated back to the tribunal's earliest years. It showed just how many liberties had been taken with rigor and responsibility. It was a heavy price to pay, and no one was spared. The judges sensed this, explaining that their decision would be "difficult to accept." But many saw that behind this decision was a desire to put things back on track before it was too late. The ruling shook the tribunal to its very core, while also attempting to fortify it.

In their conclusion, the appeals chamber judges stressed the importance of public confidence. It is what the legal system is built upon. When this trust is betrayed, the system breaks down. Trust is the source of the respect and sense of protection that justice inspires. If this source erodes, then trust, or the lack thereof, becomes the legal system's gravedigger.

Trust has another annoying tendency: its face looks different depending on which side of the mirror one stands. At the Arusha detention facility, mild euphoria obviously reigned at first following the appeals decision. Some of the accused started to entertain renewed hopes that went beyond their wildest imagination. The former minister of foreign affairs under the Kambanda government became rather ecstatic. He fervently claimed that he was also a victim of multiple violations of his rights and demanded to be acquitted and immediately released. Time passes slowly behind bars. So he used this time to devise and plan the terms of his release with meticulous attention to detail and a fair amount of cupidity. He demanded a safe conduct, someone to accompany him during his trip to Canada (and nowhere else), and, above all, monetary and "moral" damages. He calculated the amount of these damages in great detail. Had this not been indicative of a certain misery of the soul, it would have been a masterpiece of irony: over $54 million in all, in keeping with "international standards." But this fantasy was most likely not written by someone with a caustic mind. It would not be long before his hopes were dashed.[6]

In Kigali, however, it was no longer a question of trust. As quickly as a hailstorm can wipe out a harvest, the burgeoning relations between Rwanda and the ICTR, hailed by both Louise Arbour and the new Rwandan ambassador, froze on the vine.

At a cabinet meeting on November 5, the Rwandan government condemned the appeals chamber decision. The next day, Gerald Gahima, who had become Rwanda's chief prosecutor, announced that cooperation between his office and the ICTR would be suspended and immediately issued a new international arrest warrant against Jean-Bosco Barayagwiza. On November 9 the president called upon all Rwandans and the members of parliament to "rise up against this decision" and to "take all appropriate measures to ensure that this was well understood by the international community and the international tribunal."[7] In New York, by sheer coincidence of the calendar, the UN General Assembly was meeting to examine the tribunal's annual report and vote on its budget. The Rwandan representative curtly demanded a vote of no confidence. At the same time, he asked the states to review the future operations of the International Criminal Court, the ICC, which had been established in 1998. Otherwise, he said, it would be "the permanent vision of a temporary failure and for Rwanda, a permanent failure of the United Nations."[8] On November 15, survivors protested in Kigali in front of the OTP. Only the rain could disperse them. It appeared as though the worst of times under Richard Goldstone in 1996 and Louise Arbour in 1997 had returned. Rwanda's ambassador who had just been named to the tribunal was immediately recalled. He had spent only three days in Arusha. On November 16 he stated that he would not take office until the Barayagwiza decision was revised. Then, three days later, the Rwandan government initiated a more legal counterattack. It asked to be heard by the tribunal. It was no longer seeking a reversal of the Barayagwiza decision. It was asserting its right to try Jean-Bosco Barayagwiza itself. And then the government played its wild card and promised not to apply the death penalty.

In reality, Kigali's suspension of cooperation with the ICTR came about in subtle doses. The investigators' work in the field was not affected. Access to witnesses and their transportation to Arusha remained unchanged. This was the Rwandan government's lethal weapon, and it did not use it. The primary target of its wrath was the chief prosecutor. Carla del Ponte had taken over from Louise Arbour on September 15. When the November 3 decision landed on her desk, she had still not set foot in her offices in Africa. At the end of November she went to Tanzania. However, she could not go to Kigali. She had been declared a persona non grata there and was refused a visa. The minister of justice had informed her in writing that he was "not ready to meet with her at this time." The travel ban lasted two weeks.

The appeals chamber judges had no idea of the importance of this man they had ordered to be released. Sitting in The Hague, they had no specific knowledge of Rwandan history and did not know much more about the individuals the Arusha-based tribunal was trying. Of course, they had carefully weighed the responsibility of deciding to free a genocide suspect on the basis of procedural errors. But they were clearly shaken when they saw the impact of their ruling, for indeed, it had caused a minor earthquake.

The new president of the ICTR, Navanethem Pillay, was one of the few who did not get too caught up in this decision. Calm and firm, she did not make concessions. "It is an appeals court decision. It binds the trial court and we accept the decision. This decision has made us acutely aware and we want to watch out for this. We hope that other sections of the Tribunal—the Registry and the Office of the Prosecutor—will similarly look into their work."[9] Faced with pressure from the Rwandan authorities, she looked to the example of Nelson Mandela, who, following the acquittal of high-ranking apartheid leaders, declared about the judges, "That's why we put them there. We want them to be independent and fearless."[10]

But not everybody can be Nelson Mandela. The general outcry was so great that everyone understood that something had to be done to mend the broken pieces. Initiatives abounded. On November 19 Carla del Ponte informed the judges of her intent to seek a review of their decision. This measure, which is permissible under tribunal rules, was rarely used. It had to be justified by the appearance of "new facts" in the case. Be that as it may, less than a month was time enough for these new facts to surface, so the judges hastened to grant the prosecutor's request. Something also had to be done to appease Kigali. The appeals chamber therefore invited the Rwandan government to express its views before the court. Finally, the chamber had to convey the appearance of transparency and to at least feign interest in a rapprochement with Kigali. A public hearing was scheduled to hear the request for review in Arusha in February 2000.

Barayagwiza's hopes were short-lived. After the November 3 decision, he thought he could push the envelope a bit more. He immediately petitioned the appeals chamber to review the solution being contemplated for his release: returning him to Cameroon. Saying he worried that he would be without income, legal status, or family support and that he feared for his safety, he wished to be free to choose his destination and to have the tribunal's assistance to get there. By November 10 he had also issued a press release denouncing Kigali's threats, "which could result in [his] assassination." That seemed a bit paranoid. According to him, "the objective of the current propaganda and agitation by the authorities in Kigali was to intimidate the various bodies of the ICTR in order to prevent them from prosecuting current Rwandan leaders accused of having committed serious crimes." That was much more pertinent.

Then he realized that his motion concerning the country that would host him could conceivably contribute to prolonging his stay in detention, and he thus withdrew it. The rather bizarre reality was that Jean-Bosco Barayagwiza was never actually released. For three weeks, he was a free man in prison whose only newfound right was to publish regular press releases. On November 25, when the appeals chamber suspended its November 3 decision in order to hear the request for review submitted by del Ponte, there was a general sigh of relief: Jean-Bosco Barayagwiza was again a lawfully detained accused. His distribution of press releases was immediately halted.

"The last has not been heard in the Barayagwiza case," announced the tribunal spokesperson, clearly impatient.[11] "I want it to be clear that Jean-Bosco Barayagwiza has not been released and that the review process is under way. It is a legal, not a political decision," reiterated del Ponte in turn. She also wished to clarify her position: "I am not subject to any pressure. I have been a prosecutor for a little over twenty years. It is part of our job to not let ourselves be influenced. That's not something one learns from one day to the next, but with experience. I can guarantee you that I have become completely impervious to these types of attempts."[12]

In order to obtain a review, new facts must be presented. By all appearances, the definition of what constitutes a new fact is clear. However, in law, the formal realm of the codified rigor of principles and rules, interpretation is elastic. The ultimate art of lawyers is to construct a predictable world, one that is dictated to us, and to reign in an unpredictable world, one that serves them. The best formula lawyers ever invented was "in the interest of justice." In principle, this expression is imposing by virtue of its solemnity. In practice, lawyers use it to get out of a bind without having to justify themselves. When they invoke the interest of justice, it generally means they have run out of arguments. In the Barayagwiza case, the prosecution was now explaining that it was submitting new facts in the interest of justice. Nothing could have been a better indicator of the utter disarray that prevailed at the OTP.

The facts were not new at all; the prosecution had simply failed to submit them before. But they could help get it out of trouble. Now the judges had another reason to be concerned. Another case file, strikingly similar to Barayagwiza's, had been on their desks since September. It was the Laurent Semanza case, on which they had not yet deliberated. The thought had not crossed their minds when they signed the November 3 decision, but what impression would they be giving if they ordered the release of a second individual within the space of a couple of months on the basis of the same irregularities? A judge forewarned is a judge forearmed. Sometimes.

From a media point of view, Carla del Ponte was the ideal prosecutor. With her strong, firm voice and her erect, determined stance, her style was direct, without embellishment. She emitted rebel-like authority. Just as Louise Arbour commanded respect with her gentle, composed, and thoughtful style, del Ponte stood out by being blunt, raising the flag, and charging ahead without beating around the bush. Behind an often sullen and annoyed look, she was a curious mix of candor, sympathy, and a propensity to fly off the handle. She was a prosecutor both by training and by nature.

"I am a prosecutor. I have with me eight hundred thousand or a million corpses demanding justice. And that is what I am asking to be able to do," she snapped straightaway in front of the appeals judges in Arusha. Deputy prosecutor Bernard Muna was delighted with this new tone, which contrasted so sharply with that of his former boss. He seized the opportunity: "We were the ones who set the prosecutorial machine in motion. I am the one who is accusing. I am not neutral."

In the face of such zeal, it fell to Judge Shahabuddeen, as it so often did with his smooth, mildly ironic tone, to more humbly summarize what was at stake. "Could we say before an international tribunal that substance is more important than technical points?" he asked, with a keen sense of reality and sarcasm. The judge from Guyana was among those who had rendered the November 3 decision. Like his colleagues, he understood that they had to get out of it, but he wanted to give this reversal some sense of loftiness, a bit of spirit.

While everyone else (except the appellant, of course) sought to put a legal slant on this review, which had essentially been undertaken for political reasons, Carla del Ponte did not let the concern for form stand in her way. Evoking the Rwandan government's refusal to issue her a visa in December and its decision to suspend cooperation with the tribunal, albeit in theory only, she added that "this has to be taken into account." For the threat was clear, she concluded: "Either Barayagwiza will be tried by this tribunal, or the only other solution is to hand him over to the Rwandan government, to his natural judge. Otherwise, we may as well close up shop. In the end, after deciding to commit genocide in Rwanda in 1994, Barayagwiza will be the one to decide the fate of the tribunal."

It was hard to be much clearer than that. The chief prosecutor had said it with great gusto. She had even reverted to her native language to ensure she was convincing: *possiamo chiudere la baracca*. This, therefore, was the reason for the review. It was a golden opportunity for the defense counsel. They warned of the danger that the trials in Arusha would "be seen as political trials of the losers by the victors." In this case, the danger and the victor were one and the same, and he was approaching the stand. Draped in his black robes, Gerald Gahima, Rwanda's chief prosecutor, symbolized that which Barayagwiza undoubtedly feared the most. "My government appreciates what this tribunal is doing. We support it. We have had a harmonious period. We respect its decisions. If the appellant had been acquitted following a trial, we would have been disappointed, but we would have respected the decision. The Rwandan people and government find themselves in a very difficult position. Jean-Bosco Barayagwiza was one of the main masterminds of the genocide. He is an intelligent man. His crimes are well known in Rwanda. That is why we think you have jurisdiction to ensure that he stands trial. This man, who is the equivalent of a Hitler or a Pol Pot in our country, must be tried. We are ready to try him immediately, with a defense counsel and international observers, and we will not impose a death penalty."

It had taken the appeals chamber one year to arrive at its November 3 decision. It took four months to radically revise it. On March 31, 2002, the judges ruled that the appellant's rights had been violated but that the violations were considerably less serious than they had initially thought. Thus, the penalty had to be of a completely different nature: if the appellant was found guilty, his sentence would be reduced; if he was acquitted, he would receive financial compensation. For the time being, order had been restored. Jean-Bosco Barayagwiza would be tried by the international tribunal.

In November the law was all about rigor; in March it was about flexibility. The reference to "public trust" was dropped from the decision. To justify such a reversal of opinion, the judges, mindful of the suspicions surrounding them in this matter, were quick to emphasize that "the Tribunal is an independent body, whose decisions are based solely on justice and law. If its decision in any case should be followed by non-cooperation, that consequence would be a matter for the Security Council." It was no easy feat to appear indifferent to states' orders or to the pressure of public opinion while at the same time agreeing to give the exact opposite impression. Judge Nieto-Navia had trouble coming to terms with this. "I vehemently reject the suggestion that in rendering judgments, political considerations should play a persuasive or guiding role in order to appease states and ensure their cooperation so as to meet the tribunal's long-term objectives. On the contrary, under no circumstances should such considerations push the tribunal to compromise its judicial independence or its integrity. This is a tribunal whose decisions must be taken with the sole intent of applying law and guaranteeing justice for cases that come before it, and not as a result of political pressure or the threat of suspending cooperation on the part of an angry government." In insisting too much, one often ends up being convinced of the opposite. This Colombian judge, who had signed both the original decision and the review decision, was more persuasive when he described the context in which the tribunals must work: "Both the ICTY and the ICTR are at the center of a highly charged emotional environment, and they are given the task of remaining independent and transparent, pursuant to the international community's expectations, while also preserving international human rights standards." In November the judges had hoped to find virtue in being courageous. In March they settled for the courage to be virtuous.

Thus, Jean-Bosco Barayagwiza would stand trial in Arusha, but in a way that was better than he could have hoped for in terms of defending his theories. His trial began six months after the review. Barayagwiza did not participate in it. He forbade his lawyers from representing him and denounced this "parody of justice," citing the same phrase from the November 3 appeals chamber decision. He was now portraying himself as "the UN's political prisoner." Two years later, when the time came to present his evidence, he rigorously continued his boycott. "Some say that I am taking too many risks by refusing to be properly represented and defended. But I continue to believe that the risk would be real only if there was the slightest chance of obtaining a fair and equitable trial. The tribunal's sponsors have chosen their side. There is enormous pressure on the judges to make the same biased choice. A verdict of guilt is a foregone conclusion. All that remains is to decide on the sentence and to render the judgment."[13] On December 3, 2003, Jean-Bosco Barayagwiza, one of the leading ideologists of Hutu extremism, was found guilty of genocide.

His two codefendants were sentenced to life in prison. Not him. Since his rights had been violated in 1997, he now had the right to reparation in the form of a reduced sentence. But how can one reduce perpetuity? The tribunal decided that a reduced, or compensated, life sentence would be thirty-five years.

Bernard Muna's house was as empty as if he had moved in the previous day. However, he had been living in Kigali for three years. Recruited by Louise Arbour to take charge of a prosecution office on the road to ruin, he was first and foremost a symbol of regeneration and renewed ambition. Two months after his arrival, he orchestrated the arrests in Kenya, including that of former Prime Minister Jean Kambanda. He came off as someone with authority, which the prosecutor's office badly needed, and a man of action, which the investigators liked. "Muna the puma" they called him for a time. In Rwanda he skillfully managed to reap the political credit for the wave of new indictments in 1997–98. In public he eluded both charm and self-confidence. This served him particularly well in a country where much value is placed on political art. One of his staff described him as being "like the price of rubber, elastic."

Then, like so many other tribunal leaders who let power and flattery go to their heads, Muna lost in perspective what he gained in authoritarianism. His house was empty, as though he would have to leave soon.

The only things surrounding him in his Kigali villa were his masks. He owned a collection of approximately one thousand pieces. A handful of them hung on the walls, between the photographs of the reception held for him by traditional chiefs in Cameroon and of his meeting with UN secretary-general Kofi Annan. The sounds of big band jazz brightened this house that otherwise felt too big and empty. If he were a filmmaker, he said, crammed into his armchair, he would like to make a film about a peace-loving extraterrestrial who lands on Earth and is surprised to see so many monuments commemorating wars. It was April 6, 2000. As in every year for the past six years, preparations for the annual genocide commemoration had been completed, and the week of mourning had begun. It had been seven days since the appeals chamber had revised its decision in the Barayagwiza case. As Muna explained, the ICTR was born out of a twofold political equation: the UN Security Council's decision on Rwanda's request, on the one hand, and, on the other hand, the RPF's desire to use this tribunal as a tool to legitimize its power. In Rwanda, Muna suggested, there was no will to deal with the issue of justice rapidly. According to him, this explained why six years after the events, the quest for justice was still topical. Moving beyond it was never part of the picture, he concluded before dozing off.[14]

Muna was not the only victim of disenchantment. When Laïty Kama stepped down as president of the ICTR in May 1999, he stressed the "very important task" of quickly trying the accused who were in detention—thirty-five at the time. "This decision will fall to my successor," he added, like debt being carried over to the next fiscal year.[15] However, during a fifteen-month period, from June 1999 to September 2000, only one trial got under way in Arusha, a trial with a single defendant who was a simple *bourgmestre*. Even Kama, who was still a judge there, would forget the importance of the task at hand. Twenty-one months went by before he sat on another case. The new president, Navanethem Pillay, went eighteen months between trials.

The period 1999–2000, which Louise Arbour had promised would be spectacular and when everything had seemed possible at the beginning, was supposed to be a period in which all the administrative red tape, the pitfalls, and the catastrophes would finally give way to a mature, efficient, and rigorous judicial system, driven by its duty and the need to fulfill and complete its mandate. However, quite the opposite was true. It was two years of broken flight in which the tribunal was caught up in its past and became so comfortable, it forgot that its task was to respond to the demand for justice and to do so rapidly. In Arusha the problem was not the existence of a coldly strategic political awareness akin to what Muna had described in reference to Rwanda's new government. Rather, it was the lack thereof.

12

A Mayor in Turmoil

(The Doubt in Reason)

> There were some roadblocks that were not erected for the purpose of killing.
>
> Raphaël Ngarambe, Kibuye prosecutor,
> September 20, 2002

When prepared with a modicum of rigor, an initial appearance is a simple and predictable judicial event. If neglected, it can lead to a disaster, as in the Barayagwiza case, and speak volumes about the court's mindset. To complete this procedure within a short period of time, as required by law, the UN tribunal often uses a lawyer, called a duty counsel, who is available immediately and appointed for that occasion to explain the charges to the accused. During this routine procedure, the judge has a responsibility to ensure that the defendant has clearly understood the charges against him or her and then to ask if he or she pleads guilty or not guilty. On April 1, 1999, standing up behind the defense table wedged in front of the defendant, the duty counsel took the floor and introduced himself and the case.

"I am here representing Mr. Ign-ace . . ."

He paused, mouth open, felt a little dizzy, then put on his glasses, looked over his documents, and, after regaining his composure, calmly concluded:

"Ba-gi-li-she-ma."

Short but sturdy, the defendant of the day looked younger than his age of forty-three. His lower jaw jutted forward slightly, making him look somewhat unattractive when he spoke. His speech was muffled, as though he were clenching his teeth while talking. "I have a problem," he said. "For the time being, I have a duty counsel who speaks English and I speak French. We have not been able to consult with each other. I wrote to the tribunal registrar to ask him to appoint a lawyer of my choice, but I have not received a response. Yesterday, I was informed by telephone that I had to appear before the tribunal."

Ignace Bagilishema, former *bourgmestre* of Mabanza commune in Kibuye prefecture, was concerned, but he deferred to the judge's wisdom. Judge William Sekule, who spoke only English, had been presiding over this function for four years and felt the problem was benign. He disregarded the defendant's objection and ordered the indictment to be read. Armed with a red pen, Bagilishema followed along attentively as the list of his alleged crimes was read aloud. "Ignace Bagilishema was appointed as *bourgmestre* of Mabanza commune on February 8, 1980," began the registrar, trying six times to pronounce the defendant's name and butchering it every time. Then, continuing in a disciplined manner with the background summary in the indictment that was drafted in 1996, she read that the defendant was "reportedly in Zambia at present." She paused, chuckled slightly, then raised her head and exclaimed, "Which is not true."

She had scarcely begun reading the first count when the prosecutor interrupted. He thought the wrong indictment was being read. They should be reading the one that had been amended three years ago. There was confusion and discussion as the judges and registry staff compared documents. Finally, the reading continued with the new document, but only for a few seconds. In the copy of the amended indictment that the registrar now held in her hands, the names of Bagilishema's original seven codefendants had been stricken out. However, it had also been three years since the court had lifted this confidentiality measure. Major confusion, more discussion, and more comparison of documents between the judges, the registry staff, and the prosecutor followed. A solution was finally found: the registrar could include in her reading of the French version of the indictment the names mentioned in the prosecutor's English version of the document. So be it.

Bagilishema no longer knew what to do with his red pen. Which version of the indictment did he have? No one bothered to ask him. It was simply assumed that he understood the difference between the crimes of conspiracy to commit genocide and complicity in genocide, and what was covered under violations of Article 3 Common to the Geneva Conventions and of Additional Protocol II thereof. There were thirteen counts against him, all formulated in an equally lucid manner, and he had to answer to them.

"Do you plead guilty or not guilty?" asked Judge Sekule.

"I am sorry, I cannot say anything without a lawyer," replied the defendant, who in his three years of being on the run had learned the basics of being prudent.

"Do you plead guilty or not guilty?" repeated the judge. "Because in the end," he added, "your lawyer is not going to help you at this stage, unless perhaps you do feel guilty."

Standing before the court, looking at the ground, Ignace Bagilishema indicated thirteen times that he "prefer[red] to have a lawyer prior to saying anything before the tribunal." Thirteen times, the judge entered a "not guilty" plea on his behalf in accordance with the law. Then he adjourned the hearing. As they left the room, the defendant and his lawyer for a day passed each other silently. Words escaped them.

Was this hearing on April 1, 1999, an unfortunate scene in international justice that warranted a little indulgence, given that it happened so rarely? Alas, no. It was just one among so many others (and not the worst of them) that could be added to a long list, if that were not so simple and predictable.

Mabanza is located sixteen miles from the town of Kibuye. In 1994 it was the region's most prosperous commune and a strategic junction— a sort of small economic hub at the crossroads, where people stopped to buy supplies at the big market and to gas up their cars. Bagilishema had become the commune's dynamic *bourgmestre* fourteen years earlier at the age of twenty-five. Like all Rwandans prior to 1991, he was a member of the single party "by birth." Unlike some, he did not leave the party following the advent of the multiparty system. Like many, he fled his country just after the genocide. In November 1995 he was one of the first eight persons indicted by the ICTR, along with Clément Kayishema and Obed Ruzindana. In February 1999 he was arrested in South Africa and immediately transferred to Tanzania.

Contrary to all appearances, Bagilishema's case file was almost more suspect than the man himself at the start. In fact, the first indictment against this *bourgmestre* could be summed up in one, and only one, allegation: on the morning of April 13, 1994, Ignace Bagilishema allegedly sent the people who had taken refuge in the Mabanza commune office to Kibuye town, *knowing* that they would be massacred there four days later at the church and the stadium. That was it. No one really paid much attention to it, but this was probably the most benign indictment ever confirmed by an ICTR judge. When Louise Arbour took over the prosecutor's office in 1996, she made a spectacular gesture at the tribunal for the former Yugoslavia: she withdrew sixteen indictments that were deemed to be not sufficiently important for the international court. Had she had the temerity to apply this same policy to Arusha, Bagilishema's indictment would have been among the handful of those to be withdrawn. This was so true that at the time of Bagilishema's arrest, prosecutor Charles Adeogun-Phillips admitted in private that there was nothing or almost nothing in this case file and that if it were up to only him, he would reduce it to one charge: complicity in genocide. Yet six months later in August, that is, five years after the events, the case was completely overhauled.

"There was relative calm in Mabanza before Préfet Clément Kayishema arrived on April 12," prosecutor Jane Adong now declared with greater detail in her opening remarks at the trial. "When he arrived, he told Bourgmestre Ignace Bagilishema that Mabanza was the only commune where there was still 'scum and filth.' Upon hearing this, the defendant, acting at the speed of sound, implemented what can only be described as a preconceived plan." The *bourgmestre* allegedly then "tricked the Tutsis into leaving their places of refuge in order to lure them to the commune office under the pretext of protecting them." Then, "killers came to Mabanza from neighboring communes. They took aim at the Tutsis. Everyone—men, women, children, and the elderly—fled to the commune office in search of safety and shelter. The Tutsis were divided into two groups: intellectuals in one group, peasants in the other. Upon the instructions of Ignace Bagilishema, the first group was taken to Home St. Jean. They were never seen again. The second group, [still] upon Bagilishema's instructions, was taken to Gatwaro stadium," the infamous stadium in Kibuye. No figures were given as to the number of people in those convoys. But the prosecutor indicated in a general sort of way that "over ten thousand Tutsis managed to make their way to Kibuye. They were taken to the stadium, where they were packed in like sardines for three days. Those who had traditional weapons were separated out at the stadium entrance upon Bagilishema's orders. There was no water and nothing to drink. The sun was beating down on their heads. Out of desperation, they were forced to eat grass to quench their thirst and assuage their hunger." The April 18, 1994, massacres began at noon and continued until seven o'clock in the evening for two consecutive days, recounted Jane Adong. The stadium, which was surrounded by soldiers, gendarmes, and militiamen, was sprayed with a shower of bullets. Grenades were thrown into the crowd. After two days, most of the survivors were finished off with machetes, sharpened bamboo sticks, spears, hoes, nail-studded cudgels, and other traditional arms or instruments. The defendant himself killed a person named Bagambiki in cold blood. It was "the first shot fired on the first day of the stadium attacks. It also signaled the start of the attacks," stated the prosecutor.

In Mabanza, upon the instructions and under the supervision of Ignace Bagilishema, the killings did not abate. The Tutsis who had sought refuge there were hunted down and killed; women were raped, then massacred, declared the prosecutor. Five mass graves near the commune office bear witness to their fate. "It was hell on earth. As if that were not enough, death traps were laid in the form of roadblocks at every street corner to check identification cards and arrest Tutsis," Adong continued. From that point onward, an estimated twenty thousand people were killed at the commune office and the surrounding area. And that was not all. On "Gitwa Hill in Mabanza commune, Ignace Bagilishema released a large number of Interahamwe, who massacred between eight and ten thousand Tutsis," she added. Finally, there were the hills of Bisesero, the last new major charge against the *bourgmestre*. Bagilishema was seen there during the massacres. He recruited militias and supervised their training in his commune before leading the attacks.

The prosecution declared that it had twenty-nine witnesses. In six months, this case that had seemed so benign at first took on the scope of a regional genocide. It was implacable, precise, and clean cut. There was no doubt about the massacres committed at the stadium, Home St. Jean, the church, or Bisesero. The circumstances of these killings had been described at length over two years during the trials of Clément Kayishema and Obed Ruzindana. These men had just been convicted unequivocally. Then there was the Musema trial, which could only facilitate a judgment in this third instance of legally punishing the genocide in Kibuye, a repeated, albeit necessary, act.

François Roux was not present at the initial appearance of Bourgmestre Bagilishema. He had not yet been appointed by the tribunal to defend him. Six months later, in September 1999, when the trial was about to begin, he pointed out that his client had been arrested on the basis of an indictment in which the prosecution had used only five of the twenty-nine witnesses they were now planning to call and that most of these other witness statements had been gathered in recent months, even weeks. Cavalier, he boldly seized the opportunity to turn the situation to his advantage: "At this stage the defense feels that a miscarriage of justice is hovering over this case." At this stage, one could say anything.

Granted, the prosecution got off to a rocky start with this case. First, the reformulated indictment confused Gitwa Hill in Bisesero with Gitwa Hill in Mabanza. Simple and predictable, one might say. Also, at the request of François Roux, the trial chamber judges visited the crime scenes in Rwanda, a first for the ICTR. After seeing the commune office and stadium up close, they would subsequently have some serious doubts about the credibility of what some of the witnesses might say they saw or heard. Moreover, all the prosecution's last-minute witnesses gave multiple statements and often contradicted themselves. In the end, none of them wound up supporting the allegations regarding the defendant's involvement in the attacks at Bisesero. At the beginning of the second week of the trial, the prosecutor dropped some of the witnesses, even though they had already been transported to Arusha. Such was the case for witnesses C. and R. Jane Adong attempted to explain: "We were not able to call them. They will receive psychological counseling before they return to Rwanda." That was nicely put, but it was not true. In reality, witness C. was the one who had stated that Ignace Bagilishema had fired the first shot that gave the signal to begin the attack on the refugees in the stadium. However, during the two years of Clément Kayishema's trial, it was said over and over again that it was Préfet Kayishema who had fired this shot. Better yet, the court had found Kayishema guilty of this crime. All one had to do was read the judgment that had been rendered six months earlier. Simple, predictable . . .

During a press conference, chief prosecutor Carla del Ponte, who had just taken office, blamed the upset caused by the Barayagwiza case, which had turned the ICTR upside down. She stated that the trial lacked witnesses due to Rwanda's refusal to issue them travel papers. All is fair in love and war, but this was equally false. Outside the courtroom, her trial attorney, Charles Adeogun-Phillips, was more honest. "It was both a strategic and ethical decision by the office of the prosecutor," he admitted with respect to the withdrawal of witnesses C. and R. "If a witness said that Bagilishema fired the first shot at the stadium and we decided not to call him, maybe it was because we did not believe he had fired the first shot. Not all the witnesses are credible. You have to be sure that when you bring a witness to court, that person is not going to have a breakdown or simply go crazy. And I was not convinced that would not be the case with some of them." Adeogun-Phillips was known for his great aplomb. With his sidelong glance fixed halfway up a vague horizon, he could defend almost anything. To him, therefore, there was "nothing surprising about this."[1] All the same, the truth was more alarming.

In September 1999 approximately 130,000 people were being held in Rwandan prisons, according to the government. This was the largest prison population per capita in the world.[2] The president of the Kibuye district court had 7,200 genocide cases awaiting trial on his desk. To investigate all these cases, there was one prosecutor with six assistant prosecutors and twenty-seven investigators. As in Arusha, the bulk of the evidence was based on human testimony. Unlike in Arusha, witnesses here testified openly and received no protective measures other than "those that all citizens enjoy." The anonymity of witnesses in Arusha, justified by the fact that they would be in danger upon their return to Rwanda, was a source of mockery among all Rwandans, who openly discussed it without any political ulterior motives. There was one simple reason for this: in Rwanda everyone knew who had gone to testify before the UN tribunal. The "protection" that was systematically granted to the witnesses who came to testify at the international court was driven by motives of another kind. One of the most serious consequences of this practice was that it led to a complete lack of transparency in the trials. In this respect, like so many others, the Arusha-based tribunal operated in isolation, cut off from any real society and especially Rwandan society. The president of the Kibuye court acknowledged that his relations with the tribunal in Arusha were "nonexistent." He "still [did] not know exactly what procedure to follow in order for [the Kibuye court] to supply [the ICTR] evidence or for the ICTR to provide [it] with evidence." In reality, there were ties, but only with the prosecutor's office. Relations between the representatives of justice in Arusha and in Kibuye were limited to prosecutors in Rwanda handing over incriminating evidence to their international counterparts. That was it.

Not without arrogance, it was widely believed in Arusha (and elsewhere) that there was no possible comparison between the impartial justice rendered by the international tribunal, which upheld the law and was concerned with rules of procedure and evidence, and the expedited, politicized, penniless, unprofessional justice delivered by specialized courts in Rwanda. This seemed perfectly obvious at the outset. In the end, it had not been proven at all. Rwandan courts tried approximately nine thousand people between 1997 and 2002, a remarkable feat in this context, all things considered. In all these trials, the good and the bad, there were subservient judges and courageous judges, botched cases and fair trials. Had the UN tribunal shown itself to be just as impartial, rigorous, fair, and deaf to political pressure? Looking at the trials and tribulations in the Barayagwiza case and the bitter ending of the Musema trial alone, to cite but two very different examples, basic good judgment should have called for greater humility. But that was probably the least-shared feeling among the international judges.

Five years had already passed since "hell on earth." Standing a little lower down the hill, at the Home St. Jean, a priest greeted François Roux and his Mauritanian colleague, Maroufa Diabira. "You are not the first; I thought it was over," he said to his visitors from the international tribunal. "When we arrived in 1995, there were flowers. We poured a concrete slab. There, where you see the cars, there were bones. We put them in the church. Thirty-five priests were killed in the prefecture. Now there are only four of us. I was in Belgium at that time."

Naturally, Bagilishema's two lawyers had come to investigate. Following in Steven Kay's footsteps, they were especially hopeful of finding documents.[3] "Our mandate only goes as far as the goodwill of the people we will meet," admitted the French lawyer. Kibuye's new *préfet* was cheerful and direct at first. "We want justice: those who are guilty to be punished and those who are innocent to be exonerated. Ignace Bagilishema? I am not going to accuse him. It is up to you to try to find out, but one thing is certain; you will have a hard time proving that guy innocent!" he remarked, even though he had never met the former *bourgmestre*. "Justice has to be done. Maybe with mitigating circumstances, but justice has to be done," he told the lawyers straight out, without any suggestion of hatred. "I have been here for a little over three months," he explained, when asked about any documents he may have kept. "When I asked for the archives, I was shown a room, but water had leaked in there. They may be old, maybe not. The fact is it's very disorderly." Across the street, in a damp room at the former prefecture office, there was indeed a mountain of documents of miscellaneous origin. A young employee was "filing" them by handfuls into two large black garbage bags. The lawyers turned pale. "How long are the ICTR trials going to last?" asked the *préfet*, still smiling.

The next day, the greeting was more stern and the archives less accessible. "I think the way you approached the secretary was tactless," the *préfet* reprimanded. "She made an effort to come in on a Wednesday afternoon even though she has her own problems. I am speaking as a man, not as the *préfet*. I think that you have your job to do and that we have our problems. Our cousins were killed; others are in prison. The last time, people from the tribunal came to dig up bodies. Each time it is traumatic; every time a dozen or so girls go crazy. Papers do not have any meaning here. If you pay the office boy at the tribunal entrance ten thousand Rwandan francs, he will take your case file away and that will be it; there will be no trial."

The lawyers left the prefecture office to go to the Mabanza commune office. A poster in English pinned on the front door of the office promised another solution to the problem: *There would be peace in the world if all the evil mouths were shut with a padlock*. The new mayor, who had brought charges against his predecessor, seemed tense. The archives were pillaged during the genocide, he explained. Whatever was found was sent to the ICTR. He did not keep any copies and did not draw up an inventory. When he opened a door leading to the archive room, one file nevertheless caught the lawyers' eyes. The following day, in the mayor's absence, two accommodating assistants opened the offices. The lawyers got their hands on the commune's personnel log from 1994. The excitement mounted, on the part of both the lawyers and the commune assistants, who had been drawn into the game. A Garfield comic strip lying prominently on top of a pile of documents bore the title "*Don't worry.*"

In the Musema case, everyone had questioned the rigor and integrity of the prosecution investigators, who apparently had not even searched the still-intact archives of the tea factory that the defendant managed at the time of the crimes. In the Bagilishema case, the investigators also did not feel it was useful, fundamental, or even necessary to examine the commune archives, which had been preserved for the most part. Or had they concealed them? Had not a prosecution investigator who had since become a judge on the Swiss Supreme Court said in February 1998 when testifying before the tribunal that in 1995 he had "collected a few documents in Mabanza commune?"[4] Ironically, one of the few written documents that the prosecution submitted in the case—a letter from Ignace Bagilishema to Préfet Kayishema dated June 24, 1994—ended up largely being used by the defense to its advantage. During their three trips to Rwanda, the defense counsel met a few key witnesses there and, more importantly, they obtained two essential commune records: a personnel log and a correspondence log. It was a gold mine. Armed with these documents and witness statements, they portrayed Ignace Bagilishema to the court as someone who issued fake *Hutu* identification cards to at-risk Tutsis, protected other Tutsis with the help of a religious community, and, according to them, had a "deliberate policy of preventing crimes or punishing criminal acts against Tutsis." In support of this last claim, they had a decisive weapon, a sort of keystone of their version of the facts and of their client's personality: the commune correspondence logbook. Most notably, this oversized book listed the measures that the *bourgmestre* had taken against the perpetrators of crimes against Tutsis or those who illegally seized the property of Tutsis who had fled the commune. According to Roux's accounting, during the months of May and June, Bagilishema had ordered that sixteen criminal cases be transferred to the Kibuye prosecutor, written at least eight letters asking that the property of Tutsis who had left be protected, and fired two commune agents, including a police officer, for the theft of an engine belonging to a Tutsi. In the eyes of the defense, "the most that a *bourgmestre*, pastor, or police officer could do was to try to manage the situation as best they could and to save as many lives as possible using the limited means they had at their disposal." In this case, they estimated that Bourgmestre Bagilishema had saved approximately two hundred Tutsis, prevented certain crimes from being committed, and punished the perpetrators of other crimes he knew of as soon as he was able to do so, in other words, after the attacks slowed on April 25. "He did what he could, when he could," concluded Roux, stating that "in other situations, that would be called heroism," which, he stressed, was not required by the law.

In October 2000, one year after the start of the Bagilishema trial, the judges were faced with another delicate matter. Unlike with Musema, they did not have a case in which the accused claimed he was not there. This time, the defendant was saying: I was there but I was busy with entirely different matters. In the end, the prosecution called fifteen fact witnesses. However, these witnesses provided differing, even contradictory, versions of the events. "If you have two different versions, we need to know which one you are using. That is what we expect of you," explained Erik Mose, the Norwegian judge presiding over the chamber, as his Sri Lankan colleague, Judge Gunawardana, flashed a sarcastic smile.

The comment was in vain. The prosecutor's closing remarks began to take on the appearance of a penal grocery store in which the judges were free to choose one witness product over another. It was impossible for them to know what theory the prosecution was advancing, that is, what they were supposed to be judging. Their smiles faded away. Judge Mose's face grew cloudy with a mix of annoyance and supreme irritation. He was clearly frustrated. Backed into a corner, trial attorney Jane Adong finally said, "This is our theory behind the case: Bagilishema and Kayishema met; they talked about getting rid of the scum; the next day, Bagilishema sent [the refugees] to Kibuye stadium." Take it or leave it.

In my language, we say that to judge is first to understand," said Diabira in his opening remarks. But the judges had other concerns. The presiding judge interrupted Diabira's speech three times, explaining that the court had already heard experts and read reports, and he stated, "We don't need that." The defense counsel saw red. They were convinced that the tribunal was not always terribly aware of the Rwandan reality in 1994. On several occasions, Judge Mehmet Güney proved them right.

"Mr. Bagilishema was fully within his right to request reinforcements from the army, through the *préfet*. Did he do so?" asked the Turkish judge.

"Yes, on April 9, during a security meeting, he asked for reinforcements. He was given five gendarmes. On the tenth, he became aware of the situation and requested material support," replied Diabira.

"He requested reinforcements from the gendarmerie, but there was another way. If the *bourgmestre* was unable to maintain order, he could request the army's assistance!"

"I would like to come back to the reality of the situation. The country was at war and the army at the front. I do not know of any legislation that allows a *bourgmestre* to intervene at the ministry level to have the army brought in. There is some injustice in saying, 'If you were unable to stop [the massacres], it's because you did not want to.' We feel that we did everything in our power."

"The *préfet* can ask the army to intervene to restore public order," insisted Judge Güney. "Consequently, if the *bourgmestre* or *sous-préfet* were unable to maintain order, they were duty-bound to call upon the army via the *préfet*," he retorted, referring to an article in a 1975 decree from the Rwandan government. "There was not just the gendarmerie in the military; there was the army, the air force . . . ," he added.

In April 1994 Rwanda's air force consisted of four helicopters. Already irritated by the fact that he had not been allowed to come back to certain historic and contextual facts, such as the existence of a war at the same time as the genocide, Roux seized the opportunity to voice his concern. "Yesterday, when we tried to explain the context, you told us that you knew it. We were right to insist. I think that you do not realize what was happening in Rwanda. We are not here to try a man *in abstracto*. We are here to try a man *in concreto*, in a given situation. I am trying to make you understand that the front was in Kigali, not Mabanza. So for God's sake, try this man *in concreto*, not on the basis of laws that we might sit down and read together in good company. In my country, when the army was fighting—well, as best they could!—the German invader, if my mayor in Montpellier had tried to call in the army, they would have laughed in his face."

Judge Güney, a career diplomat who had never sat on a court before, save perhaps for a royal one, did not ask questions. He made statements. According to him, on April 13, 1994, the day of the militia attack on Mabanza, since there were more refugees from this commune who had fled to Kibuye than there were Tutsis left in Mabanza, the *bourgmestre* "should have been more concerned" about the fate of the former.

"He should have verified things. That was the least he could do. In one way or another, he should have been concerned about the fate of his citizens. He should have taken care of both the people in Mabanza and the people at Kibuye stadium in a harmonious way," the Turkish judge stated.

"You tell him that. You write him that. I have nothing more to say to you," snapped Roux.

"Those are surely points we will discuss when we adjourn," said an annoyed, angry-looking Judge Mose, cutting the discussion short.

Having heard the parties, the judges consulted. They were clearly in an awkward position. They ordered a break. Weary consternation had filled the courtroom. The pause in the proceedings seemed to last forever. The prosecutor and the defense lawyers were called into the judges' chambers, in an attempt to limit public exposure to the disarray. Then they returned to the courtroom. The judges wanted to give the prosecution the chance to redeem itself in the form of a written response. The prosecutor was not very enthusiastic about the idea. The defense was vehemently opposed: "The problem is very simple. The hour of truth has come for the prosecution. Since the beginning of this trial, we have been calling the judges' attention to the contradictions in their witnesses. You can give the prosecution two, three months, and they will still not resolve these contradictions. If you decide to grant the prosecutor an extension, we ask that you release the defendant this very evening." Roux's response was bold, but the near total chaos that it caused was an indication of the tribunal's utter dismay at this thought. The judges withdrew again. Then, an ashen-faced Judge Mose rendered the decision of his peers, an opinion he did not share: the prosecution would have one more chance to get its evidence in order before the judges deliberated on the case.

As in the Akayesu case, there was a pivotal date in this one. During the new round of closing arguments six weeks later, François Roux told the court, "The question before you is to decide if the prosecution has presented sufficient evidence that this man here suddenly changed from being 'good natured' and turned into a devil capable of the worst crime of all: genocide. Do we have proof that this man did a complete about-face? In the Akayesu trial, the prosecutor gave a specific date: April 18. Do you have that in the Bagilishema case?"

The prosecutor had to give a reply. Adeogun-Phillips stated that the definitive date of this dramatic change was April 12, the day when the *bourgmestre* met with Préfet Kayishema at the Mabanza commune office. "This was the meeting that formed the genocidal intent in this case. If you accept this, then everything that took place afterward naturally flows from that," he concluded. The details of this April 12 meeting were based on the testimonies of three witnesses, but only one of them spoke to the content of the alleged conversation between the *préfet* and the *bourgmestre*. According to witness O., Bagilishema supposedly said at that time, "This place is too small, and if we kill people here, the commune office will be destroyed." O. reportedly left immediately to inform the other refugees of what had been said. Judge Gunawardana noted that Clément Kayishema had testified during his trial that he was in another commune on April 12. Judge Mose asked why the refugees would have obediently gone to Kibuye the following day if they had been informed of such a plan by O.? He was still holding out hope: "Besides this conversation, is there any other element from which this chamber should infer a genocidal intent?" But with every one of the prosecutor's responses, another piece of the indictment crumbled away, as if he were trying to hold up a building and every time he moved a hand to keep one part of the foundation from falling, another column collapsed. All that François Roux had to do was note the damage. "The additional extension has ended in tragedy. I have known once and for all since last night that the prosecutor does not have a case and thus he is inventing."

At that very moment, Ignace Bagilishema had never looked so serene. Wearing a white jacket and brown shirt, oddly accessorized with a tie in shades of blue, he almost gave the impression that his trial was behind him. The time had come for him to take the floor one last time before his judges. He stepped forward and, standing before the court, stated: "Throughout my entire life, I have always fought to make this world better by doing my small part. I have always wanted to embody the pride of my children and my people. That is why during the Rwandan tragedy, I opened all the doors of the commune office and my home to take in Tutsi refugees. Very early on the morning of April 13, I made the decision to inform the Tutsi refugees of the danger that threatened us all. I affirm on this day that I saved the Tutsis who had gathered there from certain death. I decided to tell them to flee to the south. I could never have imagined what was going to happen. I did everything in my power. I held meetings; I arrested the troublemakers; I went so far as to suspend some commune staff. In order to save human lives, I even issued official documents that I tried to change, knowing full well what could happen to me. I falsified documents to save lives. I made constant requests for reinforcements. What I can say is that I am not a *genocidaire*. I did everything I could. At this point I wish to address the prosecution witnesses. I feel no resentment. They made a mistake or were misled. I pay my respects to the victims of Mabanza and of the Rwandan tragedy. As for Mabanza commune, it needs to make peace with itself and no longer cultivate hatred, because that will cause a perpetual, irreparable rift. There are no victors in war."

It was the lengthiest judgment so far, both in deliberation and in volume. On Thursday, June 7, 2001, as presiding judge Mose read a summary of the judgment and it became clear that the main count, that of genocide, was being dismissed, Ignace Bagilishema looked him in the face, then lowered his eyes. Squeezed into a dark suit, the former *bourgmestre* stood motionless, animated only by the simple blinking of his eyelids. One by one, the charges were dropped. As the verdict was pronounced, he stood, still blinking his eyes, maintaining the impenetrable look that Rwandans know how to do so well. Ignace Bagilishema was acquitted of all the charges against him. The decision was unanimous except on three counts, on which Judge Mehmet Güney found him guilty. The judges ordered his immediate release. Carla del Ponte appeared surreptitiously in the hallway. The chief prosecutor knew in advance what the verdict would be and did not wish to be present during the hearing. One other person was absent: Jane Adong, the trial attorney in charge of this case and that of Alfred Musema. She had been fired a few months earlier.

Not guilty. When a verdict is delivered, it is said that the defendant is found "not guilty." One does not say that he is innocent. This is most likely a simple choice of words. But maybe not. As soon as the judgment had been read, the trial attorney announced during the hearing that he planned to appeal the decision and requested that Ignace Bagilishema be kept in detention. This is permissible under the rules of procedure. However, this request seemed to catch everyone off guard, including the presiding judge. He hesitated a moment, then gave the parties six days to produce a written brief detailing their respective positions. "We need only an hour to respond, and we are leaving Saturday," François Roux replied dryly. The confusion that had finally dissipated returned. The judges did not wish to render a decision right away and decided to defer—at least until the next day—the release of the person they had just found innocent, or more precisely, "not guilty."[5]

Where is a person who has been acquitted by the ICTR to sleep? The question was not preposterous because the tribunal did not seem to have given it any thought. Not surprisingly, Bagilishema expressed a great reluctance to return to the detention facility. Thus the administration decided to take him to one of its safe houses to spend the night. There were several choices, but the decision was made to take him to the house where Georges Ruggiu and Omar Serushago were being held, two individuals convicted of genocide or incitement to commit genocide. The pretext was a lack of resources. Or was it rather the bureaucracy's boundless imagination at work again?

The following day, it was decided that Bagilishema could be released if he could find two people who could act as guarantors for him, report to the nearest police station once a month, not leave his country of residence without prior approval from the tribunal, and hand over his travel documents to the local police station. At the ICTR, being acquitted was tantamount to being on probation. But where? The tribunal did not seem to have thought about that either. Bagilishema wanted to go to Europe, where his wife and children were. But who would want to take in a person accused of genocide, even if he had been acquitted? To obtain "the fundamental right to the freedom of an acquitted person," as the judges had said, Bagilishema had to fulfill the conditions set by the court, yet without the cooperation of states, he was unable to do so. When asked to take Bagilishema in, France, the United States, Sweden, and Norway all refused, either formally or informally. "It is unfortunate for him. Maybe he could sue the United Nations in civil court?" stated an anonymous source at the U.S. State Department in Washington. UN headquarters in New York also washed its hands of him. "In a normal situation, a freed person has to fend for himself. That's life. It sounds harsh, but that's criminal justice," said a source there, also under the cover of anonymity.[6]

When, in June 2000, a Rwandan court made the spectacular decision to acquit Bishop Misago (who, like Bagilishema, had been on the national list of genocide suspects), it placed no conditions on his immediate release, despite the notice of appeal immediately filed by the prosecution. The prelate then left his country in a most official way to go to Italy for medical treatment for three months. Upon his return to Rwanda, he waited for his appeals judgment a free man. So between the Rwandan judges and their international counterparts, who was more independent?

Aware that his cause did not attract the enthusiasm of the crowds or human rights organizations, Roux went easy on the UN tribunal, the only entity in the end that, along with him, appeared to have an interest in finding a solution. "The problem is not the tribunal. It's the states," he said.[7]

On October 9, 2001, after four months in a safe house, where at least he was finally separated from the two other convicts, Ignace Bagilishema looked out of place sitting in the departure lounge at the Arusha airport, where the majority of the European passengers were cheerfully heading home after two weeks of being on safari. He did not have a passport. But he finally had a ticket and a safe conduct allowing him to go to France. He would await the appeals decision in the discreet setting of the Vosges Mountains. The appeals chamber opened the proceedings in record time: one year. It concluded the case in an unparalleled amount of time: one day. This time, on July 3, 2002, the former mayor of Mabanza became a free man immediately.

To remove all reasonable doubt, Bagilishema's defense team had to go well beyond what was theoretically required. It had to *prove* his innocence and not just sow the seeds of doubt like Steven Kay, who, applying the rules of his country, had found this to be sufficient in Musema's case. It was a hard lesson. However, speaking to the press, François Roux saw in this judgment proof that the UN tribunal in Arusha was "not a convicting machine." He contended, "It is a court that is there to do justice. The goal of the ICTR is not only to combat impunity but also to work for reconciliation. This decision clearly signifies, as others have said before me, that one could be a Hutu during the genocide, hold a position of responsibility, and not be a *genocidaire*.[8] This is not a decision against the victims, but a decision that gives us hope in justice."

Although Ignace Bagilishema had been a public figure, he was not as accustomed to the media as his defense counsel. A few words sufficed: "It is difficult for me to express the joy that dwells in me. I have just been freed. I have always striven for peace between the ethnic groups, the political groups, and the various religions. I will continue to fight for national reconciliation, so that my country can find the peace we all desire."

Bagilishema had to wait fourteen more months to obtain refugee status and another year before he could live with part of his family again. Since then he has lived a quiet life in western France, discreetly seeking employment as an accountant. On November 26, 2002, he spoke with journalist Laure de Vulpian during an interview broadcast on France Culture Radio.

"I talk about the ordeal that struck our country, and I wish to talk about the war that was imposed on us from outside and that we unfortunately lost; that was our misfortune," stated the former *bourgmestre*.

"You don't talk about a genocide?"

"I do not talk about a genocide for the time being because it is up to the tribunal to decide whether there was a genocide."

"But the tribunal has already made that determination on several occasions . . ."

"I think it is always in the documents, but no evidence has been found to prove that there really was a genocide in Rwanda. I am waiting for the tribunal to rule on the acts that were committed by both sides. At present, they are attacking only the Hutus. The Tutsis are innocent. They did not do anything. However, one has to assess everyone's role and draw the appropriate conclusions about what exactly happened in Rwanda."

The court had rightly found reasonable doubt in acquitting Bagilishema. However, listening to him after his judgment, it was as though justice would never be able to eliminate the doubt entirely.

13

The Principle
of Ignorance

I wonder what makes those people tick, to have done what they did. In
our culture, I thought to myself, it is not possible to behave in such a way
on this earth, but unfortunately, that is the daily lot in that region.

Judge Laïty Kama, interview in *Nouvel Horizon*,
December 31, 1998

INVESTIGATOR: Hmmm.
OMAR SERUSHAGO: I never saw that because he is not *mushiru*, he is a
Mungogo.
INVESTIGATOR: Mungogo? What does that mean?
SERUSHAGO: Someone who comes from Kingogo.
INVESTIGATOR: Someone who comes from Kingogo?
SERUSHAGO: Uh-huh.
INVESTIGATOR: Where is Kingogo?
SERUSHAGO: It's in Satinsi and Remba [phonetic] commune.
INVESTIGATOR: OK.
SERUSHAGO: But like Bahufite, he wasn't *mushiru*.
INVESTIGATOR: Hmmm. Yes?
SERUSHAGO: Bahufite, he was from Byumba. He was *kiga*, well, a
Mukiga.
INVESTIGATOR: Mukiga?
SERUSHAGO: Uh-huh. Someone who comes from the North.
INVESTIGATOR: Yes.

interrogation of Omar Serushago by an investigator with the OTP,
February 11, 1998

The universalist ideal was a powerful, and no doubt sincere,
force behind the establishment first of the international

tribunals in The Hague and Arusha and later the ICC. Since the nature of these crimes obligates the universal human community, it seemed natural that anyone who is a member of this community, regardless of origin, would be able to render justice. The premise, which seems convincing at first sight, was that judges, lawyers, legal experts, and police officers would have no problem performing their duties of investigating, prosecuting, defending, or judging, thanks to their professional expertise, which would be especially reliable since the court was to draw from the best and brightest in every nation. Following close on the heels of the tribunal for the former Yugoslavia, the tribunal for Rwanda would derive its independence from internationalization and its impartiality from its extranational makeup, which could include nationals of every country except the one where the crimes occurred. Just as the tribunal was not set up in Kigali in order to shield it from pressure or direct threats to the security of the proceedings, its legal structures are staffed solely by non-Rwandans to guarantee its impartiality. It would have been difficult not to use the services of Rwandans for translation, witness assistance, and to a lesser extent, public-relations matters, so an exception was made in these areas. However, no Rwandan was ever supposed to appear to be in a position to influence the trials, much less the judgments. This foreigner-run court system, which bases its legitimacy on the fact that the crimes were against *humanity*, was intended to ensure the fairness and integrity of this nascent international justice.

Many have highlighted the disconnect between Rwandans and the tribunal created on their behalf. Everyone recognizes that the geographical distance has had an impact. Also, the Rwandan authorities have managed to use, shake up, manipulate, and intimidate the ICTR. In a nutshell, they have had no qualms about subjecting the tribunal to their interests, and these policies have considerably weakened the institution in the eyes of the Rwandans. Another illustration of the tribunal's eroded credibility is the disdain with which many Rwandans who have been following the trials recollect and evaluate what they have seen, read, or heard.

To understand better, there is a simple but relevant way to portray how a Rwandan might perceive the proposed judicial process. Suppose you are a U.S. citizen. Imagine for one awful moment that a comparable mass crime has been committed in the United States. Everyone has been dragged into it, willingly or not, and questions about what led to the government and society's downward spiral into crime are directly related to the most complex foundations of the country's history as well as its most recent and obscure events. A tribunal is set up in Mexico City to try the main perpetrators. Three judges—a Congolese, a Chilean, and a Dutchman (the only English speaker)—conduct the proceedings on the basis of evidence gathered by Turkish, Senegalese, and Venezuelan investigators and presented by Italian, Korean, and Lebanese prosecutors. (If you are not American, simply "regionalize" the scenario to fit your own country.) Question: would we believe that "they" are capable of accurately understanding and interpreting *our* history?

Looking at the flip side does not always provide the best or only perspective. But it is a precaution that is often wise to take, and it can be a humbling experience. Granted, in this case the drawback is that this exercise is incomplete. To feel even more like a Rwandan would, one should also realize that in reality, it was not the best judges or the best lawyers or the best police officers who were recruited from every nation for this tribunal—far from it.

In order to be best able to judge something, one should see or know the least about it possible. This quickly became the judges' innovative motto. In 1997 this principle of neutrality, reinforced by minimal exposure to Rwanda's political and historical torments, took firm root at the Arusha-based tribunal, especially given the court's understandable and legitimate fear of being accused of bias. Several judges felt it was inappropriate for them to visit Rwanda or meet with its authorities, thinking that the two went hand in hand. Indeed, was it not possible that some of these same officials might be brought before the tribunal? For their part, defense lawyers unanimously claimed that their safety could not be guaranteed in Rwanda. There was real and serious tension in the country at the time, and the northwest was practically in the throes of an insurrection. All the arguments in favor of the court keeping its distance seemed to be those of a judicial system concerned about its integrity. They thus came off as the expression of a wise court, conscious of its political environment.

Judging from afar without partisan influence has its consequences on the narrative. Those who were called upon to enlighten the court on Rwanda's history, the political and military context in 1994, the meaning of various expressions, or the nature and role of various paragovernmental structures were for the most part Western experts. Thus, just as the world's history is "after all, really only the *historia mundi* as told by Europeans," as philosophy professor Alain Brossat has said, the universal history of the Rwandan genocide that imposed itself on the court was, to a large extent, a history as told by Europeans and Americans.[1] Rwandans are proud and passionate about their history, as painful and bloody as it is. Was the narrative that was being written in Arusha as offensive to them as the one that our Congolese, Chilean, and Dutch judges in Mexico City would write about ours?

The months and the years went by. The tribunal's standing and the domestic situation in Rwanda changed considerably, but the debate over the judges traveling to the land of a thousand hills not so much. The argument advanced back in 1997 based on the conditions in the country had become a sort of dogma. The judges did not go to Rwanda not only because it would be inappropriate, but also because it was not necessary in order for them to be able to try the cases properly. Proud of its first judgments, intoxicated by the flattering recognition that had suddenly surrounded it beginning in 1998, the tribunal found comfort and convenience in this. The principle of ignorance had been born and had found a new feeding ground: pride.

In 1999 it appeared this cowardly protective shell would finally crack. Standing at the defense table in March, Steven Kay brushed aside preconceived notions. Having gone to investigate in the hills of Rwanda and returned armed with a pile of documents, he upset the calm order of these long-distance trials. In June reinforcements arrived in the form of new judges. Among them, Erik Mose privately considered from the outset the most appropriate context for the court to visit Rwanda without inviting criticism. Five months later, defense counsel François Roux gave him the opportunity. Roux wanted the judges who would be trying his client to have an idea of the crime scenes, a minimal sense of this region in Kibuye that almost every judge at the ICTR would have to at least visualize in his or her mind. Judge Mose understood that a strictly legal visit conducted in the context of a trial without giving the impression of being a political compromise was an opportune way to overcome the problem of the UN tribunal being too far removed. During the first three days of November, as an opening to the trial of Mabanza commune *bourgmestre* Ignace Bagilishema, an entire ICTR trial chamber traveled to the crime scene. Three years after the beginning of the trials, this was an entirely novel initiative. In Rwanda, where the genocide trials had begun at the same time as those in Arusha, it was customary. The Rwandan courts referred to it as "traveling chambers." Rwandan judges, who could reasonably be expected to be familiar with the country and its history and language, regularly expressed the need to conduct these "on-site raids," as they called them in Rwandan French, despite the lack of resources and their extremely heavy caseloads, so as to be better able to judge the crimes in the various cases. They did so naturally, without fanfare. Their intent was not to get closer to the Rwandan people, but simply to be better able to judge.

In an incredible commotion of thirteen huge four-wheel-drive vehicles (two of which were armored) escorted by armed guards, a whole entourage of tribunal staff—judges, prosecutors, lawyers, clerks, registry staff, legal assistants—rattled down these renowned hills for the first time to see for themselves the already infamous sites: Gatwaro stadium, Home St. Jean, the Catholic church in Kibuye, Bisesero, and Karongi Hill, among others. Of course, it was all very fast, just a brief glimpse. They had to stick to the schedule, ensure that this strange, white motorized centipede stayed together as it snaked its way down the road, and avoid any unwanted contact with the locals. Upon their return, however, the verdict was unanimous: this intrepid mission into hostile territory was productive, often useful, and sometimes enlightening. And Judge Mose could therefore write to his colleagues, "[This visit] gave us a better understanding than do the photographs and videos of the alleged scenes pertaining to the case and made it easier for us to assess the value of witness statements during the trial."[2] That seems highly desirable for an institution with a mandate to try crimes.

The site visit to the crime scenes in the Bagilishema case was a first. It was a success. And it would be the last for quite some time. In the six years that followed, no other trial chamber in any of the other cases felt the need or the desire to take such a judicial initiative. It was safe to say that nearly all the judges at the Rwanda tribunal and their young legal assistants—whose role in helping draft the judgments largely exceeded their job descriptions and in many cases their professional experience—knew nothing about the country that was central to their work. The principle of ignorance had become deeply ingrained. It was no longer simply the subject of a timely debate. It had me-tastasized. Increasingly, representatives of the OTP no longer spent several long months or years in Rwanda before coming to plead in Arusha. Those who acquired a solid knowledge of Rwandan history through books were rare. The context was ripe for the Rusatira affair to come together—a vexing triumph of the virtue of not knowing.

14

The Betrayal of
the "Moderates"

I met with those investigators from the tribunal. Instead of seeking the
collaboration of direct witnesses, they use only intermediaries, and instead of trying to establish the truth, they are looking only for incriminating evidence. I refused to sign the statement. How can you restore the
trust of honest witnesses? Instead, they are bothering them. I'm thinking
of Rusatira.

Lieutenant Colonel Augustin Cyiza, interview,

September 9, 2002

There was no Hitler, no Pol Pot, no Stalin to imprint the
Rwandan genocide into collective memory. Yet, if the
two international courts established by the UN at the beginning of the 1990s
were to be symbolically identified with their primary suspect, then just as the
tribunal for the former Yugoslavia was ultimately embodied in the person of
Slobodan Milosevic, the Rwanda tribunal found its emblematic face in that of
Théoneste Bagosora.

In April 1994 this retired colonel from the Rwandan Armed Forces (FAR)
was the *directeur de cabinet* (chief of staff) at the Ministry of Defense. On
April 6 the Minister of Defense was on official travel abroad when President
Habyarimana, the FAR chief of staff, and a colonel considered to be the kingpin of the radical Hutu group all perished in the attack on the president's
plane. In the hours and days that ensued, Théoneste Bagosora emerged as the
key figure in the central government. Yet, he did not impose himself as the
country's undisputed leader. Since then, he has become, as Belgian researcher
Filip Reyntjens so accurately described him, the "prime suspect by default" in

the genocide of the Tutsis and the massacre of Hutu opponents.[1] On account of him and several other military leaders, the army found itself at the heart of the criminal conspiracy investigation by the ICTR prosecutor's office. Bringing these officers to trial was one of the tribunal's key objectives and Bagosora's trial was the most significant of them all.

During the Nazi trials in Nuremberg, several organizations, such as the SS, were declared to be criminal in essence. Fifty years later, international criminal justice advanced the principle of sole, individual responsibility. Just as the Interahamwe movement per se was not prosecuted, the FAR was not in itself declared criminal. Only individuals would be tried for their acts as direct participants or in their capacity as superiors. Recognition of this principle of individual criminal responsibility was seen not only as progress for justice. For the FAR in particular, it also reflected a crucial historical reality that was summed up by Colonel Luc Marchal, the commander in Kigali of the UN peacekeeping force in Rwanda (UNAMIR): "One can be a Hutu, have held a position of responsibility, still be alive, and not necessarily be a *genocidaire*."[2]

In investigating the crime at the highest levels, *inside* the plot, prosecution investigators had two invaluable sources of information available to them: Hutus who had been part of the political, administrative, and military institutions and who did not turn criminal, even if that meant they did nothing, and those who were also part of these structures but conducted themselves in an honorable and in some cases heroic way. The latter included even a few high-ranking military officers. Most of them were known, and several of them quickly joined the ranks of the new RPF government following the FAR's defeat in July 1994. Whether they were soldiers, politicians, human rights activists, or ordinary citizens, these Hutus were generally referred to as "moderates." The term is unfortunate and somewhat disparaging, but it has come to be commonly used. In reality, many of them formed the bulk of the democratic movement that had been developing since the end of the 1980s and began to play a role openly on the Rwandan political scene starting in 1991. At dawn on April 7, 1994, they were among the Hutu extremists' first victims. Thousands of them then became prime targets of the militias, along with the Tutsis. They were decimated by the genocidal undertaking, and in the years to come, they would end up being the biggest political losers in the civil war.

In the days following the creation of the international tribunal in Arusha, survivors from this group were among the strongest supporters of the UN court. For them, the real issue was not only a matter of recognizing the crime of which they had been victims due to their political or moral choices. It was also a matter of escaping the collective guilt that condemned the Hutu community and ultimately of establishing the rule of law in Rwanda.

In order to prosecute the most senior politicians and military leaders for genocide, the tribunal needed the cooperation of these Hutus who were in government or on its periphery but who were not part of the extremist circle. This investigation strategy developed rapidly and became more coherent under the authority of Louise Arbour. At the same time that the chief prosecutor was backing her investigators' attempts to "flip" several former Interahamwe leaders, she was supporting the efforts to establish contacts and conduct interviews with some of the FAR officers who could potentially be crucial witnesses for the prosecution. But as effective and steadfast as the investigators were in getting the militiamen to work for them, they were tragically less persuasive and consistent in approaching the former soldiers.

From 1994 to 1995, these ex-soldiers were quite willing to testify. However, the coalition government formed in July 1994 fell apart, barely a year after the genocide. Power sharing between the victorious RPF and what remained of the democratic opposition to the Habyarimana regime—the so-called Hutu moderates—had fizzled out. Many went into exile and again became opponents to a regime that they denounced as being a new dictatorship. Life in exile aggravated a political environment that was increasingly polarized and very much community based. Consequently, as the Hutu democrats who had survived the massacres were becoming permanently marginalized, their willingness to testify was dwindling. Some did not wish to jeopardize what remained of their potential political future within the new opposition forces abroad. Others were above all overcome by a great sense of bitterness, linked to the disillusionment that overwhelmed them after their hopes for reconstruction following the 1994 apocalypse had been dashed.

The soldiers among them were particularly suspicious of the UN tribunal. They were careful not to legitimize what they felt was a Manichean, simplistic, or biased version of history being developed by the OTP. Year after year, their trust in the tribunal eroded. The prospects for their cooperation with the ICTR began to fade, a victim of the high investigator turnover rate, along with the investigators' levity and ignorance, on the one hand, and, on the other, the radicalization of the Rwandan political debate. In 2002 all hopes of collaborating with these officers wound up being shattered by an unthinkable and highly politicized deviation by some righters of wrong at the prosecutor's office.

By April 2002 Théoneste Bagosora had already spent six years behind bars. He never shied away from his trial. Unlike some of his co-detainees, he did not abuse the procedural loopholes in an attempt to delay justice. He and his lawyer, Raphaël Constant, formed an odd, almost incongruous judicial couple. Stocky and solid in his dark blue suit, Bagosora sat up straight and still in his chair during the hearings, his forearms resting firmly on the table, always attentive yet impassive behind a large pair of outdated glasses that hid his small eyes, which were neither piercing nor expressionless. In front of him, Constant flaunted his laid-back attitude and his irrepressible bursts of laughter. He and his client no doubt had nothing in common. This lawyer from Martinique had the passion for history of a merry, militant, communist separatist from the French West Indies and the level-headedness that intelligence bestows on men who have managed to accept failed revolutions without becoming bitter. His professional integrity, coupled with a strong sense of humane indulgence, often led him to play the role of a sage in the restless ranks of the defense lawyers.

Above all, on this second day of April 2002, Constant had the happy and optimistic soul of a person who believed that the hour of truth was finally approaching in a trial that he had been awaiting for ages. The public and the press, which had long since deserted the trials, were back. The court drew nearly as large a crowd as on the big day of Kambanda's confession or Akayesu's conviction. At the last minute, chief prosecutor Carla del Ponte had made the trip from The Hague. In his new capacity as U.S. ambassador-at-large for war crimes, Pierre-Richard Prosper's presence gave an international flavor to an event that people had almost given up hope of ever seeing: the beginning of the trial of the main genocide suspect, Colonel Bagosora, along with three other former high-ranking officers from the FAR.

This trial was also an attempt to restore the image of a tribunal badly battered by contempt. Indeed, how was it possible that Théoneste Bagosora had waited six years from the time of his arrest to be tried? Imagine the outrage and mobilization of public opinion that would have occurred, especially among NGOs, if former president Milosevic had been made to wait even a third of that time before his trial opened. That would have been unthinkable. In The Hague, under pressure from the media and the judges themselves, the trial for the ICTY's "number 1 suspect" began on February 12, 2002, only eight months after he was arrested. This seemed normal in the eyes of everyone, an expression of the natural progression of the tribunal's priorities. Carla del Ponte had mobilized every possible resource in her office to draft the charges against the former Serbian leader, who was held responsible for three wars in eight years that led to the deaths of approximately 200,000 people in the heart of Europe.

The contrast with how the Bagosora case was handled by the ICTR, under the authority of the same successive chief prosecutors, could not be more striking. What was unthinkable in The Hague was not so in Arusha. With his six years of pretrial detention, the Rwandan tribunal's "prime suspect by default" had become the painful and unjustifiable symbol of the indifference that had drained the ICTR over the years, both on the outside and even more seriously on the inside.

If this trial was not held or continued to be postponed, then perhaps one could say that the tribunal had not fulfilled its mission. But the trial has finally begun. I hope that is what you will say," said the ICTR spokesperson, trying to defend the tribunal to a group of journalists.[3] After all the ambiguity, hesitation, and delays, this major case would finally explain the story of how the genocide was planned, or so it was thought. The stakes were high. The issue of planning was one of the hot buttons in the debate surrounding the genocide in Rwanda, and it was fertile breeding ground for fundamentalism. On one side of the debate were the fierce gatekeepers concerned about official history, who think, in short, that the genocide in Rwanda must be a tropical version of Hitlerism and cringe at the slightest hint of doubt as to the meticulous, chronologically well-organized, central planning of the Tutsi extermination. They fear that questioning whether the genocide was planned would mean the crime itself could be questioned. On the other side were those who actually silently dream of renaming this crime in order to further trivialize or deny it, and who never miss an opportunity to fan the fire by pointing out how proof of a plan continues to elude the guardians of dogma. In the midst of this ideological battle, lawyers maintain the idea, whether out of malice or a taste for exhilaration, that legally speaking, there could not have been a genocide without a plan. Rwandan history has the dark-magic ability to cause anyone who studies it to lose all reason—foreigners and Rwandans alike. In the hands of lawyers, it was bound to become complete nonsense.

Prosecutor Chile Eboe-Osuji created a sensation when he opened this long-awaited trial. He started by showing an explanatory diagram of the genocidal plan, the "tangled web of conspiracy." The drawing resembled a map of the sky where the deadly Hutu Power constellations and the isolated stars of criminal conspiracy became entangled and intertwined under the spell of RTLM's airwaves. The author of the sketch had proudly signed his work, just as one might patent the discovery of parthenogenesis. The educational intent was commendable, the artistic design somewhat muddled, and the historic performance deleterious. The sketch quickly became a prime target for mockery or condemnation.

But the prosecutor's ambitions did not stop there. He stated, in substance, that he had identified a providential Hutu equivalent of the Nazi Wannsee conference, where the final solution was planned. He was not the first to dream of possessing formal proof of a genocidal conspiracy copied from European history. In 1996 an ICTR investigator had thought he was going to be in position to announce to his colleagues that he was bringing back a video of that fateful meeting. They are still waiting for the tape. This time, the prosecutor confidently stated that the origin of the genocide plan resided in a well-known military commission set up by President Habyarimana more than two years before the crime.

Ten men sat on this commission from December 4 to 21, 1991. Their mandate was to determine "what needs to be done to defeat the enemy on the military, media, and political fronts." For a little over a year, Rwanda had been dealing with the RPF rebels, who had attacked the country from neighboring Uganda in October 1990. The president had assembled these officers in order to hear their thoughts. Colonel Bagosora was the highest-ranking among them.

Ten years later, when the ICTR identified the work of these ten officers as being the point of origin for organizing the Tutsi genocide, three of them had been indicted, including Théoneste Bagosora. Three were dead, including one who died in the attack on the presidential plane and one who died two days later, and four were still alive and at large. The paths of these four men are highly significant. Colonel Félicien Muberuka was held in detention in Cameroon for almost a year in 1996 but in the end was never prosecuted by the ICTR. He continues to lead a quiet life in that country. Commander Pierre-Claver Karangwa, who was later promoted to major, never went into hiding and lives in exile in Holland. Colonel Marcel Gatsinzi, who later became a general, was one of the best-known officers to have joined the new government in Rwanda right after the war. Since 1994 he has successively held the positions of deputy chief of staff of the new national army, chief of staff of the gendarmerie, director of the National Security Service, and minister of defense, a position he still held as of 2009. The fourth man was Major Augustin Cyiza, who also joined the new government in August 1994. He served as president of the court of cassation and vice president of Rwanda's Supreme Court before being discharged in 2002 at the rank of lieutenant colonel. Although Colonel Muberuka's actions during the genocide are not well known and could be questionable, the actions of the other three are well documented. In the case of the latter two, since 1994 their actions have largely come to symbolize the dignity maintained by a portion of the government army during the great massacres.

This was the first snag in the theory advanced by prosecutor Eboe-Osuji. How could the criminal conspiracy have originated within a commission whose members included some of the most famous senior officers in the government army who opposed the massacres in 1994? The paradox was embarrassing—for everyone but those in the office of the prosecutor. After seven years of investigation, the OTP's conspiracy theory seemed to be fraught with ineptitude.

The second hitch was that the prosecution clearly did not appear to be in possession of the full report of the infamous 1991 commission, yet it was nevertheless basing its criminal theory on this document. Or was it concealing the document? All that was known of this report was an excerpt on the definition of the enemy that was widely distributed within the army starting in September 1992. This excerpt was pertinent and real evidence insofar as it tended to designate all Tutsis and all opposition Hutus as the enemy to fight. But was it enough to attribute the objective of exterminating a portion of the Rwandan population to this commission? If that were the case, Félicien Muberuka, Marcel Gatsinzi, Augustin Cyiza, and Pierre-Claver Karangwa would have had to have been indicted immediately. Was this an absurd notion given the service records of the latter three? Not everyone thought so. The tribunal had never been so threatened by irresponsible ignorance and a taste for caricature. This would be demonstrated beyond all expectations in the weeks that followed Eboe-Osuji's perilous presentation in court.

In April 1994, Karangwa, the lowest-ranking member of the 1991 commission, was promoted to major. He served as the liaison officer between the general staff of the Rwandan gendarmerie and UNAMIR, the soon-to-be not-so-aptly-named UN "peacekeeping" force. In this capacity, he attended critical meetings of the crisis committee set up by the military shortly after the April 6 attack that decapitated the army by killing the head of state and the army chief of staff. After the genocide, Karangwa, a privileged witness to the events that had shaken Rwanda since 1990, was recognized for the integrity of his actions. For this reason, he naturally was among those who were of great interest to the office of the prosecutor in its quest to prove the guilt of other army leaders, in particular Colonel Bagosora. On two occasions, in November 1997 and in March 1999, prosecution investigators took his deposition, as good professionals do. During the first interview, Karangwa implicated Théoneste Bagosora. However, in his second deposition, a fifteen-page document, he stated that he did not wish to testify in Arusha. In military circles, distrust of the tribunal was already on the rise.

Life in exile is rarely a picnic. Karangwa was living in the Netherlands with a family to feed on a refugee allowance that covered only the bare necessities. In 2000 he was approached by the defense team of his former boss, Augustin

Ndindiliyimana, chief of staff of the Rwandan gendarmerie in 1994, who had been in detention in Arusha for a year. They offered him a job as an investigator. It was a tempting offer for Karangwa. The appeal was twofold. First, defense investigators could make as much as $2,500 per month, which was not negligible. Second, he was convinced that his former boss was innocent. On February 11, 2002, after waiting nearly a year, Karangwa received his first contract with the ICTR. Five weeks later, he arrived in Arusha to meet with his new "client." But there was another surprise awaiting him. For the past eight days, he had been under investigation and considered to be a genocide suspect by the OTP.

Of course, the tribunal's administrative staff who oversaw contracts for defense investigators had no idea who this man suddenly being targeted by the prosecution was. But within two weeks, they had determined that the contract with Pierre-Claver Karangwa, who was now labeled a suspect, had to be annulled. As far as they were concerned, there was nothing unusual about this; it was purely administrative. By contrast, for those more familiar with the Rwandan issue, it was a minor catastrophe. On account of Major Karangwa, the group of FAR officers who had not been involved in the crime were now facing public disgrace by the international tribunal. The already fading hope of ever being able to hear these unique witnesses make their contribution to the truth of what happened in April 1994 and the preceding years was quickly vanishing into thin air.

There had been an early warning sign in January 2000. The indictment and arrest of General Ndindiliyimana (the same person Pierre-Claver Karangwa would later come to work for in Arusha) had already caused a bit of a stir. This key figure in the Rwandan army had fled the country in June 1994 and was not considered by serious experts to be a *genocidaire*. Witnesses and analysts often pointed to the lack of courage or spineless opportunism that this officer from southern Rwanda had displayed. Nevertheless, Ndindiliyimana was granted political refugee status in Belgium following a thorough, adversarial proceeding. Unlike the other prime suspects on the run, who typically kept a low profile, he regularly spoke in public. He was invited to testify before highly official parliamentary commissions of inquiry in Belgium and France. He was a witness to and an ambiguous character in the tragedy, yet still considered to be the sort of person with whom one could associate. So naturally the OTP also approached this Rwandan general with a view to obtaining his cooperation and testimony. No such luck.

Four months after taking over as chief prosecutor and right in the middle of the major crisis with the Barayagwiza case, Carla del Ponte decided to brush aside all of these historical subtleties. On January 29, 2000, Augustin

Ndindiliyimana was arrested in Brussels and charged with genocide. For several months, the prosecution tried to put pressure on the general by keeping him locked up in a separate location in Arusha. Once again, their efforts were in vain. When the general eventually rejoined his former adversary Théoneste Bagosora behind bars, the UN detention facility in Arusha became a place of strange cohabitation.

Colonel Bagosora's lawyer, Raphaël Constant, had already begun to think that something much more disturbing was happening. He publicly warned that the arrest of General Ndindiliyimana was the sign of a poisonous dynamic in which, according to him, justice was being politically managed by the Rwandan authorities, and the UN tribunal was obediently following along. "The 'legal' elimination of Mr. Ndindiliyimana appears to be part of a political framework," he wrote. "In the terminology normally used to describe political forces in Rwanda, Mr. Ndindiliyimana has always been categorized as a 'Hutu moderate.' It is tempting for the authorities in Kigali to try to exclude a man like Mr. Ndindiliyimana from all political activity. This policy of exploiting justice as they please is not new. The past has already shown this. The present [has] as well; otherwise how can one explain the fact that in the latest list published in Kigali in December [1999], Mr. Léonidas Rusatira's name appeared on the list of people to be prosecuted for their involvement in the events in 1994?" the defense lawyer asked.[4]

Constant did not drop that name randomly. The man he was referring to was the first of a handful of senior Hutu army officers to publicly denounce the massacres in April 1994. He was also the first to join the RPF in July of that year and the first to go into exile one year later in opposition to the new government. Four years later, at the end of 1999, the Rwandan government made him pay the price by declaring him to be a genocide suspect. "Unfortunately, this concept of politically managed justice seems to have found a sympathetic ear in The Hague, the headquarters of the Office of the Prosecutor for the two international criminal tribunals," Constant concluded.[5] He had no idea his words would be such a premonition.

At the end of April 2002, after learning that he was suspected of genocide for the first time in eight years, Pierre-Claver Karangwa hastily returned home to the Netherlands. A gnawing sense of confusion gripped the prosecutor's office—an indication of the completely irrational machine it was becoming. It was the acting chief of prosecutions, Silvana Arbia, who had decided to mount the attack on Major Karangwa. The most puerile explanation for this initiative was that the Italian prosecutor could not stand the fact that Karangwa, whom the prosecution planned to call as a witness against Bagosora, had gone to work for the defense team of another defendant. In short, Karangwa would have to choose sides. The other, more trivial explanation was that this was supposedly a petty attempt to destabilize General Ndindiliyimana's defense in a seemingly no-holds-barred system. Regardless of which was the case, many in the prosecutor's office were embarrassed and secretly confided that they were dissociating themselves from this decision, which they described as isolated and discretionary. So who was really running the OTP? No one seemed to know anymore. Carla del Ponte was far away, absorbed in the Milosevic trial. For two years, she had been helping to create an unstable, antagonistic, and erratic system of management at her office in Arusha, and none of the people around her in The Hague had a thorough understanding of Rwanda and its key players.

Above all, Karangwa wondered where these allegations against him had come from. "For eight years I was never worried. With the position I had, they didn't discover this until eight years later? Don't you find that surprising?" he asked. Even the Rwandan government wisely kept its distance. "We were not even aware that he was an investigator," said the Rwandan ambassador to the ICTR, Martin Ngoga, who was normally quick to sow the seeds of suspicion.[6]

However, Karangwa was really only known to insiders. Consequently, the matter had about as much impact as an isolated storm. The carelessness with which individual cases were handled at the UN tribunal did not differ much from that characterizing the body of work, research, investigations, and reports that had been done since the end of the genocide. Hundreds of people had seen their names freely offered up to public suspicion. It was of no consequence. Between the license to kill and the freedom to denounce people, impunity had reigned continuously since 1994. Pierre-Claver Karangwa was not well known enough (who the devil would care about him?) to curb this phenomenon. The person who could do that was the man whom Raphaël Constant had sarcastically and defiantly singled out in his public letter in February 2000: General Léonidas Rusatira.

A graduate of the officers' training school in Kigali, in the sixth graduating class, Rusatira held the key position of chief of staff at the Ministry of Defense for twenty years. Throughout that time, he was the archrival of Théoneste Bagosora, who had graduated from the same school three years earlier. In 1988, when aspirations for political liberalization started to germinate in Rwanda, Rusatira published a book that attracted a lot of attention.[7] Indicative of the political education in which Rwandans had been submersed since the country's independence, the book is in part an apologia of the ideals and struggles of the 1959 revolution that overthrew the monarchy. Accordingly, entire pages are devoted to reminiscing about the war in the 1960s against Tutsi combatants who mounted a steady stream of unsuccessful attacks in an attempt to regain power. Rusatira extols the heroism of the national guard in an account totally in keeping with the historic mythology being taught throughout the country. Unbeknown to him, he had produced an enlightening book on Rwanda's political culture in the run-up to a war that, starting in 1990, would provoke the sudden and fatal resurgence of Hutu extremism.

But the book also revealed to the Rwandan public the well-educated, reasonable intellectual hiding behind the loyal, senior officer. Although he always praised the work of President Habyarimana, Rusatira also liked to show that he had his own store of literary and philosophical knowledge, which he drew from French culture, as did all the country's elites at the time. In his book, this soldier subtly develops an assessment of the Rwandan state that is both modern and inspired by humanism. Two years later, his political thinking would be severely tested.

In the weeks following the RPF's invasion on October 1, 1990, approximately eight thousand people, primarily Tutsis, were arbitrarily arrested throughout the country on the suspicion of being enemy accomplices. In his position at the Ministry of Defense, Rusatira was well placed to see the ethnic manipulation that was taking place. He quietly became an ally of those who were working to free these thousands of individuals who had been unjustly arrested. Beginning with this initial ordeal and throughout the period of the irrepressible rise in violence that would culminate in the genocide three and a half years later, a certain number of people who were fighting Hutu extremism learned to turn to this senior officer regularly for assistance. In the hours and days that followed the attack on April 6, 1994, there were not many emergency numbers that one could call to try to escape death. Colonel Rusatira's phone was one of the rare few that worked. It is estimated that at least two hundred people—both Tutsis and Hutus, strangers and friends alike— were saved thanks to the perilous actions of the general and the dozen or so individuals in his personal escort.

These acts were not among his best known. What was common knowledge were his official actions during the three months of terror. First, he was one of the key figures who, on the night of April 6, opposed the army takeover that Colonel Bagosora had wanted to pursue after the death of Habyarimana. More importantly, on April 12 he courageously initiated and was the first to sign a famous appeal soberly titled "Communiqué from the FAR High Command," which was broadcast over the radio without the permission of the interim government. In this communiqué, ten officers demanded that "the tragedy be ended." On July 6 he committed a second offense with the "Ki-geme Declaration," in which he and a handful of other officers condemned the genocide and called for the creation of a tribunal to try the perpetrators. Dismissed from the FAR and threatened with death, he was evacuated from southern Rwanda by French troops. At the end of July he was the first senior officer from the Rwandan army to join the new government in Kigali.

The remarkable appeals on April 12 and July 6 were not Rusatira's only re-corded actions. On April 16 and 22 he urged the government to end the mas-sacres. Finally, he approached, in vain, the RTLM broadcasters to encourage them to stop the calls for violence against the Tutsis.

After joining the RPF in Kigali, Rusatira enjoyed a unique reputation by virtue of his rank and his actions. Yet, he could not escape suspicion. Allega-tions quickly emerged regarding his alleged role in the major massacre of refu-gees at the École technique officielle (vocational school) in Kigali's Kicukiro neighborhood on April 11, 1994. ETO, as it was called, was the "Rwandan Srebrenica."[8] Approximately two thousand people who had sought refuge there with the Belgian UN peacekeepers were abandoned to their fate when Bel-gium decided to withdraw its troops from Rwanda. Most were massacred a few hours later in Nyanza, a few kilometers away. Georges Rutaganda, one of only two national Interahamwe leaders to be tried by the ICTR, was convicted of this crime.

Léonidas Rusatira first learned of these allegations against him at the be-ginning of 1995 after he officially rejoined the Rwandan army. His reintegra-tion did not go smoothly. Having been promoted to general during the geno-cide, he refused to be demoted to the rank of colonel in the new national army and was not given an influential position. He immediately reacted to the accu-sations through a widely distributed letter dated February 10, 1995, in which he called for an investigation. The matter seemed to have been forgotten when five years later the machine was set in motion again.

At the end of December 1999 the Rwandan government added Rusatira's name to its list of the main genocide suspects. "Any informed and honest observer of Rwandan affairs could only conclude that this false, gratuitous, and ridiculous accusation is purely political in nature," he wrote in response, to no avail. One year later, on April 11, 2001, on the occasion of the seventh anniver-sary of the attack on the refugees at the ETO, an organization close to the Rwandan government called African Rights published a special report com-memorating the massacre in which they interviewed witnesses and named the perpetrators. Public accusations against the ex-FAR officer reached an all-time high. "The soldier who ordered the crowd to go to Nyanza was identified by several survivors as Colonel Rusatira. Given the horrific killings which took place at Nyanza, this accusation against Rusatira is extremely serious and demands further investigation," the report claimed. The authors also stated, "African Rights calls for further investigation of Rusatira's actions at the time of the massacres at ETO and Nyanza."[9]

The message could not have been clearer. It took less than a year to reach Carla del Ponte's zealous office. On February 21, 2002, the chief prosecutor signed an indictment against Léonidas Rusatira charging him with the genocide committed at ETO-Nyanza. Three months later, on May 15, the general was arrested in Brussels. In Arusha, the chief of the press section announced the news with reckless pride. Just like the judge who had confirmed the indictment, this UN bureaucrat had no idea who Rusatira was. Neither did Carla del Ponte for that matter. He was just "one name among others" she confided soon after. One name too many.[10]

The shock produced by the announcement of Rusatira's arrest did not extend much beyond the circle of insiders. However, this time it rocked the institution from within. All the experts whom the prosecutor had been using for seven years to win over the minds of the judges—Alison Des Forges from the United States, André Guichaoua from France, Filip Reyntjens from Belgium, and François-Xavier Nsanzuwera from Rwanda—were, without exception, suddenly turning into defense witnesses. They were soon joined by several senior officials from the UN mission in Rwanda (UNAMIR) who had been announced as prosecution witnesses in some of the trials. Survivors also started to come out of the shadows, and they were not just any old witnesses. Among them was Jean-Bosco Iyakaremye, a Tutsi lawyer who had been a close friend of Rusatira for thirty years. He was among those who were rounded up in the raids of October 1990. Three and a half years later, he was among those whose lives were saved because he had called the ex-FAR officer by phone for assistance.

Iyakaremye was not an easy person. Following the genocide, some Hutu members of the group of human rights organizations in Rwanda considered him to be one of the "hard-liners" who wanted to break up the human rights movement. He later went into exile in Canada, where he continued to be an active member of survivor associations, extremely anxious to preserve the memory of the genocide. Thus, the fact that he did not hesitate to take an outspoken position—"I have a moral obligation to break my silence," he wrote ten days after his friend was incarcerated—was quite a surprise among the family of "moderates."[11] In an eleven-page document, he discussed "certain facts that completely contradict the allegations against this man," especially with regard to those crucial days, up to April 12 more precisely, when Rusatira took in dozens of threatened people at his official residence in Kigali, two-thirds of whom he probably did not even know.

Iyakaremye recounted the story of one family's arrival at the colonel's house on April 11, the fateful day of the ETO massacre, where they were placed "in a separate room." UNAMIR was supposed to evacuate this mysterious family that evening, as the logbook of UNAMIR's commander in Kigali attests.[12] In their communications, the peacekeepers referred to them as "the Rusatira package." It turns out this family was none other than that of Alexis Kanyarengwe, president of the RPF—in short, the enemy.

It took only three weeks after Rusatira's arrest was announced for the evidence to accumulate, be completed, and reveal the problem (which was as much criminal as it was psychiatric) that Carla del Ponte now faced: during those hours on April 11, 1994, in which, according to her indictment, the Rwandan officer led the massacre at the ETO, he was in fact essentially in the process of helping to evacuate eleven members of Kanyarengwe's family who were trapped in Kigali.[13] The inconsistency in the prosecution's theories, so brilliantly illustrated at the opening of the Bagosora trial on April 2, 2002, was on the verge of becoming a farce. The tribunal was now at risk of being completely discredited, relegated to "regional league justice, not even second division," as Filip Reyntjens angrily charged.[14] Regularly the butt of sarcasm, the court was now provoking muted anger and icy bitterness with respect to the political role it was playing, which one lawyer tersely summarized as follows: "We have to wonder if we are still in a peacekeeping operation or if we are moving toward preparing for war."[15]

The biggest paradox was that through its political cowardice and judicial laziness the international tribunal betrayed Rwandan democrats' hopes that the ICTR could serve as a tool for their regeneration. Of course, this infernal train wreck of 2002 would eventually be stopped. Just before committing irreparable damage, and under pressure, del Ponte pulled her office from the brink of ruin by withdrawing the indictment against the Rwandan general on August 9. But the ICTR had already marked Pierre-Claver Karangwa and Léonidas Rusatira with the curse of suspicion. There were never any official findings regarding the secret suspicions that hung over Karangwa. This court of justice, which took the responsibility of formulating such a serious accusation as involvement in genocide, never deemed it necessary to either substantiate or withdraw it. The allegations against Rusatira were not formally lifted until April 2004, when the prosecution suddenly remembered it might need the general to testify against its prime suspect, Théoneste Bagosora. Even worse: the judges disgraced Rusatira's name in their judgment against former militia leader Georges Rutaganda. Incapable of spelling his name correctly but condemning him nevertheless, they stamped this ruling with the permanent mark of their self-proclaimed right to remain ignorant. Honor is not lost but once.

A year after the "Rusatira affair," three Rwandans were recruited as full-fledged staff members at the prosecutor's office for the first time. By coincidence, one of them had been saved by Léonidas Rusatira on April 10, while another one was a survivor of the ETO-Nyanza massacre the following day. Both were "Hutu moderates," for lack of a better term, and courageous lawyers involved in defending human rights since the beginning of the 1990s. The level at which they were recruited was hardly worthy of their professional experience, but perhaps a lesson had been learned. For there was no doubt their presence was intended to prevent any new disasters following the one in 2002.

Meanwhile, Pierre-Claver Karangwa became a Dutch citizen. At forty-nine years old, he could not rejoin the police force of his country of asylum. He was hired as a "city warden," a sort of municipal security guard. Officials from the OTP never contacted him again. "They did not dare," he said coldly. Léonidas Rusatira still lives in Belgium. Unemployed, he took advantage of the time to write a book. Neither man ever appeared as a defendant in Arusha. That is fortunate. However, neither one, nor for that matter Augustin Cyiza, the other respected officer who "disappeared" in Rwanda in April 2003, ever appeared in the place where they were so eagerly awaited: at the witness stand.

In January 2009, Karangwa was convicted of genocide in absentia by a *gacaca* court, a community-based tribunal in Rwanda, and sentenced to life in prison. In November of the same year, Rusatira learned that he had also been convicted of genocide by four different *gacaca* courts in 2007 and in 2009, in regions he may have never even visited, and that he had been given three thirty-year sentences and one life sentence. After failing to materialize at the international tribunal, political vengeance through judicial means made its way to the community courts established in Rwanda, which have brought charges against more than a million Rwandan Hutus since 2002. Justice, be it in Arusha or in the hills of Rwanda, would prove to contribute little to democratic progress or national reconciliation.

In April 2005, three years after the beginning of Colonel Bagosora's trial, the prosecution finally finished presenting its evidence against the "mastermind" of the genocide and his three codefendants. None of the members of the infamous 1991 commission that the prosecutor had described in such a cavalier manner as being the origin of the genocide plan (one of whom, Marcel Gatsinzi, is still minister of defense in Rwanda) ever came to testify and the full report was never produced, even though it exists. On the defense side, all Raphaël Constant had to do was note that of the eighty-three prosecution witnesses, including some thirty soldiers, the highest-ranking was a lieutenant. "You are trying a general, two colonels, and a major. The prosecutor was not able to bring in even one high-ranking officer [to testify as a witness]. How can one prove a plot by military leaders without bringing a single one of these leaders?" he demanded to know.

He was almost right.

In fact, the highest-ranking officer to testify was a general: Roméo Dallaire, the commanding officer of the peacekeeping mission during the genocide. This Canadian general took up his post in Kigali less than six months before the genocide. A few years later, and after going through a period of major depression, General Dallaire, a nice man genuinely tormented by the past, became the Western world's impossible hero of the Rwandan tragedy. His knowledge of the UN mission's failure to prevent the genocide and of the international community's refusal to intervene was firsthand and amply illustrated. But his knowledge of Rwanda's army and politics at the time and its key players and domestic tensions was cursory, fragmented, and reconstituted after the fact. This undoubtedly explains why, among other numerous errors and speculations in his book written nine years after the events, he still systematically confused Colonel Gatsinzi with Colonel Rusatira.[16] Unlike that which prevailed at the tribunal, General Dallaire's ignorance was due more to naiveté than arrogance. But in the end, it nonetheless seemed that the history of Rwanda's military in 1994 would be written before the ICTR on the basis of this ignorance and not on the testimony of those who actually knew it.

On December 18, 2008, nearly thirteen years after his arrest, Théoneste Bagosora was found guilty of genocide and sentenced to life in prison. On the surface, it appeared the ICTR had confirmed everything that had been said and written about the "number 1 suspect" since 1994. However, a closer reading of the judgment gives a profoundly different picture. Bagosora was convicted only as a superior and over three days, from April 6 to 9, 1994. That was it. The allegations of direct involvement did not hold. All of the charges of conspiracy were essentially dismissed. On the one hand, the judgment was once again an indictment of the appalling quality of the investigations. On the other hand, it showed how, fifteen years later, a reasonable court could no longer support the official, simplistic narrative of the genocide.

From a historical point of view, it was, in fact, the most iconoclastic ruling ever issued by the ICTR judges. All of the key elements that had been presented over the years to describe the Hutu Power plan to commit genocide, including the 1991 commission, were scrutinized. What the judges eventually described was a much more checkered and dynamic course of events than the one generally told. "It is not argued that the Accused simultaneously agreed to a plan, or that such a plan consisted of a single course of equally divided or unified conduct. Instead, the proper inference to be drawn from the evidence is that at various times, each of the Accused agreed to participate in a larger, lengthier effort to increasingly homogenise Rwandan society in favour of Hutu citizens, with the object of killing Tutsi civilians, as required. It is their participation in this process—and the willingness to create or exploit various opportunities to achieve it—which is the hallmark of their agreement," the judges wrote.[17] Such discourse, which opened itself up to historical complexity and nuance, would be more challenging to use for public consumption, but it may be more helpful in understanding what happened. Having tested the evidence, carefully tried to balance facts and historical context, and chosen words as if with a pair of tweezers, the judges did not offer *the* explanation for the genocide. Rather than providing a deterministic version of history that was reassuring by virtue of an easy and clear-cut construct, the Bagosora judgment promoted the demanding task of interpreting history as a contingent— a task that was both uncertain and without promise. Surely, this was a more chaotic and unsafe path. But it was a more promising one, too.

"When viewed against the backdrop of the targeted killings and massive slaughter perpetrated by civilian and military assailants between April and July 1994 as well as earlier cycles of violence, it is understandable why for many this evidence [of preparations to commit crimes prior to April 6] takes on new meaning and shows a prior conspiracy to commit genocide. Indeed, these preparations are completely consistent with a plan to commit genocide. However, they are also consistent with preparations for a political or military power struggle," the judges said. "It cannot be excluded that the extended campaign of violence directed against Tutsis, as such, became an added or an altered component of these preparations," they concluded.[18]

The ICTR judges were aware of, and took into consideration, everything that had been published to date on the events leading up to the plane attack. And yet, based on this evidence, the conspiracy theory did not hold. The prosecution also failed to prove that the "number 1 suspect," Théoneste Bagosora, shared the intent to commit genocide before April 6. Sixteen years later, the individual who has been presented as the brains behind the genocide should be described more modestly as its first—and temporary—lead implementer.

To some, this was alarming. The Bagosora judgment raised fear that it would provide unwarranted fodder for those who denied the genocide. It should not. On the contrary, the judges' findings paved the way for attempts to understand history in a lucid and bold way to thrive. This was long and slow in coming. But to the ICTR's credit, it finally laid the groundwork for research and reflection that was more liberated from political passions and manipulation than the environment in which the tribunal had been created and had evolved. With the Bagosora judgment (despite the questions it leaves unanswered), historians and political analysts can now resolutely try to better understand how and when the preparations for the Tutsi genocide and the elimination of political opponents ended up taking the form of a plan. For there was a plan, but it was an unusual one that probably took shape as it unfolded.

15

Like a Flight of Termites

We all have in mind a question that no one who goes to Rwanda can avoid: Who sparked the fire? What criminal mind schemed up the attack on President Habyarimana's plane?

François Roux, lawyer, Ignace Bagilishema trial,
April 26, 2000

As the prosecutor has indicated, she fully intends to indict members of the Rwandan Patriotic Front, against whom evidence of atrocities has been established.

Adama Dieng, ICTR registrar,
June 11, 2001

The Rwandan authorities' reaction to the acquittal of Ignace Bagilishema consisted in a few frowns and some symbolic boasting, evidence of the fact that in their eyes, the trial of Mabanza's former *bourgmestre* held little importance. As seen in the Barayagwiza case, Rwanda's government knows how to flex its muscles when it feels its interests are being threatened. There was no better illustration of this than Kigali's ability to neutralize the only real threat that the UN tribunal could pose to it: prosecution of the RPF's armed forces for the crimes they committed in 1994.

The UN tribunal in Arusha was conceived first and foremost for the perpetrators of the Tutsi genocide. That was its primary mandate, its top priority. But one of the reasons for establishing the court outside Rwanda was that it was also supposed to punish the crimes committed by soldiers of the victorious RPF rebel force, which has been in power since July 1994. The nature of these crimes was not the same. It was not another genocide but rather repeated, large-scale massacres of the Hutu civilian population, acts that lawyers would categorize as crimes against humanity or war crimes, depending on the circumstances. Some have called this the tribunal's "second mandate"—a supplement to its genocide trials. From the outset, this second aspect has been considered essential in order for the international tribunal to appear impartial. "For justice to be seen by all to be fair, the International Tribunal for Rwanda must equally take a keen interest in reports of the human rights violations and other crimes by the RPF," as Amnesty International's legal advisor Christopher Keith Hall wrote in a letter to the tribunal's first chief prosecutor, Richard Goldstone, on December 16, 1994, one month after the ICTR was established.

There is no doubt about the RPF's crimes during the war in 1994 and the ensuing months. "The RPF committed human rights violations, war crimes, and crimes against humanity," acknowledged Rwanda's chief prosecutor, Gerald Gahima, who had been considered an RPF "hard-liner" before falling out of favor with the party in 2003.[1] However, these crimes were not nearly as well documented as those committed by the *genocidaires*. No independent observers had free access to the RPF's side of the frontline. The crimes committed by its soldiers have been only partially reconstructed, and the process has been slow in coming and a sensitive issue.

Moreover, there was a major concern after the genocide that caused some to retreat from insisting too much on the crimes committed by RPF soldiers: negation of the genocide. At the time, those responsible for the extermination of the Tutsis, such as Jean Kambanda, quickly got busy "cranking out the numbers." The double genocide theory, publicly supported by French president François Mitterrand, was an attempt to reduce the Hutu massacre of the Tutsis and the Tutsi massacre of the Hutus into an equation. However, as historian Yves Ternon writes, "Comparativism carries the risk of trivialization, and that is one of the tools of negationism."[2] Given this risk, therefore, one of the first precautions the tribunal took was to do nothing. In order to thwart the negationists, it was thought that the RPF crimes should not be prosecuted until the genocide had been clearly tried. Although understandable at first, the postponement of these investigations proved to be fatal, and in reality, it was merely the beginning of the inevitable decision to renounce them.

When Louise Arbour took over the OTP in September 1996, no efforts had been made to investigate RPF crimes, and little if any action was taken during her three years at the helm. This Canadian magistrate brought two essential elements to the prosecutor's office: a clearer, more narrow focus on prosecuting the top genocide suspects, and a sense of integrity. Passionate, yet thoughtful, Arbour personified a rare pursuit of justice that was ambitious, innovative, and concerned about rigor at the same time. But she was also very pragmatic. That was undoubtedly why she renounced the two most politically sensitive matters at the ICTR: investigations into RPF crimes and, first and foremost, those into the April 6, 1994, attack on President Habyarimana's plane.

Time and time again since the start of the trials, survivors testifying on the witness stand never really got to the heart of the matter until they were asked the question: "Where were you on April 6, 1994?" On that day, at 8:25:50 in the evening, the airplane carrying the president of Rwanda, the president of Burundi and two of his ministers, the chief of staff of the Rwandan army, and the Rwandan president's security advisor was shot down by missile fire upon its approach into Kigali.[3] At dawn the next day, the presidential guard assassinated several opposition ministers in their homes. Then the systematic massacre of Tutsis in Rwanda's capital began. The genocide had started. The triggering incident had indeed been the attack on the president's plane the previous evening. Moreover, this chain of events in the execution of the crime was precisely what pointed to the Hutu extremists as being behind the attack. According to this analysis, the attack was part of the plan to exterminate the Tutsi population.

But this was only one suspicion. On the opposite end of the spectrum, another leading theory blamed this act on the RPF rebels, who allegedly wanted to use the attack to revive the civil war, which was their only hope for a total victory. Herein lies the great enigma of Rwanda's contemporary history. The mystery is certainly fascinating: it is not every day that two heads of state are assassinated by unknown perpetrators. It is even more unusual for such an act to be followed by genocide, an undertaking in human destruction that engulfed approximately one million people in three months.

Today, the mystery remains. One thing is certain: it will not be solved by the Rwanda tribunal. Early on, Louise Arbour publicly explained her lack of interest in what the rest of the world nevertheless wanted to know. She maintained that legally speaking, the attack on President Habyarimana did not fall under the scope of crimes she was authorized to investigate. It was not a crime of genocide, a crime against humanity, or a war crime, she insisted. Technically, her argument had some merit. But in substance, Arbour's position was not convincing. On the one hand, lawyers can be quite creative when necessary; also, the legal impediment was never clearly demonstrated. On the other hand, if the prosecutor's office thought the attack was in fact an element of the genocide plan, it indubitably would have gone to great lengths to prove it, thereby immediately removing the legal barrier cited by the prosecutor. The attack would have been central to establishing that the crime had been planned. Consequently, the prosecution's disturbing lack of interest in investigating the incident only gave fodder to the theory that this investigation had been ruled out or abandoned for political reasons because the evidence pointed more to the RPF, that is, the ruling government in Kigali.

At the beginning of 2000 the suspicion grew and caused a bit of a stir. At the time, a Canadian newspaper revealed that the UN archives contained a confidential investigation report concerning the attack on Habyarimana. The report was signed by Michael Hourigan, a former ICTR investigator. Hourigan stated that in 1997 three Tutsi informants disclosed to the ICTR prosecutor's office that they had been part of a ten-member commando unit, referred to as "the network," that had planned and carried out the missile attack responsible for bringing down Habyarimana's plane. According to these sources, the person behind this operation was the RPF military leader General Paul Kagame, who became Rwanda's vice president in July 1994 and has been president since April 2000.

The report did not stop there. It also stated that Louise Arbour called the investigation off after she learned what these three informants had disclosed. The accusation was serious: the prosecution leadership, in possession of potentially crucial information, had allegedly decided to keep it quiet because it implicated the government in place.

When the controversy broke, Louise Arbour was no longer the international tribunal's chief prosecutor. She had moved on to the much calmer and quieter world of the Canadian Supreme Court. Concerned about her former and present duties, she did not respond to the revelations in the *National Post*. Naturally, the indictees at the Arusha detention facility were quick to react. "This report is critical to the defense of the accused and shatters the prosecution's premise that the 'genocide' was meticulously planned," they wrote, taking special care to put quotes around this word that bothered them so much. Some of the defense lawyers hastened to announce that based on this report, they could request that the proceedings before the ICTR be suspended. Rwandan authorities denounced it as a campaign of disinformation organized by revisionist groups. "This is not the first time that such allegations have been leveled against the government. Their goal is to deny the genocide and that is why the Rwandan government feels obligated to reply," stated the Rwandan ambassador to the ICTR. During a press conference, ICTR deputy prosecutor Bernard Muna cast doubt on the value of the report and called its author, one of his former investigators, a "pyromaniac."

In terms of credibility, the report was indeed shaky. None of the information it contained had been corroborated. Several senior investigators who were present at the time explained that the lead provided by the three informants had not been pursued because it had seemed to be either a booby trap or far-fetched. "There was no credibility and no possibility of investigating. At the time, there were questions about the credibility of the witnesses, how this information was obtained, how the informants were identified, and how to verify the documents. We did not know if it was a trap," explained Mohamed Othman, one of the two highest-ranking officials at the prosecutor's office from 1996 to 2000.[4] Added another lead investigator: "It was the stunt of the century. If these people had really been involved in something that was so professional, so major, the three of them would not have just walked in with a file and told someone from the tribunal, not even the top brass. That seems so crude, like such a con that Arbour had to say: this simply does not hold water. There are risks that should not be taken."[5] Louise Arbour did not put a stop to an investigation that in reality had never been ordered. She simply decided clearly to refrain from following a lead that was both tempting and perilous.

On the defense side, theatrical requests for a stay of the proceedings were as overly dramatic as they were pointless: regardless of who committed the attack, the crime against the Tutsis remained. One did not erase the other. It also did not change the definition of the crime. What solving the mystery of the attack could do was provide a historical understanding of the sequence of events leading up to the genocide and, if necessary, reassign political responsibility for triggering it. Herein lies the significance of the attack: amid the great violence and extreme tension in Rwanda at the beginning of 1994, the person behind the attack had to have known that thousands of Rwandan Tutsis would forfeit their lives. Whoever that person was, his or her criminal cynicism was undeniable.

There had been many anti-Tutsi pogroms prior to April 6. But it is not at all clear whether the forces of extermination would have been unleashed without the death of Habyarimana. French sociologist André Guichaoua, who served as an expert witness for the prosecution, summarized this dilemma best when he testified in November 1997: "I have the impression that history has largely been rewritten, as though fatality has been inscribed into every event, that the planning may have been in place since 1989 and that all the events were linked together to arrive at this fatal outcome. The triggering incident, with the attack on the presidential plane, was certainly a decisive act, which, from that moment on, inevitably made the ensuing series of events fatal. However, I think that up to that day [April 6], there were still alternatives and that a certain number of people thought—in a country where people were used to playing at the edge of the precipice and where politicians had a long tradition of intense clashes to the point where they all ended up toppling together—that many imagined that the worst was not always fatal. However, from the moment the president's plane was shot down, I believe that those who had taken the initiative did in fact raise the stakes to a very high level, which meant that political mobilization eluded a large portion of the politicians as they were no longer in a position to weigh in on the events or to control the forces that were being unleashed with this assassination."[6]

Herein resides the utterly explosive nature of the mystery of the attack. The prosecution was not the only one it frightened. It clearly bothered the judges as well, who were always very careful to avoid the subject. In the Akayesu judgment, the three judges borrowed the prosecutor's formulation, which was neutral to the point of being ridiculous, stating, "On April 6, 1994, a plane carrying President Juvénal Habyarimana of Rwanda and President Cyprien Ntaryamira of Burundi crashed at Kigali airport, killing all on board." The attack was an established fact, but to say so in writing was apparently a little too risky. The judges were not always as cautious: these same three judges did not hesitate to write in another judgment that Léonidas Rusatira was guilty, without knowing whom they were talking about.

It took the brouhaha following Hourigan's report to prompt three other judges at the ICTR to finally take up, purely for the sake of form, a motion to order the prosecutor to conduct an investigation into the attack that had been filed by one of the defense teams a year and a half earlier. It was also this report that led the judges in the Bagilishema case (except Judge Güney, of course) to acknowledge that the attack had indeed been the event that had triggered the massacres and not "a simple fact of history," as a representative of the prosecutor's office had once argued.

Thus, the dissemination of the UN investigator's report dissipated some of the prevailing hypocrisy and reopened the debate. Carla del Ponte had just succeeded Louise Arbour. Initially, she advanced the same argument. In December 1999 she explained that "if the tribunal was not dealing with the matter, it was because it lacked jurisdiction to do so."[7] In April 2000, in a Danish newspaper, her position changed. She announced that she was taking a hard look at reopening the investigation "if [they had] proof or strongly suspect[ed] that the assassination of the president was an act linked to the genocide."[8] Given the apparent difficulty of solidly establishing such a link, her approach was prudent. However, it did mark a turning point, as evidenced by the fact that she authorized a French judge to question some of the ICTR accused.

French anti-terrorism judge Jean-Louis Bruguière took up the question of the attack via a lawsuit filed by the families of the French plane's three crew members. He came to Arusha twice, in 2000 and 2001. For three years, del Ponte said that she would base her decision on whether to take up the case on Bruguière's findings. In April 2001, when the French investigation was already in an advanced stage, she announced that it was highly likely that she would open an investigation. But she never did anything further. In the end, Judge Bruguière's investigation was the only one ever conducted to determine who perpetrated the attack on April 6, 1994, with the eternal and inevitable suspicion that always accompanied any of France's initiatives in Rwanda, including judicial ones. In March 2004, one month before the tenth anniversary of the attack and the genocide, the results of the French investigation were widely reported in the newspaper *Le Monde*. Not surprisingly, they pointed to the RPF, which vehemently denied responsibility for the attack and in retaliation promised to mount an investigation into France's role in the genocide. Meanwhile in Arusha, the UN tribunal had long been enjoying the timorous tranquility of risk-free justice.

The jurisdiction argument may have served as an excuse to avoid dealing with the attack, but it could not prevail with respect to investigating the killings committed by RPF troops—the much talked-about "second mandate." It was impossible to say that these crimes were outside the scope of the tribunal's jurisdiction. At the beginning of 2000 Carla del Ponte announced that she had opened these investigations in December 1999. That was nearly true. In fact, Louise Arbour had actually initiated them in utmost secrecy in February 1999. Jean-Paul Akayesu and Jean Kambanda had been convicted six months earlier. The genocide was now solidly recognized, and the fear of revisionism was greatly reduced. Arbour also knew she would be leaving in a few months. With no risk to herself, therefore, she set the "second mandate" in motion. Still, she did so belatedly and in a measured way: the strike force consisted of only one investigator. Later, she candidly told journalist Carol Off: "The Rwandan government was reading my mail. We were infiltrated. They knew what I was doing. So if I sent someone off to do an investigation of the RPF, they might be killed. I wouldn't do it."[9]

In this respect, Carla del Ponte was by far the most enterprising of all the prosecutors who held this position. At the end of 2000 she publicly pledged to conduct these investigations in a transparent manner and with President Kagame's promise to cooperate with her office. For eighteen months, and no more, three men—only three compared to the eighty-some people who were assigned to investigate the genocide over ten years—would make up the so-called special investigations team in charge of prosecuting officers from the RPF army. They at least worked on three relatively well-documented cases: the massacres committed after RPF forces took the city of Butare in the south of Rwanda; the execution of three bishops and ten priests in Kabgayi on June 5, 1994, to which the RPF admitted; and the killings in Giti, a commune that was particularly relevant given that it had become famous in 1994 when it posted a sign at its entrance that read: "The commune where there was no genocide." The chief prosecutor later said that these special investigations covered a total of fourteen sites.[10] That was as far as it went.

General Kagame probably never had any intention of handing over any of his men to the UN tribunal. He indicated as much in little doses. "We cannot confuse the victims of the genocide with the people who were killed in our attempt to prevent them from committing the genocide. Why should someone who fought [the criminals] be treated on equal footing? His actions would be justified. Anyone who is a victim of having saved human lives should be considered a hero," he declared, for example, on April 7, 2002, on the eighth anniversary of the genocide.[11] He also conveyed his message through other means.

The Rwandan government had a supreme weapon it could wield to pressure the tribunal: access to witnesses. Almost all the prosecution witnesses came from Rwanda. Without Kigali's cooperation, there would be no witnesses. Without witnesses, there would be no trials. At the time of the Barayagwiza trial, Rwanda was already talking about no longer allowing witnesses to go to Arusha. That was just a warning. In June 2002 it carried through with its threat. For several weeks, Kigali prevented witnesses from traveling to Tanzania and caused an immediate suspension of the trials. By the following month, both del Ponte and the president of the tribunal, Navanethem Pillay, had alerted the UN Security Council. The council did not react until five months later, affirming its commitment to "full cooperation by the states" and calling for a "constructive dialogue." Meanwhile, Rwanda's ultimatum had already started to bear fruit. Publicly, the tribunal's chief prosecutor denounced the government's use of witnesses for blackmail. In private, she immediately halted all investigative missions related to the RPF cases. Then, in September 2002, she just as discretely ordered the outright suspension of the special investigations. Naturally she did not publicize her decision. Some thought, perhaps, that it was just a way to calm things down again. But the burial certificate for the RPF investigations was already being drawn up.

In order to reach an agreement on this burning issue, discussions between the chief prosecutor and the Rwandan authorities were initiated under the aegis of the U.S. government. The first meeting scheduled in December 2002 did not take place. Then the second meeting was postponed as a result of the beginning of the war in Iraq. The critical meeting wound up being held in Washington on May 14 and 16, 2003, mediated by a man who was very familiar with the matter: Ambassador Pierre-Richard Prosper, former trial attorney in the Akayesu case.

Four representatives of the international prosecutor's office were in attendance, including Carla del Ponte and her new South African deputy. The Rwandan government was represented by its own chief prosecutor, Gerald Gahima, and its ambassador to the ICTR. The Rwandan proposal was simple: Kigali would take over the cases against the soldiers in its army, on the premise that the ICTR and Rwanda's national courts should share the burden. This proposal was doubly backed by the U.S. government: on the one hand, Washington wanted to resolve this problem with the Arusha tribunal once and for all, and, on the other hand, this approach was totally in keeping with its new aggressive policy of promoting criminal proceedings at the national level and limiting the expansion of international criminal justice. Finally, as an International Crisis Group report noted at the time, now that Rwanda was "an integral part of U.S. counterterrorism measures in central and eastern Africa, the American government clearly wanted to offer its ally guarantees of impunity from prosecution by the UN tribunal in Arusha. Incidentally, on July 30, 2003, the U.S. government announced that it was lifting the arms embargo on Rwanda that was imposed in May 1994."[12]

Carla del Ponte agreed to the proposal. She has always denied it, stressing, rightly, that she did not sign anything. But the principle set forth at the Washington meeting had been endorsed. For Kigali, it was a flawless victory that had been cinched under the leadership of the American superpower. As for Rwanda's pledge to initiate proceedings, it would largely be disregarded in short order. First, the government asserted that it had already punished some of its soldiers, which is not true concerning the crimes of 1994. Second, it made a play for time: all it had to do was wait for the tribunal to close down in 2008, which was the deadline at the time. Eventually, one trial was organized in Rwanda that pertained to the Kabgayi massacre, which the RPF had admitted to committing back in 1994. Four officers were tried. In February 2009 a general and a major were acquitted, and two captains, who had pled guilty, each received a five-year sentence. There was no sign of any other attempt.

In September 2003, a few months after the agreement in Washington, Rwanda won another victory: henceforth, the ICTR would have its own chief prosecutor. Carla del Ponte would continue to serve only as the chief prosecutor for the tribunal for the former Yugoslavia. Prior to being ousted, del Ponte stated that if a "deal" on the RPF crimes were reached, "that would mean the Office of the Prosecutor had failed completely; that would mean that I am partisan and politicized."[13] For someone who had allegedly consented to this agreement, she was certainly not lacking in self-criticism.

In December 2004 the ICTR's fourth chief prosecutor, Hassan Boubacar Jallow, announced, as planned, the conclusion of his office's investigations after ten years of work. By the time he inherited the hot topic of the special investigations, he had very little room for maneuver. It was patently obvious that the international community had long since given up hope of salvaging the appearance of independent justice. Everyone's top priority was to close out the books and ensure that the tribunal's work was actually completed in 2008. The dual pitfall of lost time and the little time remaining was closing in on the illusory prospect of implementing the "second mandate." One last time, the medicine was administered with a spoonful of sugar. Jallow stated that the genocide investigations were indeed closed, but that those concerning the RPF army remained open and were in the process of being "evaluated." No one was fooled.

Every year in Arusha, transient and seasonal swarms of winged termites come to die on the neon lights. Their mad rush toward the light begins at dusk, but they do not last long. Before long, hundreds of wings and the worms that lost them litter the ground in front of homes where the exterior lights were left on. The tribunal's main entrance, with its bright lights, thus became the site of tremendous carnage, which the birds and geckos, after eating their fill, left behind for the wind and brooms to sweep away. It was a strange scene when the death of these isopterous insects was thoughtlessly interrupted as passers-by, annoyed by this chaotic attack, would start to bat wildly at the air with their hands, unintentionally slapping themselves in their attempt to shoo away the bugs, before taking cover by simply stepping away from the beam of light. Within the international community, the embarrassment caused by dropping the cases against the RPF was like this ephemeral, light-sensitive, and somewhat epileptic flight of the termites.

16

Loser's Justice

The ICTR, in view of the delicate balance between justice and reconciliation, is cautious to ensure that it is not a victor's court.

Judge Navanethem Pillay, president of the ICTR, "African Dialogue II" conference,
May 2002

Everyone who supported the creation of the tribunals for the former Yugoslavia and Rwanda and later the ICC dreaded the thought of these courts giving the appearance of victor's justice. The Nuremberg military tribunal created just after World War II hung like a specter over the proceedings. To the extent that it had succeeded in replacing vengeance with justice, it was embraced as a revered ancestor. To the extent that it perpetuated the now archaic notion that the vanquished must submit to the laws of the victors, the tribunal at Nuremberg was eschewed as a bogey. Fifty years later, international law activists were hoping this justice would embody "true" impartiality—the result not of a discretionary decision on the part of a victorious alliance, but of a higher moral standard established by the human community as a whole.

Yet, the tribunal's failure to prosecute the RPF would inevitably lead to the objective conclusion that the ICTR was a form of victor's justice. The facts speak for themselves. As of 2009 the tribunal had indicted ninety individuals. They were all from the forces of the former regime, which as they committed genocide in 1994 simultaneously lost the war in the process. Thus, it was clear that only the vanquished would be among the defendants. No member of the RPF has been charged to date, and it is unlikely that any ever will. Even if a few end up being indicted at the last minute for appearance's sake, no one will be fooled: the proceedings will be marginal and likely inconsequential. Any attempt would only be a ploy. The die has been cast. The RPF's crimes will not be tried, at least not here and not now. The Rwandan government has successfully defended its legitimacy as a victor. This victory is twofold: escaping judgment by others and avoiding legal scrutiny of its own crimes. The few who find this troubling are voices in the wilderness. Everyone else was prepared for this inevitability and has accepted it.

Every mass crime is unique. No two genocides are alike, even though their ultimate objective—the extermination of a group of people whose only crime is having been born—forges a common label. One can note their common techniques, such as the implementation of a process to dehumanize the victims or the use of the media, or highlight the similarities in the executioner's discourse: "I was following orders," "I was powerless." But no genocide or crime against humanity is exactly the same as another. Each has its own history and its own dynamic.

The same holds true for the courts tasked with trying these crimes. Lessons learned from one can be applied to others. The rule of ignorance is, in principle, just as great a threat to the ICC that is succeeding the UN ad hoc tribunals. Its foreseeable distance from the societies it is and will be dealing with raises real concerns about its relevance and flexibility. Similarly, witness protection measures threaten to jeopardize the public nature of its trials. However, every international tribunal is also the fruit of a unique historical context, which may help explain some of the failures and shortcomings. The ICTR, therefore, is the product of a history that distinguishes it from all the other international tribunals.

In the former Yugoslavia, NATO forces, and by proxy the UN Security Council, were the strongest in the end. This enabled the UN tribunal in The Hague to try Serbs, Croats, Bosniaks, and Kosovars. In Sierra Leone, peace was imposed, albeit belatedly, by the UN and the British. This authorized the UN court in Freetown to prosecute the three main armed factions in the civil war, including the one that had supported the democratically elected sitting president.

But in Rwanda in 1994, there was only one military and political victor: the RPF. The Hutu Power extremists were defeated. They had committed the crime of all crimes, and they had lost the war. The UN was completely discredited for having withdrawn its peacekeepers and left tens of thousands of Rwandans in the hands of the militias. Belgium, which was criticized for having sowed the seeds of racism while still a colonial power, lost all authority when it withdrew its battalion deployed under the UN banner at the height of the massacre. France's reputation was tarnished like none other for having supported a genocidal regime to the very end. The United States was disqualified for both its strong support of the UN troop withdrawal and its obstinate opposition to using the genocide label to describe what was happening in Rwanda so as to circumvent its obligation to send troops. The international community emerged covered in shame due to its refusal to intervene and stop the extermination of Tutsis, a failure that produced a rare and obsessive feeling of guilt.

Since then, whenever one meets with a Rwandan official in Kigali, before there is any hope of discussing the events of 1994, one question must first be answered: who stopped the genocide? There is only one right answer—the RPF—and it is inevitably accompanied by an unequivocal, implacable look that intimidates you into lowering your gaze and signals the end of the discussion. After all, the art of politics consists in limiting the debate to that which is indisputable. This art is second nature in Rwanda. It is practiced at the highest levels with a rare mastery.

Rwanda disconcerts, surprises, and intimidates foreigners who come into contact with it. On the African continent, it is a very unusual situation when Westerners find themselves in a position of weakness. Yet, the Rwandan authorities' constant use of the genocide to advance their interests on the international scene since 1994 has been a model of political efficiency. What other former African colony has been able to prompt commissions of inquiry in Belgium, France, and within the United Nations and the African Union? What other nation so devoid of strategic interest has managed to get a sitting U.S. president to come to its country to apologize? What other country as minuscule as Rwanda has been able to put the date marking its anniversary of horror, April 7, on the calendar as the world genocide commemoration day? The enormity of the crime committed in Rwanda in 1994 is not the only explanation, nor is this simply a sign of the times. Part of the credit must go to Rwanda's leaders.

The RPF was the only victor in 1994, and yet the tribunal established shortly after its victory was not the one it desired. It was a tribunal created and operated under the aegis of the "losing side," that is, the international community, the UN Security Council, and its most powerful members. It is therefore paradoxical and misleading to call the ICTR victor's justice: it was neither designed nor run by the victors. In reality (and this distinction is as unique as it is critical), it is the exact opposite: loser's justice.

This fact was not easy for the tribunal's creators or its protagonists to accept. And yet it is important if we are to understand some of the failures and errors. The Arusha-based tribunal is probably the only international tribunal that was not designed and run by powers who could at least count themselves among the victors.

This is exactly how the RPF sees the international community and its members, as a community of the defeated. Accordingly, what government that single-handedly won a military and political battle at the cost of so much bloodshed would agree to be held accountable for the crimes attributed to it by a community of losers? The ICTR was created by powers that failed, on the moral level if nothing else. Thus, it had to render a justice in their image. It had to be a court of remorse.

Those who were in charge of the court—the prosecutors and the judges— could not change that. They could not aspire to impartiality because they were the product, not of a mark of power, but of an act of contrition. Sooner or later, most of the tribunal's leaders internalized this feeling of guilt, either through logic or out of weakness. There is no better explanation than this contrite conscience for the hesitation and the crippling fear that gripped the judges as the Bagilishema trial came to a close, at the thought of setting free the person they had just acquitted. There is no better explanation for the judges' inability to dismiss the rape charge against Alfred Musema. And there is no better explanation for the fact that the Rwandan tribunal was able to keep some of the accused in pretrial detention for six years, without even contemplating what a more self-assured court would have granted in the face of such lengthy delays—conditional release, a practice that the tribunal in The Hague generously and unaffectedly applied. There is no better explanation for the fact that no respected human rights organizations ever publicly expressed any concern over all these violations of rights. And of course, there is no better explanation for the failure to prosecute the RPF.

An international court derives its authority from those who create it. Officials at the ICTR failed to master this precept of power. They thus taught that it was possible to have a form of justice that was even more partial and less courageous than victor's justice. At the slightest deviation from what they expect of the tribunal, Rwandan leaders have always managed to remind these representatives of the international community of their duty to press on, head down, walking the walk of the vanquished. Allowing nothing to interfere with their undivided victory, they made sure that the tribunal in Arusha would be the stooped, shameful shadow of a world that had failed.

17 | Giving and Taking Back

What we are trying to do is contribute to peace and reconciliation. The ICTR can do something that a national system cannot: establish a historical memory of what happened.

Judge Gabrielle Kirk MacDonald, interview,
June 11, 1998

The entire staff is there solely to assist the judges in the trials and with the judgments. And not for any other reason. Not for peace. Not so that Hutus and Tutsis get along. Not for any of that; it is a tribunal.

Judge Lennart Aspegren, interview,
April 16, 1998

On December 31, 2004, the ICTR prosecutor officially closed the genocide investigations. The decision was not his. It was imposed on him by the countries that had created the court and were financially supporting it. According to President Pillay's projections in 2001, if Carla del Ponte had been given free rein to implement her work plan, the trials would have lasted until 2021. The states firmly indicated that this was utterly unreasonable. They demanded that the trials be completed by 2008 and the appeals procedures by 2010. The same deadlines were imposed on the tribunal for the former Yugoslavia in The Hague.

The deadline was never met. Initially given a four-year mandate, the ICTR will have lasted for approximately twenty years by the time it closes down, in 2013 at the earliest. Since its inception, it has tried forty-five individuals. Seventeen were sentenced to life in prison; nine others were sentenced to twenty-five years or more. Eleven, including nine who pled guilty, received between six and twenty years. Eight were acquitted.[1] In December 2009 the trials of twenty-nine additional accused were in progress or pending. Eleven fugitives were still at large. In all likelihood, only a few of them will be arrested. To have completed all appeals by 2010, the court would have had to try twice as many people as it had since it was established, in one-third the amount of time. To no one's surprise, it failed to meet that deadline. The conditions for closing up the Arusha-based tribunal remain uncertain. But the length of its existence and that of the ICTY is already unprecedented (the Nuremberg trials were spread over only four years).[2]

With a total of ninety individuals indicted, the Arusha-based tribunal represents a symbolic justice that was supposed to formally mark the community of nations' refusal to allow the crime to go unpunished and its primary perpetrators to have a say in the political debate. It was also symbolic in its selective prosecution of prominent suspects and key groups (the military, politicians, the media, etc.). In Rwanda, with tens of thousands of suspects in prison since 1994, the courts wanted to ensure that there was also mass justice. Symbolic justice and mass justice normally fall within a limited time frame. By being spread out over fifteen to twenty years, the two forms of justice rendered in both Arusha and in Rwandan courts have not only departed from what was envisioned in 1994, but their very purpose has also changed.

The year 2002 was a turning point in the quest for justice following the genocide. In Arusha, the Rusatira case and the suspension of the investigations into the RPF dealt a fatal blow to the tribunal's moral function and marked its forced entry into the era of "realjustice" (analogous to the concept of realpolitik). Since that time, the tribunal's strategic direction has been dictated by its completion deadline. Its priorities and legal proceedings are no longer dominated by the moral duty and the political need to meet an urgent demand for justice. They are governed by administrative requirements—the prosaic need to process pending cases within a fixed period of time. There are no longer any expectations of a historic nature. Rather, it is simply a matter of planning for the institution's closure.

That same year in Rwanda, genocide trials in the national courts began to slow at first and eventually stopped altogether for at least ten months in 2004.[3] This slowdown, followed by the temporary suspension of the judicial process, was initially intended to allow the so-called *gacaca* courts to get off the ground across the country. The government had decided to set up these community courts three years earlier in response to the 130,000-some suspects still in prison awaiting trial. Between 1997 and 2002 approximately 9,000 Rwandans were brought to trial in their country for their alleged involvement in the genocide. Approximately 9 percent were sentenced to death, 36 percent sentenced to life, and 20 percent acquitted.[4] The Rwandan effort to try the perpetrators via the conventional legal system would have been remarkable in scale. But starting in 1999, the government was forced to admit that the criminal justice system was not adequate to handle such a massive caseload; that would have taken a century or two. Refusing to resort to amnesty, it opted for a novel solution to this enormous challenge: the *gacaca* courts. In 2001 some 250,000 judges were elected by the people to lead roughly 11,000 community courts on the most remote hills in the Rwandan countryside.

Rwanda was no different from the other countries facing mass crime: in December 2000 chief prosecutor Gerald Gahima had stated that the time had come to "put the genocide behind us," not because of a moral failure, but out of political necessity.[5] Thus, these *gacaca* courts had five years to determine the fate of approximately 100,000 accused in prison, leaving the biggest suspects in the hands of professional judges. To advance this process, the law governing the *gacaca* encouraged prisoners to admit to their crimes with the promise of substantial sentence reductions in exchange for full confessions.

At the beginning of 2002 part of the prosecution staff was assigned to preparing the cases to be transferred to the future *gacaca* courts. Shortly after some of these courts were launched in June 2002, however, they became bogged down. It took three more years for the trials to get under way. Between 2002 and 2005, at the height of this enormous logjam, the *gacaca*'s only major accomplishment resided in confessions: at least thirty thousand prisoners had decided to confess to their crimes. But for the court to accept their confessions, they had to give the names of all their accomplices. *Gacaca* justice was designed to clear out the overcrowded prisons and quickly reduce the backlog of pending cases. However, the clause requiring denunciation of accomplices produced a radically different outcome: in mid-2002 the minister of justice was informed that there were now 250,000-some people who had been implicated by those who had confessed. Instead of whittling down the caseload, *gacaca* justice was now threatening to increase it tenfold. The challenge was judicial: the credibility of these repentant criminals' testimony was questionable to say the least. And it was, above all, political: in lieu of the stated objective of national reconciliation, *gacaca* was in danger of deteriorating into a mass criminalization of the population.

Two years later, the government unveiled its choice. It announced that at least 550,000 people were now suspected of having taken part in the genocide through killing, supporting the killings, or simply stealing victims' property. At the beginning of 2005 it cited a possible figure of 1 million suspects. By 2009 more than 1.1 million Rwandans had officially been charged before *gacaca* courts. In 2002 one out of every fifty-five Rwandans was being prosecuted and held in prison on account of the genocide. Seven years later, one out of eight Rwandans had been a suspect. *Gacaca* justice had been assembling a disturbing and massive police record of the population.

In four years, from 2005 to 2009, the *gacaca* tribunals dealt with an exorbitant number of cases, offering a totally unprecedented experiment in mass justice. But the logic behind this people's justice has changed. Hundreds of thousands of "suspects" have been living under the threat of being prosecuted at any time, at the slightest false move. Mass justice has been doubling as an instrument of mass political control. In 2009 Rwandan authorities announced that the *gacaca* courts would be completed in February 2010. In the end, the need to "put the genocide behind us" that Gerald Gahima had recognized in 2000 took nine years to be met.

In both Kigali and Arusha, 2002 was a year of peaks and valleys and major policy changes—all at the same time. The quest for justice went from being a moral and social requirement to being a matter of essentially political or administrative management. In 1994 Rwanda was the only state to oppose the creation of the international tribunal. Fifteen years later, it was the only one dissatisfied with the results of the ICTR's work. In its eyes, the tribunal had not done enough.

The paradox is all too obvious. The tribunal's existence, an expression of the international community's feeling of guilt, helps the Rwandan government dodge accusations about its own violence by reminding the major powers of their original sin: having abandoned the Tutsis in 1994. As long as the tribunal exists, the Rwandan government can also impose the idea that justice is a never-ending obligation.

Since the Rwandan government never wanted to end the work of justice after the genocide, it can hardly be said that the tribunal impeded Rwanda's reconstruction by not doing its job swiftly either. But, the UN tribunal clearly reinforced the idea that the time had not come for either symbolic justice or mass justice to "put the genocide behind us." In fact, it will have forced the Rwandan people to face up to their crime and the lingering shadow of punishment for twenty years. It thereby fuels the vague but real suspicion of "neo-imperialism" that hangs over an international justice largely influenced and shaped by Western powers. And it illustrates the natural tendency of lawyers to ignore priorities other than their own.

International justice was entrusted with many tasks: to judge, impose peace, deter future conflicts, contribute to national reconciliation, and establish a historical memory. No doubt flattered, always proud, it lacked common sense, taking all the tasks that were naively or calculatingly handed to it. One of the paradoxes of the Rwanda tribunal is that two of its most obvious and commendable achievements were either not judicial at all or only indirectly so.

The first of these accomplishments was that it helped politically silence all supporters of the regime that had overseen the genocide. The tribunal in no way brought peace to the Great Lakes region in Africa. It also lacked the credibility to make various armed groups curb their systematic violence against civilian populations. Judge Laïty Kama had already recognized this by 1999: "After the Rwandan genocide, we thought this would open the eyes of African states to the abominations that could happen in their countries. But we've seen what happened in eastern Congo and in Sierra Leone. The [UN] Security Council had established a certain dialectic relationship between the convictions and the fact that these convictions could be a deterrent. I do not think the tribunal has played that role. Moreover, the convictions never played their intended role as a deterrent. Otherwise, these crimes would have never been repeated. After Nuremberg, there were death sentences and people said 'never again.'"[6] Nonetheless, the marginalizing of Hutu Power brought about by the ICTR's prosecutions was vital to the prospects for political stability in Rwanda and the region.

The tribunal's second tangible success was that it emphatically reinforced the recognition of the crime committed in Rwanda in 1994. From the beginning, the genocide of the Tutsis has been the unending subject of an exceptionally lively and abundant literature. The production of documentaries continues apace. Even the movie industry has seized on the topic. Out of all the mass crimes that have disfigured the African continent, the Rwandan genocide is probably the only one—along with slavery and the specific case of South African apartheid—that can claim to be inscribed in the universal conscience. Thus as applied to Rwanda, the notion of a "forgotten genocide" is erroneous. Yet this recognition of the genocide was not so apparent in 1994. It did not come about solely through the ICTR's efforts, but the UN tribunal certainly contributed to constructing the memory of the genocide. In June 2006 the ICTR appeals chamber ruled that the genocide against Rwandan Tutsis in 1994 was a fact of common knowledge. It no longer has to be proven.

The pursuit of truth was certainly not the key point of the trials. Giving judges the power to help write history is not a new danger. In Arusha, they by and large confirmed this risk. The stakes and the history that intermingle in such trials also go well beyond legal issues. Just as Clemenceau, who was hardly inclined to shy away from a battle, said that war is too serious a matter to be left to soldiers, so also can one say that justice for state crimes is probably too important to be left to lawyers alone. Nevertheless, the tribunal has assembled a collection of previously unavailable records, some of which have true historic value. Several of these documents are kept under seal. There is no clear mechanism to indicate who will keep them after the tribunal closes and who may eventually decide to make them available for public access. If the disturbing cloud of judicial opacity in Arusha ever lifts, these records will serve as a unique source of information for a more thorough and comprehensive understanding of how the 1994 genocide unfolded. Although the Bagosora judgment in December 2008 did not contain conclusive findings on how the genocide unfolded, it reflects a valuable effort to accept history's complexities.

Shortly before his death in 2001, Judge Kama reflected on the tribunal and its legacy. "I think that there was a choice: let things go unpunished or render justice, hoping that we can learn from it. We opted for that. The alternative is very simple: it means letting things happen, never rendering justice, bringing vengeance into play. I think we have to look at it the other way around. Just because convictions do not prevent repetition of the crime does not mean that we should not convict. In the case of Rwanda, if the only justice that can satisfy the victims is a justice of vengeance, I think there is no possibility for national reconciliation. The illusion is that conviction will bring instant reconciliation. In all societies of the world, people expect too much from justice."[7]

Acknowledgments

This book was mainly inspired by my coverage of the ICTR from May 1997 to October 2002 in Arusha. It is also the product of the work of those with whom I shared this task. I first wish to thank my colleagues and friends Jean Chichizola, Arnaud Grellier, Franck Petit, and Lars Waldorf, with whom I had the great privilege of working and who, inadvertently, allowed me to use their writings.

Relations with the UN tribunal were inevitably delicate and sometimes antagonistic. I also met a number of remarkable people there who cannot be named here. Many placed their precious trust in me over the years, and some became friends. In many respects, this book is the result of sharing their passion, their questioning, and their openness to reflection. May they find an anonymous recognition here that is both deep and sincere.

The ICTR's press room was an unattractive place to work, but my heartfelt thoughts go out to my fellow journalists there who managed to embellish it with their warm presence over the years. Tanzanians, Kenyans, Rwandans, Europeans, and Americans turned it into a small "press club" that was guided by a spirit of great tolerance. Julia Crawford, Jean-Marie Gasana, Coll Metcalfe, and Farah Stockman were vital companions.

I thank the courageous and friendly team at International Crisis Group in Nairobi, with whom I had the great pleasure of working from 2000 to 2003. My thanks to Victor Peskin from the University of California, Berkeley, now at Arizona State University, for so generously agreeing to share the fruit of his research.

In France, Christophe Gargot's support and critical eye were crucial to making headway in writing this book, and his friendship was infallible. Catherine Duvillard also contributed her input as well as her helpful editing comments. I also thank Antoine Garapon for his advice and constant support. In the United States, thanks to Shantha Rau for her affection.

This book was written over several periods and in several places from 2003 to 2005. I wish to thank Rose Moss from Harvard University's Nieman Foundation, who gave me invaluable advice for beginning this project, generously provided feedback on the first proofs, and did not say a word when I put the book on hold. When I resumed work again in earnest, in the fall of 2004 in the northern part of New York, Marek Waldorf was a valiant writing mate at first. Philip, Larissa, and Clio Gourevitch then offered me the forest, a fireplace, and solitude for a retreat that was both decisive for the book and unforgettable for its intense serenity. May they find here the expression of my deepest friendship. In France, the sweeping view of the sea that Jacques and Fanny Cadène offered me made it possible to finally finish the work I had begun. Thank you so very much.

At the University of Wisconsin Press, Gwen Walker's support, trust, and stamina were both remarkable and decisive. My most sincere thanks to her and to the always kind and professional people at UW Press who worked on this publication. I am also very grateful to Chari Voss for her patience, gentleness, and dedication in translating the original text and going through the edits.

I would never have been able to cover the trials in Arusha for so long had it not been for the indispensable, unfailing, and radiant presence of a man who cared nothing about Rwanda or international justice, who had moved to Tanzania from Kenya before the international tribunal existed, and probably hoped to leave after it, or perhaps never. This book would not exist without the fraternal friendship of Aziz Hajee. May he know that I am eternally grateful.

Finally, I wish to thank Yann for being the best brother, an indispensable editor, and a great advisor on ethics. I owe the rest, that is, nearly everything, to my parents, Christine and Yves, for having always talked to us about history, conscience, and free will.

Notes

Most of the information contained in this book comes from notes the author took while observing hearings before the tribunal for Rwanda and from the numerous formal and informal interviews of those in charge of the trials that he has conducted since 1997. Part of this information was published as the events unfolded, from 1997 to 2005, in articles available on the International Justice Tribune Web site, http://www.justicetribune.com.

Prologue

1. Excerpts from the hearings are generally a retranscription of notes taken by the author during the hearing and not a reproduction of the official ICTR transcripts. In some cases, however, the author used the official transcripts to complete his notes.

2. André Sibomana, *Gardons l'espoir pour Rwanda: Entretiens avec Laure Guilbert and Hervé Deguine* (Paris: Desclée de Brouwer, 1997), 166.

3. Telford Taylor, *The Anatomy of the Nuremberg Trials: A Personal Memoir* (New York: Knopf, 1992), 4.

Chapter 1. The Addis Ababa Departure Lounge

1. *Le Monde*, November 10, 1994.

2. The story of Froduald Karamira's transfer to Kigali is based on three main sources of information: AP, AFP, and Reuters newswires; the remarkable interviews of Richard Goldstone, Gerald Gahima, and Filip Reyntjens conducted in 2002 and 2003 by Victor Peskin, professor of politics and global studies at Arizona State University, who very generously gave the author access to these interviews for this book (see also Victor A. Peskin, *International Justice in Rwanda and the Balkans: Virtual Trials and the Struggle for State Cooperation* [New York: Cambridge University Press, 2008]); and letters written in 1996 by prosecutor Richard Goldstone, Belgian lawyer Johann Scheers, and Kenyan lawyer Kennedy Ogetto. In addition to these sources are the author's

interviews in 2000 with an ICTR investigator who met with and questioned Karamira in prison in Rwanda, as well as the documents and proceedings from the Rutaganda trial in February/March 1998.

3. Richard Goldstone, interview with Victor Peskin, April 2003.

4. Letter written by Richard Goldstone to Johan Scheers, July 10, 1996.

5. Goldstone, interview with Peskin, April 2003.

6. Gerald Gahima, interview with Victor Peskin, May 2002.

7. Goldstone, interview with Peskin, April 2003.

8. Filip Reyntjens, interview with Victor Peskin, December 2003.

Chapter 2. The Eagle Eye

1. Carol Off, *The Lion, the Fox and the Eagle* (Toronto: Random House Canada, 2000), 284.

2. Ibid., 289.

3. Ibid., 11, 313.

4. UN Office of Internal Oversight Services, *Audit and Investigation of the International Criminal Tribunal for Rwanda*, A/51/789, February 6, 1997, 2, 22; see http://www.docstoc.com/docs/6809477/A-51-789-UNITED-NATIONS.

5. AFP, February 27, 1997.

6. Jean-Bosco Barayagwiza, *Rwanda: Le sang hutu, est-il rouge? Vérités cachées sur les massacres* (Yaoundé, Cameroon, 1995), 307.

7. Statement made during a panel discussion at Coordination SUD, Paris, December 12, 1997.

Chapter 3. At the First Judgment

1. André Sibomana, *Hope for Rwanda* (London: Pluto Press, 1999), 56.

2. This quote and subsequent quotes from Prosper are taken from the author's interviews with Pierre-Richard Prosper in 1997, 1998, 2001, and 2004.

3. The 6 other states that voted against the Rome Statute were China, India, Israel, the Philippines, Turkey, and Sri Lanka; 21 countries abstained, and 120 voted in favor.

Chapter 4. Lines of Defense

1. Michael Karnavas, "Rwanda's Quest for Justice: National and International Efforts and Challenges," *The Champion*, May 1997.

2. Author's interview with Luc de Temmerman, August 25, 1997.

3. Ibid.

4. Author's interview with John Philpot, Arusha, September 7, 1999. See also *Living Marxism*, no. 103, September 1997.

5. Ibid.

6. Alison Des Forges, interview by Arnaud Grellier, June 6, 2002; see http://www.justicetribune.com.

7. Jean-Marie Biju-Duval, in "Médias de la haine, crimes contre l'humanité et Génocide: Les occasions manquées," a document prepared for the symposium "The Media and the Rwanda Genocide" at Carleton University's School of Journalism, Ottawa, Canada, March 13, 2004.

Chapter 5. The Fool's Game

1. The account in this chapter is based primarily on documents filed by Jean Kambanda in his appeal case. The rest was reconstructed from the author's interviews with prosecution investigators in charge of this case. The links between Bernard Muna and Oliver Michael Inglis come from the author's interviews with the two men in May 1998.

2. Alain de Brouwer, former political advisor for Internationale démocrate chrétienne, in a letter to Carla del Ponte on January 12, 2001.

3. Author's interview with Alain de Brouwer, December 26, 2002.

4. William Schabas, "Clemency and Historical Truth," *Ubutabera*, no. 46, September 28, 1998, htttp://www.justicetribune.com.

Chapter 6. Counting Up the Interahamwe

1. Concerning Dieudonné Niyitegeka, see the Jean Kambanda appeal file. The rest of the story was reconstructed on the basis of numerous interviews with primarily six staff members at the office of the prosecutor over the period 1998–2005, as well as several other public or confidential court or investigation documents.

2. The account of the Nkezabera case is based on numerous interviews with staff from the office of the prosecutor from 2000 to 2005, as well as documents from the ICTR.

3. All of the information concerning the Serushago case was taken from court documents and public hearings, with the exception of the quote "was unacceptable," which comes from a telephone interview with the author on March 14, 2000.

4. Omar Serushago's mother and second wife are Tutsis.

Chapter 7. The White Man's Grave

1. The account of Georges Ruggiu's story is based on documents produced in court during his trial and during his subsequent appearances as a witness, augmented by numerous interviews conducted during the confession process from 1999 to 2000 with Ruggiu's lawyers and the people in charge of this case at the prosecutor's office.

2. This scene took place in the presence of the author.

Chapter 8. A Little Murder among Friends

1. The action committee was RTLM's board of directors and executive committee, of which Ferdinand Nahimana and Jean-Bosco Barayagwiza were members.

Chapter 9. Opening Up Kibuye

1. The trial was held before Trial Chamber II, composed of the judges William Sekule (Tanzania), Yakov Ostrovsky (Russia), and Tafazzal Hussein Khan (Bangladesh).

Chapter 10. Be like the Arab

1. The entire account, which is based on court hearings and the dozens of documents filed in this case, is supported by the author's observations during visits to the
various crime scenes in Rwanda and coverage of the defense investigation in Rwanda
from March 14 to 21, 1999.

2. Sibomana, *Hope for Rwanda*, 78.

3. The prosecutor is obligated to disclose all exculpatory evidence to the defense.

Chapter 11. Closing Up Shop

1. Hirondelle News Agency wire, August 7, 1999.

2. Martin Ngoga, press conference, October 1999.

3. Author's interview with Augustin Cyiza, September 9, 2002.

4. Barayagwiza, *Rwanda: Le sang Hutu est-il rouge?* 217, 219, 236, 287.

5. Author's interview with prosecution investigator, November 5, 1999.

6. Reference to a motion filed by Jérôme Bicamumpaka, former minister of
foreign affairs.

7. President Pasteur Bizimungu, Radio Rwanda, November 9, 1999.

8. Rwandan ambassador Joesph Mutaboba in New York, quoted in *Ubutabera*, no.
75, http://www.justicetribune.com.

9. Author's interview with Navanethem Pillay, November 18, 1999.

10. Nelson Mandela, quoted in the UN briefing by the president of the Rwanda
War Crimes Tribunal; see http://www.globalsecurity.org/military/library/news/1999/
11/19991109-rwanda-brf-doc.htm.

11. ICTR spokesperson Kingsley Moghalu, press conference, November 26, 1999.

12. Carla del Ponte, press conference, November 29, 1999.

13. J.-B. Barayagwiza, press release, September 2, 2002.

14. Author's interview with Bernard Muna, April 6, 2000.

15. Laïty Kama, press conference, May 20, 1999.

Chapter 12. A Mayor in Turmoil

1. Interview with Charles Adeogun-Phillips by Franck Petit, quoted in *Ubutabera*,
no. 76, December 7, 1999, http://www.justicetribune.com.

2. In 1999 Rwanda had a population of about 8 million. Therefore, approximately
1 in every 55 inhabitants was in prison, compared with 1 out of 210 in the United States
and 1 out of 1,100 in France or Belgium, i.e., twenty times fewer than in Rwanda.

3. The account of the site visit to Rwanda and the coverage of the defense team's visit to Rwanda are based on reports by Franck Petit at the time, supplemented by information gathered by the author during his trips to Rwanda.

4. Alain Ribaux, Kayishema/Ruzindana trial, February 1998, quoted in *Ubutabera*, no. 31, March 2, 1998, http://www.justicetribune.com.

5. Up to at least the end of 2006, the official Web site of the ICTR listed Ignace Bagilishema as a "released accused." He was later moved to the "detainees acquitted" list.

6. Sources at the U.S. State Department and UN headquarters, interviews with the author on July 26 and 27, 2001.

7. Author's interview with François Roux, August 2, 2002.

8. See chap. 14, p. 137.

Chapter 13. The Principle of Ignorance

1. Alain Brossat, "Massacres et génocides: Les conditions du récit," in *Parler des camps, penser les génocides*, ed. C. Coquio (Paris: Albin Michel, 1999), 167.

2. Judge Mose, internal memorandum, December 8, 1999.

Chapter 14. The Betrayal of the "Moderates"

1. Author's interview with Filip Reyntjens, March 21, 2002.

2. Luc Marchal, *Rwanda: La descente aux enfers; Témoignage d'un peacekeeper, décembre 1993–avril 1994* (Brussels: Labor, 2001), 299.

3. Kingsley Moghalu, press conference, April 2, 2002.

4. Raphaël Constant, *Une gestion politique de la justice*, February 2000, http://www.justicetribune.com.

5. Ibid.

6. Author's interviews, April 26, 2002.

7. Léonidas Rusatira, *l'Armée pour quoi faire* (Kigali: Pallotti-Presse, 1998).

8. Concerning the ETO affair, see in particular the letters sent by Léonidas Rusatira to the RPF secretary-general on June 10, 1999; to Rwanda's chief prosecutor on February 8, 2000; and to Carla del Ponte on October 22, 2001. See also the African Rights report *Left to Die at ETO and Nyanza: The Stories of Rwandese Civilians Abandoned by UN Troops on April 11, 1994*, Witness to Genocide 13 (London: African Rights, 2001).

9. African Rights, *Left to Die at ETO and Nyanza*.

10. Author's interview with Carla del Ponte, May 30, 2002.

11. Jean-Bosco Iyakaremye, "À l'intention de tous ceux que cela pourrait intéresser" (letter in author's possession), May 26, 2002, and interview with the author, May 21, 2002.

12. Colonel Luc Marchal's logbook, information provided to author by Marchal.

13. The author spoke with several members of the Kanyarengwe family, including Alexis Kanyarengwe, in May and September 2002.

14. Author's interview with Filip Reyntjens, May 16, 2002.

15. Author's interview with Jean-Marie Biju-Duval, May 17, 2002.

16. Roméo Dallaire, *Shake Hands with the Devil: The Failure of Humanity in Rwanda* (Toronto: Random House Canada, 2003).

17. ICTR, Bagosora judgment, December 18, 2008, http://www.ictr.org.

18. Ibid.

Chapter 15. Like a Flight of Termites

1. Author's interview with Gerald Gahima, December 5, 2000.

2. Yves Ternon, "Le sens des mots: De mal en pire," in *Parler des camps, penser les génocides*, ed. C. Coquio (Paris: Albin Michel, 1999), 105.

3. This is the precise time that the presidential airplane's distress beacon went off and was recorded by the control tower at Kigali airport.

4. Author's interview with Mohamed Othman, April 4, 2000.

5. Author's interview with an ICTR senior investigator, March 30, 2000.

6. Kayishema/Ruzindana trial, hearings from November 3 to 6, 1997.

7. Author's interview with Carla del Ponte, December 3, 1999.

8. *Aktuelt*, April 17, 2000.

9. Off, *Lion, the Fox and the Eagle*, 331.

10. Information regarding the "special investigations" comes from the author's numerous interviews with staff at the OTP, including Carla del Ponte, between 2000 and 2005, as well as with Rwandan representatives and Pierre-Richard Prosper, U.S. ambassador-at-large for war crimes.

11. Paul Kagame, speech, Nyakibanda, April 7, 2002.

12. International Crisis Group (ICG), *Tribunal Pénal International pour le Rwanda: Le compte à rebours*, August 1, 2002, available at http://www.unhcr.org/refworld/docid/3c0c968d7.html [accessed January 27, 2010].

13. Author's interview with Carla del Ponte, June 3, 2003.

Chapter 17. Giving and Taking Back

1. In December 2009, of the forty-five individuals who had stood trial, nine still had cases pending before the appeals chamber.

2. The trials of the main Nazi dignitaries by the four Allied powers lasted only one year. However, eleven other trials were held in Nuremberg between 1946 and 1949 before U.S. military tribunals. From 1945 to 1949, 5,025 Nazi criminals were convicted in Germany by U.S., British, and French tribunals. See http://www.memorial-delashoah.org.

3. The data concerning the genocide trials in Rwanda is primarily from the Ligue pour la promotion des droits de l'homme au Rwanda and Human Rights Watch.

4. Only twenty-two of those who were convicted, including Froduald Karamira, were executed on April 24, 1998. Also, several thousand other accused died in prison

before standing trial, although they are never included in the statistics on postgenocide justice.

5. Author's interview with Gerald Gahima, December 5, 2000, quoted in International Crisis Group, *Justice Delayed*, June 7, 2001, http://www.crisisgroup.org/home/index.cfm?id=1649&l=1.

6. Author's interview with Laïty Kama, June 5, 1999.

7. Ibid.

Index

THIERRY CRUVELLIER, an investigative journalist, covered the International Criminal Tribunal for Rwanda from 1997 to 2002. Since then he has reported on tribunals in Sierra Leone, Bosnia-Herzegovina, and Cambodia. Cruvellier also founded the *International Justice Tribune*, an online magazine covering international criminal justice.

Photo credit: John Vink / Magnum Photos

CHARI VOSS is a French–English interpreter and translator based in Washington, D.C., who spent two years interpreting the genocide trials at the United Nations International Criminal Tribunal for Rwanda (ICTR).